Creative
Process

in
Gestalt
Therapy

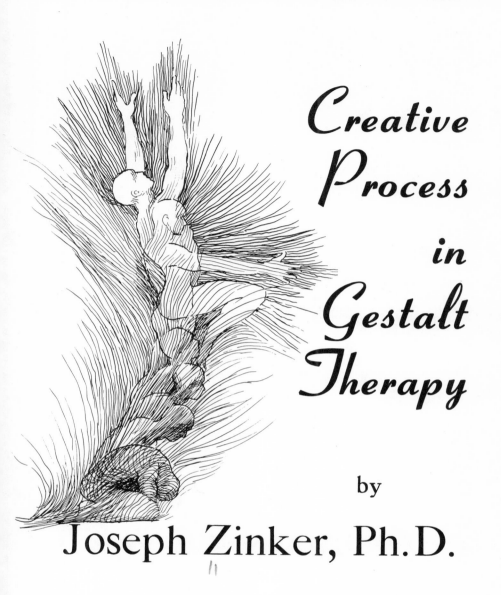

Creative Process in Gestalt Therapy

by

Joseph Zinker, Ph.D.

Brunner/Mazel, *Publishers* • New York

Library of Congress Cataloging in Publication Data

Zinker, Joseph Chaim.
    Creative process in Gestalt therapy.

    Bibliography: p. 271
    Includes index.
    1. Gestalt therapy. 2. Creative ability. I. Title.
RC489.G4Z56   616.8'917   76-49430
ISBN 0-87630-140-5

SECOND PRINTING

Designed by Susan Barrows

MANUFACTURED IN THE UNITED STATES OF AMERICA

To my parents.
For the singing and laughter,
for the joy for life you gave me.

Preface

It has become almost a tradition among clinicians in psychology to write books about the nature of creativity and the creative process of great artists. Freud wrote a number of pieces about art and creativity. Two of the most recent books which have described the nature of the creative process are Rollo May's *The Courage to Create* and Silvano Arieti's *Creativity*. These three authors are or were psychotherapists, and all made inspired efforts to understand the world of the artist and how the artist produces his work. Yet it seems to be a common malady among therapists that they do not see *themselves* as artists involved in a creative process.

This book is an exception. It is written about my experience as a therapist in the realm of creativity in the therapeutic process.

I enjoyed writing the book. I learned how to write better and to clarify my own ideas. It gave me great pleasure to make some of the drawings in the book and to solicit my artist friends to contribute their work as well.

I hope the reading of this book will stimulate you to become more creative in your own work.

JOSEPH ZINKER
January, 1977

Acknowledgments

I feel like the astronaut who gratefully acknowledged the contribution of hundreds of people on his flight to the moon. There were many people who loved me enough, and tolerated my craziness, and concretely supported me in this project. Among them, of course, are the members of my family—Florence, my wife, and my daughters, Judy and Karen. Myrna Freedman, my secretary, gave me a lot of encouragement and support, besides typing portions of the manuscript. Viki Williams contributed to the initial editing work. Most importantly, Shirley Loffer did a masterful job in helping me organize the manuscript, edit and type it in its final form.

I also want to acknowledge the contributions of the following artists to the book: Barbara Balbot, Tomi Ungerer and Greta Waldas. Finally, I would like to acknowledge the support, help and contributing ideas of the Professional Staff of the Gestalt Institute of Cleveland, and especially my friends Julian Leon, and Erving, Miriam and Sarah Polster.

Contents

Preface vii

Acknowledgments viii

1. Permission to Be Creative 3

2. The Creative Leap 21

3. The Creative Stance 37

4. Roots and Assumptions 76

5. Goals and Aspirations 96

6. The Experiment 123

7. Groups As Creative Communities 156

8. Polarities and Conflicts 195

9. Art in Gestalt Therapy 236

10. Castanedian Vision 257

Appendix 269

Bibliography 271

Index 275

Creative
Process

in

Gestalt
Therapy

Chapter 1

Permission to Be Creative

Creativity is a celebration of one's grandeur, one's sense of making anything possible. Creativity is a celebration of life— *my* celebration of life. It is a bold statement: I am here! I love life! I love me! I can be anything! I can do anything!

Creativity is not merely the conception, but the act itself, the fruition of that which is urgent, which demands to be stated. It is not only an expression of the full range of each person's experience and sense of uniqueness, but also a social act—a sharing with one's fellow human beings this celebration, this assertion in living a full life.

Creativity is the expression of the presence of God in my hands, eyes, brain—in all of me. Creation is each person's statement of godliness, of transcending the daily struggle for survival and the burden of mortality—an outcry of anguish and of celebration.

Creativity is the breaking of boundaries, the affirmation of life beyond life—life moving beyond itself. Out of its own sense of integrity, life asks us to affirm our own intrinsic nature, our essences as human beings.

Finally, creativity is an act of bravery. It states: I am willing to risk ridicule and failure so that I may experience this day with newness and freshness. The person who dares to create,

3

to break boundaries, not only partakes of a miracle, but also comes to realize that in his process of being he *is* a miracle.

It does not matter what field of endeavor we are talking about. In every field it is the same act of celebration, the same fullness of expression that justifies our purpose of living.

My goal as a therapist and as a person is to treat the whole of my life—the manner in which I move, work, love and live—as art, as a creative process. Each act of creation is like a unit of inhalation and exhalation, an expression of the fullness of my life as well as the support for my liveliness. Each creation is the expressed, behavioral outcome of a multitude of images, fantasies, musings, and thoughts. It is a process of longing for more complete, sharper experiencing and expression.

And so it is in my work as a therapist. Each therapy session has an intrinsic flow and structure. It begins with simple, mutual sharings of awareness which are narrowed toward and distilled into a meaningful theme. The theme is then elaborated and still later transformed into a new concept or behavior. Participating in this process of transformation, even on the smallest scale, gives me great pleasure. A simple translation of a person's metaphor into a new concrete experience helps him reveal himself to himself. If a client lifts an ashtray and speaks of its simple, unpretentious beauty, I may ask him to imagine the ashtray as a mirror, to test out "simple" and "unpretentious" and "beautiful" as self descriptions. The unfolding process can be electrifying.

Each working unit becomes a forum for exploring life themes in an environment which is both congruent and challenging for the client, keeping him perking at his growing edge. Yet a work of art is never completed; it is brought to a ripeness which the creator cannot improve upon at any given moment. A poem can be rewritten a thousand times, each attempt a new way of experiencing the process of one's thoughts. The new words themselves modify one's experience, one's ideas, words, and images. Analogies and metaphors move fluidly into one another like the conversation of good friends. Each rewritten poem, like each unit of an ongoing relationship, has its own internal validity.

ASPECTS OF CREATIVE THERAPY

Therapy is a process of changing awareness and behavior. The sine qua non of the creative process is change: the transformation of one form into another, of a symbol into an insight, of a gesture into a new set of behaviors, of a dream into a dramatic enactment. Thus creativity and psychotherapy are interconnected at a fundamental level: transformation, metamorphosis, change.

Although this book primarily focuses on the therapist as an artist—a person who uses inventiveness to help people shape their lives—it is clear that any relationship between two people becomes a creation when their encounter has the flow and feel of mutual transformation. The therapist lends a structure, a form, a disciplined process to the formulations constantly generated by the relationship between himself and his client. The therapist creates an ambiance, a laboratory, a testing ground for the client's active exploration of himself as a living organism. This is the therapist's primary responsibility to his client.

It is out of the mutual richness of this experience, as well as the technical know-how of the therapist, that the threads of each life experience are given elegant development and substantive completion. Creative therapy is an encounter, a growth process, a problem-solving event, a special form of learning, and an exploration of the full range of our aspirations for metamorphosis and ascendance.

As A Loving Encounter

The making of art is intoxicating, one of the great joys of life. In the creative process, as in falling in love, we contact our sweetness, longing, powerful intention, and profound thoughtfulness. Arthur Rubinstein said, "Playing the piano is like making love, it fills me completely with joy."[*]

---

[*]from an interview by Barbara Walters on the NBC Today Show, 11 February 1975.

Authentic love for another is experienced as ecstacy in the very being of the other, as rejoicing in the loved one's existence. It is non-manipulative, non-clinging, non-demanding. We let the other be. We do not wish to violate his unique human integrity. The "purest" kind of love (pure, not in the puritanical sense of being clean, but in the sense of prerequisite clarity of rejoicing in the other's being) involves the total experience of the internal tension or energy which is part of one's responsiveness to the loved one.

Thus, we can speak of love as a kind of creative tension. "Staying with" this tension—letting it permeate one's whole being—is an enormously difficult task, particularly since our society has a tendency to sell canned pleasure for immediate satisfaction.

My love for the client is agapeic—more a feeling of good will toward humanity than a romantic, sentimental, or possessive love. I seek my client's good, whether I like him or not. Agape love for me is thoughtful, prudent, just, benevolent, gracious. The term "brotherly love" has been used in this sense. My own image is of "grandparently love." Unlike a parent who directs his children passionately and sometimes egoistically, my grandparent asks for nothing, yet takes pleasure in learning, observing, and understanding the life experience of another just as it is. When I experience my love passionately, as a parent, I am wary of losing my perspective and objectivity in clearly perceiving my client.

Agape love from the therapist engenders trust. Because the process often deals with the most vulnerable parts of the person, trust must always be there for both parties to allow the unfolding of their feelings. It is this "love" in all its forms which lubricates the creative process between client and therapist.

Yet one does not have to love someone to respectfully attend to that person. As Martin Buber put it, "One cannot command that one *feel* love for a person, but only that one deal lovingly with him."[*] And so must the therapist act lovingly with his client.

---

[*]Buber, Martin. *Ten Rungs: Hasidic Sayings.* New York: Schoken Books, 1962.

The experience of being loved is one of acute receptivity, of taking in the gift of another. It necessitates readiness to let the other person penetrate one's deepest stratum; it requires openness and lack of defensiveness and suspiciousness that the loving person will be injurious. In the experience of letting the other person love us, we willingly take the risk of being hurt. The fact that the loving other has the power to hurt (to reject) and chooses not to gives the experience a sense of magnetism.

When we feel totally loved by someone who really "matters," the ecstatic receptive experience makes us feel beautiful, perfect, graceful, profound, and wise.* Our deepest, most profound stirrings of self-appreciation, self-love, and self-knowledge surface in the presence of a person whom we experience as totally accepting. It is as though we say, "When I know your total acceptance, then I can show you my softest, most penetrable, delicate, beautiful, and vulnerable self."**

---

*Maslow, Abraham. *Toward a Psychology of Being.* Princeton, N.J.: D. Van Nostrand Company, Inc., 1962.
**Rogers, Carl. *On Becoming A Person.* Boston: Houghton Mifflin, 1961.

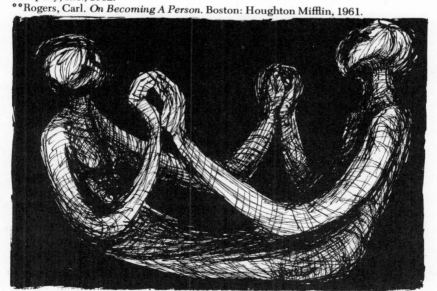

The experience of being loved is one of acute receptivity, of taking in the gift of another.

The clients' love for the therapist varies with their stages of development as well as with each person's specific life circumstances. Often a client projects ghosts of his past onto the therapist: I am seen as the critical or loving parent, the sadistic villain, the seducer, the teaser, the wise old man, the Christ-Rabbi, a sex object, a potential lover or spouse. As Freud pointed out long ago, psychotherapy is in some ways a working out of the patient's perception of the therapist.

At higher levels of development, the client can appreciate and love me in the same grandparently way in which I strive to experience him. At the most advanced levels of the relationship, both people take turns grandparenting; each uses his individual competence to enhance the life of the other. Said Martin Buber, "When a man is singing and cannot lift his voice, and another comes and sings with him, another who can lift his voice, the first will be able to lift his voice too. That is the secret of the bond between spirits."*

As A Growth Process

The creative process is therapeutic in itself because it allows us to express and examine the content and dimensions of our internal lives. We live full lives to the degree to which we find a full range of vehicles which concretize, symbolize, and otherwise give expression to our experiences.

The depth, duration, and extent of cultivating each medium of expression are the other significant factors in defining the fullness of life. I have known many people who have spread themselves so thin that their lives took on a shallow, translucent, and sadly contrived quality. In the frantic flight to touch all we can in life, we wind up feeling like harried tourists, snapping pictures of everything and seeing nothing.

We can either spread ourselves too thin or become too concentrated, looking for the universe under the lens of a microscope. In our age of specialization, there is great danger of leading a constricted life; we take comfort in our specialized

*Buber, Martin. *Ten Rungs: Hasidic Sayings.* New York: Schocken Books, 1962.

competence and righteously sink into a morass of narrowly
directed awareness. A life of limited exposure to the world
and its potential experiences has little possibility for creativity. Creativity is impatient with stasis of experience; it cannot
flourish in a meager sprinkling of topsoil.

Making art is a way of concretizing our need for a broader
and deeper range of living. In the process of creating, we
stretch our psyches, touching both personal and archetypal
aspects of our origins. The creation of art as a professional
activity and academic discipline, the development of mu-
seums, galleries and concert halls, and the narrow methodology of teaching the arts to young children have intimidated
people into thinking that art is an activity of the educated, the
sophisticated, the credentialed. Art-making as a playful, life-
supporting activity thus becomes the province of the professional. In his book, *Art and Alienation,* Herbert Read said,
'Common to both sophisticated and simple people is the assumption that whatever art may be, it is a specialized or professional activity of no direct concern for the average man."*

The act of creation is as basic a need as breathing or making
love. We are driven to create. We must take the risk of projecting the most idiosyncratic, personal imagery upon objects,
words, and other symbols—the same sort of risk we take in
loving another person.

As Problem-Solving

Every creative encounter is a search for and partial resolution of a "problem" in the broadest aesthetic meaning of that
term. If I make a red, round mass in the middle of a blank
canvas, and then want to make a painting beyond that initial
mass of color, I have a problem to solve. Where do I go next?
What color? What shape? How to balance or to make asymme-
try work for the painting? So it is with therapy, but a thousand
times more complex.

I want to share a particular experiment with you. Ron, an

*Read, Herbert. *Art and Alienation.* New York: World Publishing Company, 1963.

engineer in one of my groups in Florida, wants to work with me in the group. He is thin and delicate; his movements are very fine, almost fragile. I think about these things before he opens his mouth to say that he wants help in understanding a dream. I experience his recounting of the dream as a delaying action—the telling of it has no apparent energy for him. Why jump on a lifeless dream? I feel he is using the notion of the dream merely to initiate contact with me. As we work together, I visualize us on a journey in search of a problem, one which is perhaps at the center of Ron's concern.

I think about homosexuality, about the mother who flatters and wants to swallow her son, and about the father who is absent, reflective, crude or angry in the rocking chair. At the same time I am looking at the man before me. He is, in my estimate, a beautiful man. I like him. I have a fantasy of myself as his father—how I would love him and have fun with him if he were my son.

I do not share most of these thoughts and fantasies. I listen, I watch, I question:

> *Joseph:* Where is your energy now?
> *Ron:* In my face—it's hot and burning. I am afraid of what people will think of me, of making a fool of myself.
> *Joseph:* You sound like you fear "losing face."
> *Ron:* Yes, I do.

All of my previous thoughts are temporarily filed away—perhaps for use at a later time. I decide to work with Ron's face, thinking to myself that he always looks so serious, his face so controlled, mask-like. I suggest an experiment: "Could you 'lean into' losing your face by contorting it? Could you literally 'give up' your face by making faces at other people?"

Ron agrees to the experiment, and once he lets go a bit, he is masterful at making faces—especially at the women. After making faces some more, he reports, "I feel better, more relaxed, not as afraid of what people will think."

Now my formulations about Ron are coming into focus, and

I continue working with his face and the notion of taking women in through his face. He tries to take one woman in through his eyes, partially succeeds, and feels wonderful about his efforts. Later Ron tells the group about his mother, his anger with her, his fear of her, and his inability to look fully into her face. The experiment began with Ron's facial immobility and lack of expression, moved to his remoteness from members of the group, and finally led to his lack of direct expression of anger toward women.

Ron's problem was multifaceted; working toward its solution involved trying to understand different levels of his awareness, as well as making a whole range of choices about what to say and do in response to Ron during the course of our work. Table 1 shows how I conceptualized the dynamics of Ron's inner life and then attempted to create a situation in which he could concretely experiment with modifying his own behavior. This process involved three overlapping, and at times simultaneous, steps: 1) following the nature of Ron's immediate experience; 2) making silent, theoretical formulations about him, and 3) inventing some ways in which he could permit himself to concretely explore his relationship to women (and men, too).

The therapist's "problem" is to establish an adequate cognitive map which includes the client's experience of himself and then to point to action steps to make the solution possible for the client. Like a good guide, the therapist must know the lay of the land so his path will take the person where he wants to go—at the time he is ready to go there.

As Tao Learning

Tao learning takes place when an individual experiences his own force of movement and exploratory possibilities. Unlike deficit learning,* which takes place on a verbal-concep-

---

*I am thinking of learning which is motivated by needs for survival, security, and other basic human wants, rather than by higher level, self-actualization needs. For more information in this area, read the works of Abraham Maslow listed in the bibliography.

TABLE 1
Formulation of Ron's Dynamics and
Development of Experiments

Observations of Ron
his delicate, almost fragile movements;
his manner of telling the dream as if it were a precious jewel.
↓
My Personal Fantasies
I want to father Ron—he is my beautiful son;
a feeling that my gentleness with him is a novel experience for him.
↓
Ron's Theme—"Losing Face"
his burning face and lack of facial expression;
his concern about what others might think of him.
↓
My Inner Formulations
his father is coarse and his mother wants to control, to swallow him;
his consequent discomfort with women.
↓
Development of Experiments
"making faces"—especially at women;
taking women in with his own face.
↓
Outcomes
more comfort and confidence with women;
expression of anger and freeing of energy.

tual level, Tao learning is initiated by the individual who then moves gracefully from one minute step in his process to the next. This step-by-step movement of imagery, muscular tension, verbalization, and release gives the person an awareness of the ongoing creation of his own destiny. He gradually begins to value his process for its own sake, *as process,* rather than bypassing the scenes on his way to a puzzling and unclear goal—one which is often experienced as belonging to "them," to the other, to the parent or therapist.

It is important that a person learn to value and enjoy his fluidity within the movement and trajectory of his growth; it is also important that he experience the therapist (or teacher) as his lubricant, rather than his source of knowledge. Many months of valuable time are wasted when therapist and client collude to make the therapist the source of knowledge and the client a pseudo child-cripple in need of a wise man's answers.

It takes immaculate discipline (and joyful curiosity) on the part of the therapist to stay with another person's process, to forego prematurely "pinching" it off with half-formed statements of explanation or clarification. These premature moves generally come from the therapist's own anxiety to justify his role as helper and sage; they do not come from respect for the aesthetic nature of the client as a unique individual moving through time and space in a valid pathway. When the therapist can lean into this sort of aesthetic appreciation, he is a naturalist—a lover of human nature.

Enabling the process to unfold does not deprive one of potency. The therapist is always there pushing, prodding, enjoying, laughing, and flowing in a sense of wonderment and fascination. This stance gives one the freedom to be a learner and to play with hypotheses, rather than becoming fixed in stale eternal truths and routine self-righteousness.

As Projection

Creative projection involves a dialogue with the self which is then concretized into a concept, a painting, a sculpture, or a behavior. We created God, Christ, Buddha, heaven and hell out of our most profound projections. Our holy places are manifestations of man's inner struggle for transcendent metamorphosis. It is no surprise that during the Renaissance a symbiotic relationship existed between artist and church.

Every person is pregnant with projections, yet fearful of the frightening delight of fully expressing them. Making music, sculpture, pictures, or creating change in another's or one's own life is taking the risk of releasing one's self, one's heart and soul, into the world.

Every person is pregnant with projections, yet fearful of the frightening delight of fully expressing them.

Projection is a form of escapism. It is easy to relinquish ownership of one's talents, one's color, one's prejudices— most anything that appears unpleasant or that we have learned to distrust or dislike in ourselves. Commonly we look out into the world as the perpetrator of these qualities, rather than looking inward to develop insight into their nature in ourselves. In pathological projection, the impotent person colors the world castrating, the angry person colors it destructive, the cruel person colors it sadistic, the person who fears his homosexuality sees a world of marching faggots. Every person colors the world with his inner life. The disturbed inner life searches for and locates nightmares, even if it must hallucinate them.

The difference between the pathological projections we so fear and the creative projections of Michelangelo, Shakespeare, and Bach is the creator's relation to and power over the environment. Psychotherapy allows an individual to dialogue with and take ownership of frightening projections, turning them around into creative ones.

Projection becomes creative in three steps. First, the individual learns to own what he fears in the world, e.g., "I am frightened of my cruelty." Second, he begins a dialogue between his cruelty and his gentleness or some other polarity within himself:

Cruelty: Animals are animals. They don't feel the pain of a bullet the way *we* do.
Gentleness: But I am an animal, too. I am made of flesh and blood, too. And I feel pain.

In this way, the person establishes friendliness with all the polarized forces within himself and begins to experience his wholeness.

Finally, the person transforms his dilemma into a concrete product or act. He writes a play or joins a political movement or paints a picture in which the subject of cruelty is being investigated, coped with, understood with a sense of full awareness. In the process, he may, for example, become deeply aware of man's fundamental goodness as well as his actual evil acts. The creative projector harnesses the energy of his conflict in the service of a deeper understanding of self and a more active relation to his fellow human beings. The pathological projectionist's energy is tied up in his conflict. He cannot act.

Creative therapy does not excise conflicts the way a surgeon removes a tumor. It allows the person to contact the energy which is frozen in conflict and to make it available for self-actualization and the actualization of humankind.

As A Transcendent/Religious Experience

Art is prayer—not the vulgarized notations handed down to us in the scriptures, but a fresh, vital discovery of one's own special presence in the world. Marc Chagall was once asked if he attended a synagogue; he answered that his work is prayer.*

In the process of making anything, a person not only illuminates and illustrates his inner life, but moves beyond personal expression to make something which stands by itself. The work acquires its own internal validity, its own integrity. It is in this process of making something which stands on its own integral structure that the creator contacts a concrete reality outside his subjective life and moves into the realm of the transcendent. In touching and letting go of his product, the creator touches and lets go of his personal identity.

This process is the same when a person becomes the art medium. It is not easy to stay in touch with another person, to give one's attention to another person's awareness without deflecting from that process by talking about oneself. I don't mean that we should leave ourselves behind, but that we appreciate the other person with all of our inner resources. This process of fully engaging oneself with another without losing one's sense of identity, without losing one's boundaries, can be a profoundly moving experience. Quite aside from making

*McMullen, Roy. *The World of Marc Chagall.* New York: Doubleday, 1968.

a direct impact on another person's behavior, being fully present for each other in a given hour or two is like worshiping together.

> When I experience the other fully, acceptingly,
> when I experience the flow of his feeling,
> the beauty of movement, of expression, of longing,
> then I know the meaning of reverence, holiness,
> and the presence of God.

It is an interesting paradox that we discover our most important inner ecstacies in the process of moving beyond ourselves into other lives. It is only after such an intimate transaction with another human being that we can enter into more ascending, religious transactions. To speak with God one must first give up one's narcissism, and to give up one's narcissism one must enter into an authentic dialogue with a fellow human being: To speak with God one must speak with humankind.

In the realm of psychotherapy, one begins with this kind of relation to one's client. Even if I do nothing more than be a real presence for someone, I at least affirm the other person's experiential validity. This affirmation is "therapeutic," not only because the person grows to appreciate his intrinsic nature, but also because he develops the courage to push against his boundaries and test new behaviors.

GESTALT AS CREATIVE THERAPY

"People-making," as Virginia Satir calls therapy, has the same quality as making music or painting pictures. Creative therapy treats a person as an art medium—sometimes discouraging, jarring, stubborn, boring or abrasive, and often humbling and inspiring. The creative therapist sees the client in his completeness: his plasticity and rigidity, brilliance and dullness, fluidity and stasis, cognitive punctuality and passion. The creative therapist is a choreographer, historian,

phenomenologist, a student of the body, a dramatist, a
thinker, a theologian, a visionary.

Gestalt therapy is really permission to be creative. Our
basic methodological tool is the experiment, a behaviorist approach to moving into novel functioning. The experiment
moves to the heart of resistance, transforming rigidity into an
elastic support system for the person. It does not have to be
heavy, serious, or even precisely fitting; it can be theatrical,
hilarious, crazy, transcendent, metaphysical, humorous. The
experiment gives us permission to be priest, whore, faggot,
holy man, wise witch, magician—all the things, beings, and
notions hidden within us. Experiments don't have to grow out
of concepts; they may move from simple playfulness into profound conceptual revelations.

In my work I always begin with what exists for the person
(or the group) rather than with some arbitrary notion of what
should be there. I try to understand and feel—to psychologically gargle—the other person's mode of being in the world.
Like a sculptor attending to the odor, shape, and grain of the
wood he carves, I try to stay with the configurations of the
other person's experience. Even though I respect the validity
of his experience, I am tempted to whet his appetite toward a
formulation of new visual or cognitive or motoric perspec-
tives of himself. The new perspective or dimension does not
have to be dramatic; it merely needs to move the existing
system into a slightly fresher view of itself.

For example, a woman says she feels childlike. Upon ques-
tioning, she explains some of the ways in which she knows
about her childlike nature. I then ask her to act out her childlike behavior with me or with the group. The reason I ask this
is that, usually, she only has a conceptual notion of what
"childlike" means, and she needs a more expansive view of all
that "childlike" implies for her.

I also ask her to do something which is anchored in her own
immediate experience, to her view of herself right now. I start
with the surface acceptance of the woman's experience of her
"child." It is a given. I don't try to persuade her that it isn't so;
rather, as the work develops and she begins to feel a sense of

readiness, we can move into more resistant aspects of herself —parts which were originally difficult to bring into awareness or share with others.

The implications and possible outcomes of such a simple experiment are enormous. They involve exaggeration of one polarity of the self, observations of posture, language, voice quality, and breathing, as well as the therapist's silent, theoretical formulations about, let's say, the undeveloped adult behavior or experience of this particular person. So this little experiment is only the beginning of work—a mere behavioral extension of the words presented to the therapist at that moment.

Experimentation is powerfully effective in groups as well, because it is supported by the varied creativeness of a total community. No one person gets depleted and everyone is nourished. In one group I worked with, experimentation made it possible to transform a simple Christmas carol into what felt like a Bachian choral work. Its immediate impact was not even clearly appreciated by the therapist-participants, but somehow we knew we had created something beautiful and transcendent of our own personal limitations.

Gestalt therapy is permission to be exuberant, to have gladness, to play with the nicest possibilities for ourselves within our short lives. For me it stands for all that is in front of me, for all that promises completeness of experiencing, for the things to come which are awesome, frightening, tearful, moving, unfamiliar, archetypal, growthful. For me it means the full embrace of life—the savouring of all its subtle tastes.

If Fritz Perls were alive today, he would be disappointed to see a multitude of therapists parroting his work as if it were the last word in psychotherapy. What many of us didn't have the courage to learn from him was his sense of inventiveness, his way of creating dramatic learning in the human situation. For Fritz, the Gestalt constructs of the "hot seat" or the "top-dog/under-dog" were momentary insights to be explored, then moved aside so that other experiments and metaphors could take their place.

If Gestalt therapy is to survive, it must stand for this kind of integrative growth process and creative generosity; it must keep intertwining discoveries about our musculature, our archetypal origins, and our primal screams into novel conceptions. If we, the teachers of the craft, forget this basic principle of creative experimentation, of evolving novel concepts out of our own sense of daring, of being unabashedly bold, then Gestalt therapy will die with the rest of the contemporary therapeutic fads.

Chapter 2

The Creative Leap

Creative process in psychotherapy has basically two elements. The first is the therapist's relationship with the client's existing integrity. Every person enters therapy with a unique personal integrity. This means that he has developed, over a span of many years, modes of moving in the world which have structural and functional unity for him. This unity also includes his "symptoms," complaints and behaviors which, in the therapist's view, hamper the client's capacity to change. This whole bundle of feelings, physical stances, and verbal styles comprise the person's integrity, and he comes to a group or into individual therapy not so much to change this sense of being himself as to exercise it.

Establishing contact with this integrity involves using one's whole being in a study of "what it is like to be a person like this"—to bend one's shoulders, tighten one's ass—to get into the client's posture of being in the world. This is a kind of loving curiosity, a lively state of naturalistically learning the other's life space.

The second element in the creative process is revolutionary molding. Here, the therapist identifies with the most radical aspects of his client's personality, that part of him which is waiting for permission to experiment with novel or truly startling ways of experiencing himself.

The client is constantly experiencing the existential dilemma of being torn between the painful comfort of his existing integrity and his need to change. Generally, creative process is hampered when client and therapist unwittingly identify with the separate parts of the client's personality: The therapist begs for change and the client fights for his "integrity." In this collusion, the "revolutionary" in the client is projected onto the therapist, and the client then conveniently "fights" with his own projection.

In the creative process, the therapist enables the patient to join with him in an adventure in which the pair can constantly play all parts of this conflict drama. The therapist helps the client to be the experimenter, the teacher, the active modifier, while maintaining an attitude of understanding and respect for his client's existing stance. It is in this process of rhythmic sharing and active exploration of the client's inner life that his original personal structure begins to change.

GROUNDWORK

I am fond of saying to my students, "Look at the person the way you would look at a sunset or at mountains. Take in what you see with pleasure. Take in the person for his own sake. After all, you would do that with the sunset also. Chances are you wouldn't say, 'This sunset should be more purple' or 'These mountains should be taller in the center.' You would simply gaze with wonder." So it is with another person. I look without saying, "His skin should be more pink" or "His hair should be cut shorter." The person is.

The creative process begins with one's appreciation of what is there—the essence, the clarity, and the impact of what is around us. I would like to approach people the way Henry David Thoreau saw and understood nature: "The brilliant autumnal colors are red and yellow and the various tints, hues and shades of these. Blue is reserved to be the color of the sky, but yellow and red are the colors of the earth-flower. Every fruit, on ripening, and just before its fall, acquires a bright tint. So do the leaves; so the sky before the end of the day . . ."*

The therapist, like the poet, is able to appreciate the full scope of life around him, including the landscape of his patient's existence, his physical being, his grimaces, gait and walk. In order to help someone, you must love him in a basic, simple way. You must love the person who is before you and not a goal you set for him. You cannot love future images of the other without absenting yourself from the person sitting in front of you.

Valuing the Process

I go up to my studio to paint. I get up there and realize I don't *feel* like painting. So I putter around. I clean brushes, or prime canvases, or look at pictures in magazines. I do the things that are possible for me at that moment and allow myself room to build my imagery and excitement until I become ready to make something. It may only be a paper cutout, but it is just what I am ready to do at this point in my creative process.**

One cannot "push the river" to make art. And so it is with me as a therapist. The client must be taken through a graded series of experiences before he is ready to grasp a new notion of himself and to behaviorally move in that direction. You can order the client to do things for you, and he may even cooperate, but if the process of building readiness has not occurred, nothing significant happens—other than perhaps getting into an argument, or feeling flat, or feeling that we are not, somehow, communicating with each other. Much of therapy consists of stoking the fire, nurturing a particular theme, building support in areas of verbalization or action where support is

---

*Quoted in Porter, Eliot. *In the Wilderness is the Preservation of the World.* San Francisco: Sierra-Ballantine, 1962.

**For more information on priming the creative process, I suggest you read *Creative Person and Creative Process* by Frank Baron (New York: Holt, Rinehart & Winston, 1969) and *The Act of Creation* by Arthur Koestler (New York: Dell, 1964).

needed. It is like priming the canvas and cleaning the brushes.

Another part of the process in psychotherapy is that of staying open to the myriad possibilities available to the person or group. Every new hypothesis or exchange or experiment should be considered an exploration, a possibility which, if it "catches fire" for the person, will be taken further and further to the deepest layers of the personality.

Although I may envision two or three hypothetical outcomes somewhere out there, I cannot squeeze these outcomes from my client. I must be willing to count every shrub and pebble on the road before I get to the color and excitement of the city. When the person reaches resolution at the end of such a respectful journey, the insight and satisfaction are whole and obvious to him, his group, and his therapist. It takes time to be reborn. It takes patience to be a good midwife.

Generating and Transforming Energy Systems

Psychotherapy is a lively process of stoking the client's inner fires of awareness and contact. It involves exchanges of energy with the client—exchanges which stimulate and nourish the other person but do not deplete one's own vitality and power.

In order for a person to "work" in therapy and, consequently, to change, he needs energy. Generally, he has enough energy to come to my office or to a weekend group, but that does not guarantee that he has the energy to work on himself. Often his energy is locked in the muscular (or systemic) frigidity of his character structure, or, as most people like to see it, in his "resistances." Actually, there is no functional or structural difference between character frozenness and resistance. A resistance is what the therapist experiences. The client is merely the person he thinks himself to be; his experience is that of taking care of himself.

So the person's energy and the focal point of that energy may not be in his awareness, or it may be experienced in a negative way—e.g., being aware of stiffness in one's knees or pain in one's chest.

The therapist's job is to locate, mobilize and modify this energy in the service of new, more adaptive, more fluid behavior. In my work with student therapists, I have found that it is very important to teach them to use their eyes and hands in order to locate where the client's energy is perking, and also where energy is blocked. These two phenomena may often occur within the same person at the same time. For example, a person may experience a great deal of liveliness in his upper chest, but may feel blocked in his pelvis, or the person may feel a great deal of fluidity in his pelvis and a mask-like frozenness in his face.

In an exercise I do with student therapists, I divide them into pairs and have each person silently observe the other for both lively and blocked areas of invested energy. The investigator is urged to get up and walk around the person or ask him to move in particular ways in order to use his fullest powers of observation. He may even tactually check out certain muscle groups in order to see if his visual experience is congruent with what the person feels like. I encourage the student therapist to really get into his boldness and his grandness, to assume he can see and feel much more than he has allowed himself to in the past. Following the observation period, the student therapist is asked to write down his observations, and then to ask exploratory questions regarding the other person's awareness of his body, where he feels the liveliness of energy flowing within him, and where he feels dammed up or frozen or blocked.

Although there is the problem of time lag between observation and inquiry, the therapist gets an opportunity to explore and test his capacity for locating and evaluating energy systems. The exercise gives the student confirmation of his capacity to see, and I have often been surprised by the enormous sensitivity and visual power the therapist can exercise in just watching the ways in which a person is breathing or the way in which he stiffly articulates the muscles in his face. Once feedback from the client-learner is forthcoming, there is a lively exchange of feelings and ideas about his inner experience; at this point work can begin.

The second part of the exercise involves "warming up" the musculature in which energy is blocked in preparation for its expression in the therapy session. This may be done either by asking the client-learner to rub parts of his body or by the use of a hot towel or heating pad.

The next stage of work in this exercise is crucial, for it asks the client-learner to become aware of flashes of memory or feelings which may be involved in a particular part of his body. Such feelings may be facilitated by asking the person to exhale into that part of the body which feels stiff or frozen, or by physical movement of the body part.

Image or feeling is tranformed into vocalization, screaming, walking, running, jumping, arching the back, bending, pounding pillows, or some of the classic stress positions developed by Alexander Lowen, in which the individual becomes aware of the amount of energy vibrating within his body. The process is that of changing tension systems into clear, fluid actions.*

Students are also taught how to work with resistances to such contactful, muscular movement. Work with resistance is a central part of all dynamic therapies, and the student is taught to feel friendly with resistance, rather than frustrated by the person's lack of cooperation. Resistances arise naturally at many aspects of this exercise, and I encourage the client to flow with the resistance, to lean into it, to exaggerate it. Exaggeration of tension states in the joints, pelvis, or anus, for example, usually leads to a fuller positive expression of movement in those parts of the body.**

Finally, the client-learner is allowed to rest and be physically comforted. If he has been pounding a pillow and using his back in a whip-like motion, a hot towel may be placed on this area to give him comfort, avoid future development of

---

*Lowen, A. *The Betrayal of the Body.* London: Collier Books, 1967.
**This work is technically known as the "undoing of retroflections." In retroflection, the person tightens a part of himself, rather than using that part to express a feeling in the direction of other people.

muscular stiffness, and to facilitate a close feeling between the therapist and client as partners in a creative venture. The hot towel is also a positive reinforcer for the client's efforts to be fully in touch with his energy, excitement, and physical expression.

Much of therapy relies on verbal exchange, yet often there is little energy in the client's verbalizations; they have become habit tapes, well-rehearsed and impenetrable. The therapist often falls into the trap of exchanging energy-depleting, sterile words with the client, with a resulting sense of heaviness and even depression for both therapist and client. The client does what is easiest for him, but the therapist can't afford this luxury, simply because he becomes more and more removed from the client's liveliness—where the action really is within the arena of therapeutic change.

I am talking with Betty. She feels flat and immobilized. She feels she cannot survive in this competitive world. She goes on and on. I am beginning to feel drained. My energy depletion tells me that Betty's energy system is frozen and she is sucking sustenance from me. At this point I stop listening to her words and watch her body. Her arms and legs look bloated and stiff. When I bring her attention to her body she says, "I feel tight in my legs and my arms."

At this point I ask her to imagine what she could do with her sensations—how she could use the muscles which are stiff. She relates an image of running and I ask her to close her eyes, go back in her life and visualize that experience. The following story emerges: Betty is ten years old. She is in camp and there is a running contest. Everyone in her tent believes that she will be the winner for her tent. She feels increasingly pressured and frightened of failure, and in the end she loses the contest for her tent.

After telling the story, Betty begins to get in touch with her anger at the kids in camp for pressuring and pushing her. I ask her to see if she can use her arms and legs (where the energy is frozen) to let out the anger on some large pillows. Betty is flying high at this point, ready to express her anger: She kicks and punches the pillows repeatedly; her voice strengthens as she yells at the kids. She returns to her chair breathing heavily: "I feel so loose and strong. I feel like I can go out there and do what I need to do for myself. I am not going to let people step on me."

Betty's frozen energy was freed up and mobilized in the service of adaptation, behavioral flow, and a general sense of well-being. My reward was not only getting her off her stuckness, but that I, myself, felt more enlivened and less drained.

If energy is nowhere to be located in a person, then it can be "pumped up." In another case, I asked a client to run in circles in my room. He said it was silly, so I offered to run with him. We ran together for what seemed like ten minutes, until I fell back exhausted in my chair. But my client was revivified and proceeded to work on a serious problem involving his sexuality. Apparently, the running had stimulated sexual sensations in him and sexual anxieties as well.

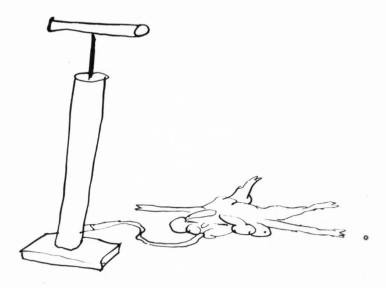

If energy is nowhere to be located in the person, then it can be "pumped up."

°Ungerer, Tomi, *The Underground Sketchbook of Tomi Ungerer,* Dover Publications, New York, 1964.

One needs "juice" to make creations, and if the juice is not in the person's feelings or language, then it is surely somewhere in his body. The recovery of body energy feeds the person's spirit and puts color into the content of his language.*

REVOLUTIONARY MOLDING

The beauty of Gestalt therapy is that it allows me to be true to what is there for the client and, at the same time, permits me to translate my hunches into experimental acts. At best, these experiments have the possibility of breaking through existing character patterns, and at worst, they fall flat or backfire.

Under proper conditions, one is able to jump into an experiment without lengthy preparation. It is as if one feels a "soft spot" in the person's system which can be permeated directly. Yet, one must have a good feeling for (and with) the client or group in order to jump the gun and ask them to do or think something brand new. One should have some sense of good taste, or perhaps one might call it the sense of the acceptable aesthetic in the particular system within which one finds oneself. Asking the person a coarse or ugly question, or an insensitive one, may not only be tasteless, but puts one in a position of bullying, bulldozing, and insulting the other; then the therapist must deal with unnecessary conflicts of his own making.

The creative leap is the culmination of one's clinical hunches and outrageous inventiveness. For example, at one point in my work with Ron,** I said to him, "Tell me about your hate for your mother." Although I had a sense that he "had to" have difficulty with this woman, nowhere in the previous work had we discussed this, nor did I prepare him for it. I was ready to be told that I was full of beans. But I was also ready to respond to Ron's heightened feelings—his shar-

---

*For further reading on retroflection, I suggest *Gestalt Therapy Integrated* by Erving and Miriam Polster (New York: Brunner/Mazel, 1973).

**The beginning portion of my work with Ron was described in Chapter 1.

ing of blocked anger with his mother by stiffening his face toward her and, indeed, toward everyone else. It was a chance to take. I was hesitant and yet excited at the same time as I allowed these words to slip out of me. This time it worked in the right direction and as a result we moved into a series of experiments which resulted in important revelations for Ron.

One experiment of looking at a woman and trying to take her in through the eyes and mouth was a behavioral extension of the initial thrust of new energy in Ron:

> *Joseph:* Ron, look at Bev and try to relax your whole body while you are looking.
> *Ron:* Bev, do you mind my experimenting on you?
> *Bev:* It's OK with me. I am kind of enjoying it so far.
> *Ron:* (To Joseph) I am feeling tight in my stomach . . . queezy.
> *Joseph:* Having trouble swallowing what you see?
> *Ron:* I didn't think of looking that way.
> *Joseph:* Keep looking at Bev and take in only what pleases your eyes. You don't have to swallow everything you see. Be in control of your own seeing.
>   (Long pause while Ron looks.)
> *Ron:* I am beginning to feel more comfortable looking at you, Bev.
> *Bev:* That's good, 'cause I was beginning to feel nervous . . . like an object in a museum.
> *Joseph:* Ron, did you look at her that way? Tell Bev.
> *Ron:* (To Bev) Well, at first I sort of looked at you objectively and critically. Maybe that's what you felt. I looked at you the way my mother might look at me. "The blouse doesn't go with the color of that skirt," I said to myself. Now I am not doing that.
> *Joseph:* Perhaps you could share with Bev how you are taking her in now?
>   (Long pause)
> *Ron:* (To Bev) I am looking at you as if there is more softness in my eyes. You have a lovely figure. I like your eyes very much; they seem so dark and so deep.

> I can tune in to the taste of you—as if I can taste you. I
> imagine you to taste like honey, but with a hint of
> tartness. A very pleasant sensation, indeed. I am glad
> I stayed with looking at you. I want to try this with
> Shirley next.

This experiment was a creative leap from Ron's merely dis-
cussing his mother to an active encounter with a living, breathing woman in the group.

Creative process exists in a balance between the experiential base of what is there on the one hand, and behavioral
jumping to strange territories on the other. The creative leap
breaks the rules of constantly staying with the process. To do
it well, one must take chances and be prepared to momentar-
ily fail, shift gears and move on to something else that seems
to work better, or shift to that which the client finds more
palatable.

Innovation often calls for the breaking of rules. One must,
after all, attend to and respect one's own inventiveness and
intellectual "jumps," as well as one's capacity to shape the
ongoing action. It is this aspect of psychotherapy that keeps
me most enlivened. This jumping over possible objections
and resistances is one defining characteristic of the creative
process in all areas of living and working, not just in Gestalt
therapy.

Context and Metaphor

A man says he has a problem with his son, so I think of him
as a teacher, a babysitter, an animal with a litter; I think of
him as a child. Maybe I should have him behave as if he is the
troublesome child he describes and see what happens, because I already know that his context, his metaphor, and his
literal, nonplayful approach do not work. That is why he is
asking for my help.

So he plays like the kid that keeps doing "bad" things to
attract attention. Then he says, "Dad, I want you to take me

with you on your next trip." He realizes, with this statement, that on one level he has not *heard* his son before, and is neglecting the inner voice of his own child on another level. The new metaphor in which the man is himself a child turns out to be more helpful than I had originally expected, because he begins to understand his son's isolation and loneliness and anger.

I did not start out with an answer for this man; I just played with a new way of experiencing his particular dilemma. There is no magic in it—just a kind of emotively intellectual boldness that puts the data on a different conceptual channel and allows the person to examine it afresh.

Someone is telling me a very serious story and his face is a mask, or his voice is whiny, or he is hunched over, or he is not breathing, or he is sweating like hell in an air conditioned room, and so on and on. As long as I can be there, listening to my own songs, seeing my own hallucinations, inventing my own peculiar humor without falling into the other person's limited view of the situation, then I stay alive and he has a chance of coming to life by moving into a new channel of himself, by seeing himself in a brand new mirror.* One must be free from attachment to the client's perspective or the material he produces so that one's awareness can become illuminated.**

In order to make new metaphors, one must also be free from attachment to one's own needs: needs that limit one's intellectual scope, needs for success, approval, or sexual satisfaction. In order to invent new contexts for the other person, I must learn to listen to him without wanting, to touch without desiring, to love without squeezing, to gaze without becoming overly pedantic. It is this inner freedom which enhances the creation of yet unexplored experiential channels for my client, for myself, and for both of us as we encounter each other.

In short, the process of Gestalt therapy is not only the continuous invention of new models of seeing oneself. It is also a continuous behavioral testing of these innovative models in the safety of a creatively permissive environment.

*Gordon, W. *Synectics*. New York: Collier Books, 1961.
**Ram Dass. *The Only Dance There Is*. New York: Anchor Books, 1974.

Novel Integrations

Another part of the creative process in Gestalt therapy is the integration of polarities within the client's personality.* We often identify ourselves with one characteristic and not its counterpart, e.g., I see myself as peaceful and not aggressive, or stingy and not generous, or honest and not devious.

It is simple enough to question the client's view of himself or challenge and stimulate his thinking in another direction. These verbal exchanges lay the cognitive ground for changes in the person's restrictive self-concept. But they need to be reinforced and driven home by experiments. The experiment not only offers an exaggeration of the person's polarized behavior; more importantly, it makes for creative integration of his polarities and for greater wholeness of experience and expression.

After many months of therapy, Katherine Miller, a professional singer, confesses to me that she has not been able to achieve an orgasm during the seven years of her marriage. I begin to fantasize about the orgiastic feelings she must get when she sings as a soloist with a large chorus and full symphony orchestra. After a tentative inquiry, she volunteers to sing for me, and for a number of sessions we work on her body awareness while she sings. In the process, she discovers enormously intense feelings in her abdomen and vagina while singing. I then suggest that, as she sings for me, she close her eyes and visualize having intercourse with her husband. She feels embarrassed, so I volunteer to turn around. This makes the experiment more comfortable for her, and she proceeds. At the end of the session, she informs me, "I almost came while singing today and thinking about John." Several months later, John and Katherine Miller came to a session with a bottle of wine to celebrate Katherine's first orgasmic experience during intercourse.

In another case of integration the client is a priest. He doesn't want to be called "Father" because, he says, "It makes

---

*For more information about polarities in Gestalt therapy, I suggest a paper by Rainette Fantz entitled, "Polarities: Differentiation and Integration" (Gestalt Institute of Cleveland, 1973).

me feel impotent. It makes me feel like I have no balls." So I ask him to bless everyone in the group with his right hand, while he holds his crotch with his left. As he begins to get into his potency, his blessings become more and more inspired and beautiful; with each person the blessing develops more sensitivity, giving recognition to the other person's area of need. The priest becomes lively; there is more color in his face. The blessings are like spiritual explosions, and as he nears the last person, I notice several people are weeping.

What seemed like a crude and vulgar suggestion turned into a deeply insightful experience for this lovely man. As he finished the experiment there was a long silence in the group. He looked around, gazing warmly into our faces: "I think I would not mind if you called me 'Father' from time to time."

Resistance: Stability Versus Change

All movement engenders resistance. Since experience is in constant flux, it too takes place against an inner resistance. This inner resistance of mine I experience as a reluctance to change my own ways of doing things, of behaving as I typically do in daily life. I take comfort in the me that has constancy. I also take comfort in my flow, but this change needs to move at a rate which is safe and clearly lubricated for me, a change which enhances the experienced me.

Resistance is a term that connotes an external observation of my state of reluctance. Although I may be observed to resist some behavior, idea or attitude, my own experience is that I am acting to preserve, maintain, and enhance my self, my integrity. And what appears to you, on your observing surface, as a casual reluctance to change may be an inner crisis for me, a fight for my life. This is the phenomenological definition of resistance, a definition which stresses the validity of my inner experience, my inner life.

A few comments at the level of "plumbing" may be helpful here. My process of being and experiencing is constantly colored by my needs, their frustration and satisfaction. As a complex and yet easily programmed organism, I can learn to block my own need satisfaction. This blocking can occur at every level of the ingesting and assimilating process including my sensory inputs, glands and other internal organs, muscles, and various other vital, supportive functions like respiration. Blocking also occurs on the cortical level in the form of ruminations, obsessions, repetitive stereotyped thoughts, ad infinitum. This is a form of fixation. Fixation blocks the continuous development of the organism.

All pathology may be understood as an extensive, chronic interruption of the process by which the person moves to fulfill his full range of needs. The person is not robbed of his integrity; his integrity or his experiencing changes to accommodate this halted state of affairs, a condition which Kurt Goldstein described beautifully.* Crippled behavior has its own special characteristics, and what appears "sick" to us is a state of accommodation to blockage in the other person. I develop a stiff muscle in my neck. Quite naturally I find myself holding my neck rigid to lessen the pain, with the rest of my body accommodating itself to my neck. I walk stiffly in the street and someone perceives me as walking like a zombie, but I know that as long as I walk this way I am relatively free of discomfort.

Even though the person is complex, his neurons and other cells are discrete, finite. To the degree to which I am manipulable, conditionable, and capable of relatively permanent storage of information, I have a tendency to retain my own functional stability: I perpetuate my way of functioning.

All human processes include polar forces. For example, all fluid movement involves intricate cooperation of opposing muscle groups. If it were not so, a person would become gelatinous or frozen and incapable of highly differentiated activity. One of the central polarities of our existence is that of stability versus change, the need to know versus the fear of knowing. Whether we like it or not, we are habit-bound and behaviorally repetitive beings. We are constantly struggling to improve

---

*Goldstein, K. *The Organism.* Boston: Beacon Press, 1963.

our lot and modify our future. Much of our energy is used up in the tension between these two forces. And any therapy which intends to modify behavior must deal with these polar phenomena as being in the foreground of behavior. It stands to reason, therefore, that whether we deal with the "cooperative" or the "resisting" sides of the person, we have a tendency to move toward his motivational center. All parts and forces in the person are integrally connected, and each minute aspect leads us toward a fuller sense of the whole person.

                ✿   ✿   ✿   ✿   ✿

The creative therapist, as I see him, is a lover of nature. He feasts himself on everything around him—like a sensitive novelist he relishes and tastes the other person's hoarse voice, his structured language, his curly, unwashed hair, his way of leaning forward when he is excited.

He should gaze at the client rather than stare at him, taking him apart. With childlike wonderment, he can gaze at the chair he sits in, the paintings on the wall; he can reach down and fondle the thick green carpeting on the floor. Everything has aesthetic value. There is goodness even in "ugly" things.

A naturalistic outlook gives one freedom to take in the person's experience without evaluating or judging him. In this context the therapist experiences the "symptoms" the client tells about as ways in which he takes care of himself in his world.

One must have patience. The creative therapist can appreciate the process of his ongoing experience without "pushing" the river. He can attend to the small and seemingly insignificant units of his experience. From these emerge novel constructs and special visions of his world.

Chapter 3

The Creative Stance

> What a piece of work is a man, how
> noble in reason, how infinite in
> faculties, in form and moving, how
> express and admirable in action,
> how like an angel in apprehension,
> how like a god: the beauty of the
> world, the paragon of animals.*

For me, doing therapy is like making art. The medium is a human life. Whether admitted or not, the effective therapist shapes lives. Too often the therapist is not honest about his powerful influence on others and unwilling to take responsibility for his behavior.

Every human life has an integrity of its own. A human being is already a dynamic work of art when he invites another person, a therapist, to insert himself into his integrity— to affect it in some meaningful way. One must learn to maintain one's strength and technical skill as a therapist without losing respect for the other person. The therapist cannot afford to be carried away by his power over others any more

---

*Shakespeare, William. *Hamlet* (Act II). Edited by Cyrus Hoy. New York: W. W. Norton & Co., 1963, p. 35.

than he can afford to abdicate that power. Working with human lives is a privilege and must be approached with the knowledge, respect, and humility it is due.

The creative therapist provides the milieu, the thick, rich atmosphere within which a person's integrity can become more fully realized. As Maslow put it: "Self-actualizing creativeness is 'emitted' like radioactivity, and hits all of life . . . it is emitted like sunshine; it spreads all over the place; it makes some things grow (which are growable) and is wasted on rocks and other ungrowable things."*

It is because of my belief in the impact of the therapist as a presence in another person's life—an impact which transcends whatever methods he uses—that I want to share with you my thoughts about the characteristics of a creative therapist.

THE THERAPIST AS ARTIST

In the process of writing this chapter, I made a list of the characteristics of the creative therapist. Two overlapping categories emerged: 1) essences of the therapist as a person—his values and attitudes; and 2) his capacities, abilities, and techniques.

Essences, Values and Attitudes

I was a refugee most of my youthful life. I learned never to take anything around me for granted. Every moment had a precious quality. Over the years I also learned to combine this sense of preciousness with an attitude of hanging loose, of flowing with the action. The notion is to enjoy, to take in fully what is right there in the moment without clinging to anything.

Living my life involves this combination of being there,

---

*Maslow, A. *Toward a Psychology of Being.* New York: Van Nostrand, 1962.

taking in whatever is available, and at the same time letting go of the passing scenery—getting hold of and letting go. In this way, living a full life is a constant rehearsal for giving up one's life: Eventually we must give up all which is precious to us. It is a simple existential reality.

The dangers in having been a refugee are that one has a tendency to cling to one's possessions, to hoard and devour everything around without assimilating—to live *for* the moment rather than *in* the moment. During a catastrophe, if you cling to your home and belongings when you should get the hell out, you wind up dead in short order. In this society we have a tendency to do this anyway—not from past traumatic experiences, but out of a need to fill an empty spiritual hole in ourselves.

We hunger for self-actualization, for ascendance. Too often we solve this problem by filling ourselves with the ethics and values of gimmickry, passing fads and fashions, and shiny new belongings. We long for rapid completion, for fast results: Twenty minutes of meditation in the morning and twenty more in the evening and we're all set. (This may be an exaggeration, but the substance is true.) Other examples in psychotherapy are Rolfing and primal screaming; both methods, although useful, may neglect the complexity, richness, and full scope of a human life.

Quick inspirations burn up rapidly when they are not articulated, developed, and concretized. We tend to jump over this difficult developmental stage of creation—one involving confusion, hard work, and getting one's hands dirty in the process.

A creative life demands hard work. The outcomes, the products of the work may or may not be rewarding; when they are not, one is still nourished by the ongoing process. Process itself is the main course of the feast of creation.

The creative therapist has a rich personal background. He has experienced a great deal in his life—not only in terms of his own emotional and intellectual development, but also by his exposure to a range of life experiences.

The creative therapist celebrates life. He celebrates another person's essence, beauty, goodness, capacities, and future possibilities. This basic attitude of celebration permeates his attentiveness and full involvement in the details of the other person's experience—a simple gesture holds exciting possibilities.

He is driven. He is fully immersed in his work, undistracted by irrelevant events. My own experience is an example: While I was working on my doctoral dissertation I was in a daze for months. I looked at my family and didn't see them. When I shared the problem with my teacher, Dwight Miles, he said, "Good. It is difficult to carry out a piece of work like this without being obsessed with it." This obsession takes place not only in relation to the process itself, but with respect to its structural integrity, its excellence. In the interview I mentioned earlier, Rubinstein listened to himself performing Liszt's Liebestraum in concert. When Barbara Walters asked him if he liked it, he replied, "No, too much bass . . . when I play a concert, it is just a lesson for the next concert."

The inventive, experimental therapist has rich inner imagery. "The shape of that man's inner life," he says to himself, "is perfectly round like a pink balloon. The space is small and shallow. The rubber is stretched thin. The balloon is wrapped in a conglomeration of stories impatiently woven together to create a sense of substance. Here I am," he continues, "feeling like another weaver making stronger wrappings for him." The imagery is vivid and sometimes frightening, but it always has possibilities: "If I trust my imagery of this person, I will not treat him with a scalpel; the sharpest instruments should be knitting needles."

An aesthetically sensitive person, the creative therapist has a sense of grace, structure, order and rhythm of life. Grace is not an abstract notion for him; he knows it in the movement of his own body, in the movement of reeds in the meadow below his house. He can feel a piece of work becoming awkward or ungainly; it bothers him, and he is compelled to deal with it.

Love of play is an essential aspect of creative life. Playfulness is not conjured up; it is not contrived to see what happens. Rather, it is an intrinsic part of one's life. As I am writing this, for example, I am playing with different ways of crossing out almost every line I have written before. The wiggly cross-out lines are most interesting because they look like the ocean—I can sail or swim on them. I love to play with my friends, my children, and by myself. I enjoy the playfulness of others. In therapy, to "play around" means to move to the outer edges of the literal, to invent outrageous contexts for situations which hypnotize with their flatness. To play means to come to life, to experience another with lively eyes.

Another characteristic of the innovator is his excitement about the unrevealed mysteries in himself and others. He is aroused by unknown possibilities beneath the surfaces of human lives. Like an archeologist or a Sherlock Holmes, he searches for clues, cues, and inroads into another person's unknown spaces. Like a child untainted by the prejudices and values of elders, the creative therapist likes to investigate even the most obvious situations. No action or appearance is taken for granted. This investigation involves a sensory curiosity and involvement, and the seeking of sensory clarity.

A sense of humor is central for someone who hears stories of woe all day long. Humor is a friend, a homunculus sitting on my shoulder chuckling at the action whenever he gets a chance. Humor is my wise court jester, making it possible to stand aside and laugh at my own self-importance. It begins with general statements of grand contradictions in life and ends with little bits and pieces of whimsy. It is another way of superimposing a thousand contextual templates on the existing action, another way of transcending the obvious.

I am reminded of Michael, a 27-year old clinical psychology student, who comes in with a long face—it feels like for the thousandth time. (This is his 15th session.) His presence in my office makes the air heavy. I feel his artificial somberness in my chest and shoulders.

"Michael," I say to him exuberantly, "take off your mask and make yourself comfortable!"

"I wish I could," he says with a droning voice.

"Tell you what," I continue, "let's work on your mask together—you massage one side of your face and I'll help with the other. Once we get the flesh warmed up, we'll start making faces." We proceed to work on various expressive movements in his face and their effect on his inner experience.

On another occasion, the following transpires between Michael and myself when he again walks into the office with a very heavy face. (This is session # 20.)

Joseph: Michael, don't become a therapist. It's foolish. You will have to listen to all these suffering people, all these masochistic people. And then you will take on the sadness and carry it with such pain. It's a pain in the ass.

Michael: (Looking wooden, his face mask-like as usual) Glad you mentioned that. I'm feeling real low.

Joseph: Oh shit! I just got through with a phobic man, and now I've got to deal with your depression. This is too much for one day.

Michael: (Pretending not to hear me) I wonder what my depression does for me.

Joseph: Michael, I have an idea. (We are beginning to pace back and forth in the room.) Michael, you tell me one thing that your depression does and I'll match you with a statement of what my depression does for me.

Michael: My depression makes me feel like I take care of myself.

Joseph: My depression makes me feel like I'm stroking myself.

Michael: My depression makes me feel like somebody is playing with my cock. And I can get everybody to surround me and stroke me and play with me and be attentive to me.

Joseph: My depression makes me feel so sweet and sentimental.

Michael: My depression makes me feel like I'm a little boy and I gotta be taken care of.

Joseph: My depression gives me permission to withdraw

and have privacy and rock and write sad poems, and
listen to the most schmaltzy Russian music. I can feel
like Romeo and Juliet.

Michael: My depression makes me feel like I can neglect
myself. And I can walk stooped over. And I can exaggerate my wooden face—be an old man in a dry
month.

Joseph: My depression is like a song. Like a sad love
song. (I begin to sing a song in the praises of our
mutual depressions.) Oh how sweet it is to be sad, to
be special. All these people in the streets are walking
with smiling faces having a sense of purpose in life,
able to do their jobs. But you and I are special because we are sad and down. (Michael joins in repeating this song.)

Michael: Why do you do this to me? I'm not feeling depressed anymore. Why are you insisting on poking
fun at my sadness?

Joseph: Look, if I take on your sadness, if I listen to one
more piece of sadness, I'm gonna get a headache.
And if I get a headache I'm gonna feel heavy. And if I
feel heavy I'm going to get so depressed, and *then,*
you sonofabitch, you will feel better and you will
leave this room with a little smile on your face feeling perfectly all right. And I will be the one who will
get stuck with your depression. I refuse to carry your
sadness for you.

(We continue talking and feeling closer to each other.)

Michael: You know, the way we were singing that thing,
it sounded like Gilbert and Sullivan—like an
operetta.

Joseph: Poor Michael, poor Michael, he is really sad. Oh
Michael, oh Michael, he is really sad. He can't do
this, he can't do that. He can't move; he is so slow.
He can't even make love because he is so very very
sa-a-ad, so very sad.

(To my great surprise, Michael joins me in singing coun-
terpoint to this.)

> *Michael:* I'm sad, I'm sad, I'm very, very sad. Yes, I'm very very special 'cause I'm very, very sad.
> (The lyrics are not especially imaginative, but with the singing voices they sound grand. In the meantime, the two of us are beginning to feel happy together. I mean, we're really having a good time.)
> *Michael:* (Laughing) Look, 1 am no longer feeling depressed and now I'm feeling silly. I'm feeling stupid. I don't know what to say.
> *Joseph:* You don't need to feel knowledgeable. Why don't you be dumb. Be stupid.
> (The operetta changes to a new reverie)
> *Together:* Oh how stupid, how stupid we are. We are very stupid men . . .

Later, we talk about how important it is to be stupid sometimes: what Michael stands to lose by being dull and what he stands to gain. By the end of the session, Michael feels exhilerated. The mask has disappeared and his blue eyes are lively. He gets up and makes a gesture as if he is going to punch me in the stomach.

> *Michael:* You sonofagun. (Instead of punching me, he gives me a big hug.)
> *Joseph:* Are you coming back next week? I hope you're coming back because I wouldn't want you to be deprived of being teased.
> *Michael:* I'll be here. (He laughs.)

Michael came to me because he was stuck with a certain perspective which was no longer useful to him and kept him in a frozen position. Too often the therapist becomes stuck in the same serious role in which he nods, scowls, and quietly groans. He accepts the other person's experience in one flat perspective—the literal perspective. He does not allow himself to create other images and other kinds of backdrops against which he can see a particular piece of behavior or concern for the client.

*The psychotherapy situation is a laboratory, an opportunity to look
at oneself in a variety of mirrors.*

The psychotherapy situation is a laboratory, an opportunity
to look at oneself in a variety of mirrors. Humor allowed us to
turn the world upside down, to make the familiar strange. It
gave Michael the opportunity to stand above himself, look
down, and take into account not only his own existential dilemma, but the dilemma, the nature and complexity of the
human race. He could then look at his depression out of a
broader perspective.

Often the therapist assumes the other person wants him to
extricate his symptom. To see one's work as a symptom-re-
mover is limiting. In the session with Michael I assumed his
sadness was a way of supporting himself—a style of being in
the world and dealing with a particular set of problems. By
moving into the validity of the sadness and taking it to its
extreme position of celebration, Michael was able to accept
his experience and see me as a fellow traveler.

There is a whole list of characteristics of the imaginative therapist related to how he thinks and what he believes in. These characteristics border on the techniques and methods to which he is attracted.

The creative therapist has a capacity for detached involvement in another person's life experience. He is able to be empathic and to assimilate and follow another person's experience without giving up his own inner reminiscences and independent thinking. It is this quality of being attached and receptive to the other person as well as detached and attentive to his own internal process that makes the therapist useful to his client.

The therapist's greatest enemy is that state in which he finds himself deeply identified with his client, embedded in the other's psychological skin. The psychological boundaries —what we call contact boundaries—begin to merge. This state is called confluence: the loss of differentiation between two people. The characteristic result is that they can no longer disagree and rub against each other. Creative conflict, or simply good contact, is sacrificed for routine interactions which are flat, static, and safe.

Once the therapist loses his independent perception of his client, he is sunk. He does not stand solidly as an independent visionary consultant. Freud spoke about the analyst's ability to float above another person's content in order to free associate and be in contact with his own deeper processes. Such associations often produce brilliant and original understandings of the ongoing process.

An attitude or stance which I value very much in my work is a kind of pleasure in anticipating a solution or insight. I am optimistic about the success of the outcome. I anticipate great things, and there are moments in my work when this optimistic anticipation is very clear. And usually, the clearer the pleasurable anticipation of the process, the more predictable the successful outcome. It is as if I am responding to an unconscious process which picks up clues of the anticipated outcome. In his book, *Synectics,* William Gordon names this phenomenon "the hedonistic response" and gives a number of examples of famous creative insights which were preceded by this sense of optimism and pleasure. For example, an intimate of Franz Kafka's described him as "constantly amazed."*

Related to the pleasure of anticipated success is the love of the process as such. Sometimes the process itself takes on a kind of functional autonomy. The artist/therapist experiences himself as a mere witness within the movement of his work. Brewster Ghiselin quotes Carl Jung having remarked, "The work in process becomes the poet's fate and determines his psychic development. It is not Goethe who creates *Faust,* but *Faust* which creates Goethe."**

Despite my anticipation, I do not rush a desired, prefabricated result of a therapy session. I am willing to stay with the situation no matter how difficult, and to pursue its detailed exploration openly enough such that a variety of factors may intrude. Generally, this exploration does not frustrate and confuse me. I am still able to maintain a sense of thematic direction in the therapy session. This capacity to follow the theme and development of the session is called "tracking." The therapist is like a complex radar machine, able to consolidate material, see its direction, and keep moving with it until the person is able to surprise himself with an insightful experience.

The creative therapist has an important quality which I identify as the capacity for wonderment. This sense of wonderment makes it possible for me to be surprised by a special quality that I'm experiencing in another person. It is a sense of *Wow!* about some seemingly insignificant way in which the other person sees the world. It is the ability to partake with pleasure another person's special experience.

The creative therapist is a risk-taker. He is willing to move into an experiment, a way of looking, or a piece of behavior which is often chancy, if not dangerous. He has enough skill and predictive understanding that if the work goes sour, his timing is precise enough to rescue the situation.

*Gordon, William J. J., *Synectics.* New York: Macmillan, 1961.
**Ghiselin, B. *Creative Process.* New York: Mentor Books, 1952.

The creative person is filled with characteristics which would seem contradictory to each other. For example, although he can comfortably enmesh himself in complexity and obscure details, he is also attracted to and seeks order and elegance: "The modern aesthetic motivation, when faced with two notions of equal instrumental value has its source in the Pythagorean reverence for form, for simple whole numbers, in Pythagoras' intoxication with the music of the spheres. Deriving from this notion of 'economy' is the concept of pleasure in the elegance of solutions to such problems."*

Every artistic form I can think of combines love of detail with development of strong, almost monolithic themes, explosion of passions modulated and harnessed by disciplined structural integrity. Mozart and Bach stand out as beautiful examples of this phenomenon. Creative psychotherapy is no exception.

Capacities, Abilities, and Techniques

The creative therapist is experimental. His attitude is one of using himself, his client, and objects in the environment in the service of inventing novel visions of the person. A man begins by telling of his father's recent death. His voice is soft with sadness. His body looks stiff as if bracing itself against a blow. All the characteristics of the mourning process are laid out in his language, his softness, the frozen anger in his arms. After five minutes of sharing, I formulate our therapy session in four movements. This formulation flashes inside me in its totality, its language clearly identifying with my client:

1. My father's death: my shock and sense of disorientation; our life together before his illness.
2. My rage with him: he was a busy man, or a neglectful parent, or he didn't understand how lonely I was; my rage with him for leaving me now that I was ready to be closer.

*Gordon, W. J. J. Synectics. New York: Macmillan, 1961, p. 153.

3. Breaking through the rage into sadness: the mourning proper—woe is me, I lost my dad; the experience of tenderness and of forgiving.
4. The final farewell and burial: my sense of inner substance and self-affirmation—I am now my own father.

The sudden insight of the four movements came upon me with pleasure and was backed by my enormous energy.

The literature on creative process is filled with examples of sudden automatic flashes of insights by artists and inventors.* The implication is that the insight has magical qualities, a miracle sent by the gods. What is often not stated is that the inventor spent months or years working his material, that he has been obsessed with it, that its ingredients have been incubated in his brain.

So it is with this case. For years I have familiarized myself with the process of mourning and experiences of loss in general. I have investigated the stages people live through when significant others die. I have worked with many individuals living through such predicaments. Now this particular man comes with his story. My sudden "flash" is no miracle, although it feels like it at the time. The incubated information is waiting to be used. It has been stored and unconsciously "worked" inside, and has now emerged out of hiding, pointing itself at this event. This process is illustrated in the diagrams entitled The Development of an Insight and The Birth of an Insight.

What looks like magic to the novice is a highly developed and carefully exercised set of skills practiced by the artist. It is the suddenness of the formulation, as well as its sense of urgency and "rightness," which gives the insight its dramatic quality.

I don't burden my client with all the details of my insight. Somehow there is a silent contract that he is in good hands, that the process will be elegant, good, beautiful, moving, dramatic. I know that there will be minimal "talking about" various events surrounding the father's death. The client will be

*Ghiselin, B. *Creative Process.* New York: Mentor Books, 1952.

THE DEVELOPMENT OF AN INSIGHT~

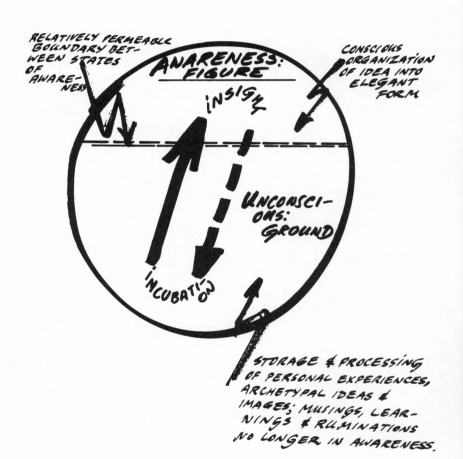

RELATIVELY PERMEABLE BOUNDARY BET-WEEN STATES OF AWARE-NESS

AWARENESS: FIGURE

INSIGHT

CONSCIOUS ORGANIZATION OF IDEA INTO ELEGANT FORM

UNCONSCI-OUS: GROUND

INCUBATION

STORAGE & PROCESSING OF PERSONAL EXPERIENCES, ARCHETYPAL IDEAS & IMAGES; MUSINGS, LEAR-NINGS & RUMINATIONS NO LONGER IN AWARENESS.

The birth of an insight.

encouraged to enact each developmental stage in the immediacy and urgency of the here and now, e.g., "Dad, I think you're not breathing . . . call the nurse. Dad? I can't believe you are gone . . . this feels so unreal."

The master plan is not rigid, nor are the transformations between the stages. The "movements" may in fact be modified to fit developmental changes which carry energy and meaning for the client. I don't make interpretations of what his actions mean. I rely on the natural process of learning that takes place for him as he works. I don't push him to squeeze out meanings for himself prematurely. Everything has its time, its rightful place.

As we work together I envision all the instrumental steps for each movement. The story-telling quality of the first movement is followed by the rageful voice or the pounding of pillows or the enactment of shaking his father's shoulders and telling him off. Each act is clearly self-revealing to my client. He surprises himself with his own expressed wisdom.

I am there with my client while he screams at his father and pounds his fists on pillows. I watch the movement of his hands change pace. He slows. The clenched fists open. His eyes become moist. At this moment I know that we are entering Stage 3, the breaking into sadness. The open hands begin to gently caress the pillow and sounds of deep sobbing emerge from his belly: "I love you daddy . . . I'm gonna miss you so much."

As the time ripens, we invent a ritual burial scene—shoveling the hard earth and saying prayers. No matter that it was done before. This time it may be more complete, more profoundly whole than before. My client and I cry together as he says a final farewell to his father.

I see the last stage of our work as my client's resurrection, the celebration of his own identity and inner substance. I visualize one generation leaving a legacy to the next. How do we concretize this notion of self-affirmation? I ask him to consider taking over the job of parenting himself, of being his own father.

"Yes," he says, "I'm a grown man, I have my own family; it's time to be my own man."

I answer, "Start with the words you just said and continue describing yourself in a way that enumerates how substantial you are, how solid you are, what a loving person you are."

My friend seems to rise from his weariness, speaking praises to himself, to his own goodness as a human being, as a man: "Papa," he turns to an empty chair, "I don't promise not to make mistakes—all of us do that. You made yours. Papa, because I can stand on my own feet, I can now forgive you and love you."

For the time being, the drama ends. I try to leave enough time to "debrief" my client. Mainly, I want to know what he feels and what learnings are in his awareness. I don't assume he knows all the learnings at that moment, but I encourage articulation of whatever awareness is available. I share my awareness also.

In order to be innovative, the creative therapist needs to touch the concrete underpinnings of his client's abstract statements. He is able to separate the word from the experience, to listen to the word, and to visualize the event. By seeing experiences in front of words, the therapist can create dramatic events which transform the client's life right in front of him. The drama of mourning just described illustrates this point. Feelings of rage or warmth or forgiveness which were only vague sensations before are now tested out and fully illuminated. What fits is underscored, and what doesn't fit fades out of the action.

There is a whole category of awareness and sensitivity to language—the manner in which the person uses analogies and metaphor in describing himself—that is a valuable capacity of the creative therapist. This kind of linguistic sensitivity grows out of one's intimate contact with the poetry in oneself. The Gestalt therapist uses metaphor in his client's expression as a vehicle for detailed analysis of the underpinnings of his experience. If I say, "I was clinging to the notion of boating with my family when the others resisted," my therapist might focus me on the term "clinging" and have me explore it in a more concrete sense of clinging to an object, clinging to him, clinging to my family. He may offer himself for me to cling to physically.

I take him up on it and grab on to him, my arms around his torso. At first I feel comfortable and secure. As I stay with it, I am suddenly surprised by a new feeling: a discomfort of being clung to—as if my therapist is holding on to me. When he asks how this applies, I tell him that I must be confusing clinger and clingee with my family as well. I am struck by an old complaint that they are holding on to me when, in fact, I am clinging to them. This revelation opens up a whole area of all the intricate collusive elements in my family.

The Synectics people refer to this process as making the familiar strange and the strange familiar. When I learn to look at myself as a clinging person outside of my casual use of that word with respect to a particular situation, I am making the familiar strange in the sense that I am looking at myself in an unusual way. Having explored that special use of metaphor with respect to other parts of my life, I can then make the strange familiar again.

William Gordon has formalized this process and identified four mechanisms for making the familiar strange, each metaphoric in character: personal analogy, direct analogy, symbolic analogy, and fantasy analogy.* In *personal analogy,* the individual attempts to identify with the concept. If the concept is a "molecule"—"I feel like a molecule in this vast universe"—he may be asked to imagine himself as a molecule—"I am floating in space, bumping up against my neighbors." The *direct analogy* is "the actual comparison of parallel facts, knowledge, or technology."** With respect to "clinging," one might think of the properties of all things that cling.

In the *symbolic analogy,* the person has an opportunity to use impersonal images in describing an idea. Clinging may be seen as a relationship to a doctrine, a political system, or a system of stars in the Milky Way. In Gestalt therapy, the analogy may be followed through by asking the person to personalize and act out a particularly enticing image evolving from this process. The *fantasy analogy* is most directly applicable

---

*Gordon, W. J. J. *Synectics.* New York: Macmillan, 1961.
**Gordon, p. 42.

to our work and we are quite familiar with it. We ask the person to have a fantasy of being this or that and he reports the imagined event. Usually, if the fantasized event looks promising in helping the person gain insight, he may be asked to act out each segment of the fantasy.

In making such analogies to the notion of "clinging," a personal analogy might be "tying up the use of my arms and legs." A direct analogy might be, "holding on to, holding on for life, a child holding on to his mother . . . certain things stick to other things naturally—glues, paints, plastic tapes, tar." A request for a symbolic analogy might yield, "Cling . . . to give away one's freedom, to adhere to a principle, to be bound together, ball and chain, living in a totalitarian state, relationship between prisoner and guard, not having clear boundaries." Fantasy analogy of clinging might be, "The strongest image I have is of swimming and someone is drowning. This person is in a panic. In a frantic effort to save himself, he grabs me around the neck. I feel like we'll both sink if he doesn't loosen his hold."

The Gestalt therapist may extend this technique for his own purposes. He may ask me to act out my fantasy analogy as the rescuer as well as the drowning person. The direct analogy of "glue"—"There is glue between us"—may be used to explore the client's relationship to his family. Just after he hears this statement and before he makes the following intervention— "Suppose you are the glue that is between you. How would you feel and behave as this glue?"—the therapist engages in "float thoughts": glue is a filler, or a barrier, or an insulator; glue can mean love, devotion, caring, loyalty; maybe glue is something artificial holding them together; I wonder if he feels like he acts as a bond between members of the family? The therapist's last hunch is most attractive to him so he takes it on as a hypothesis, saying to himself, "I'll test that out by asking him to act as if he is the glue and we'll see what happens." All these float thoughts happen fairly quickly. The process of selecting the "right" intervention is illustrated in the diagram on the Therapist's Use of Direct Analogy, "Glue" and the Forming of an Intervention.

THERAPIST'S USE OF DIRECT ANALOGY, "GLUE" & THE FORMING OF AN INTERVENTION.

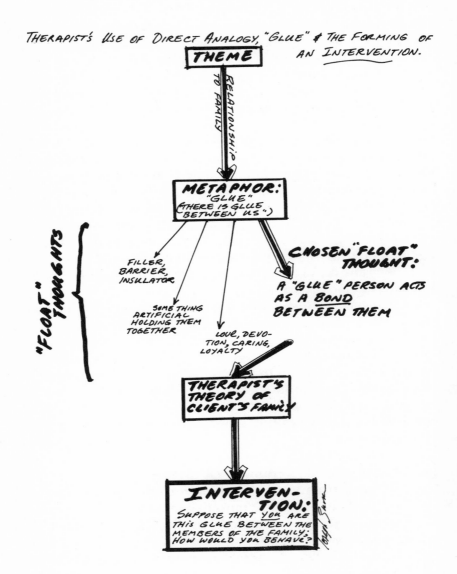

Attentiveness also contributes to the creative process.*
"What is necessary," says Brewster Ghiselin, "is to be able to
look into the wings where the action is not yet organized, and
to feel the importance of what is happening off stage. It may
not seem to be much. The young artist is likely to feel that it is
nothing, and go on imitating. Yet it is there, behind the scenes
. . . that the new can be prepared. No matter how meager, dull,
disorderly and fragmentary the off-stage action, it must be
attended to."**

In his effort to secure a clear theme in the work of his client,
the novice therapist often ignores "irrelevant" comments by
his client, perceiving them as mere "resistances" to work.
Obviously, the irrelevant action must be used selectively,
rather than as a way of distracting oneself with useless
bullshit. The clever therapist has a hunch about a particular
bit of data that will yield results. When seemingly useful distractions are woven into the theme, they can enrich its meanings. Let's say a client is talking about his mother and in the
course of the discussion he mentions how warm the weather
has been; natural curiosity alone should bring this comment
to the therapist's attention. With proper instruction from the
therapist, he may wind up talking like this: "My mother is
sick . . . and the weather is hot. My mother has been making
unreasonable demands on me . . . and the weather is hot. My
mother likes to kiss and hug me all the time . . . and the
weather is stiffling. . ."

Several other work-related characteristics of the creative
therapist are:

— a good sense of timing;
— the capacity to detect where the person can be
   reached, energized, moved emotionally;
— a knowledge of where the psychological "buttons" are
   and when to push them;
— the ability to shift gears—to let go of some things and
   move on to other, more lively areas;

*Gordon, W. J. J. *Synectics*. New York: Macmillan, 1961.
**Ghiselin, B. *Creative Process*. New York: Mentor Books, 1952.

— the willingness to push, confront, cajole, persuade, energize the person to get the work done;
— and the wisdom to know when to let the person stay confused so that he may learn to evolve his own clarity.

It is difficult to illustrate these characteristics. Ideally, we should have a videotape which could be played to illustrate such subtle aspects as timing, so the viewer could see the transitions between events and how the therapist influences them.

Let's go back to the man who is mourning his father's death. His energy is in his relationship with his father and its unfinished qualities. Any work initiated in this direction will find enormous responsiveness. I address myself to specific energies frozen in his body, attending to the stiffness in his arms and what these arms may need to express before the drama is over. I know that getting him to do something expressive with his hands and arms will yield results, not only because of their stiff appearance, but because my past experiences tell me that dead parents tend to leave angry children behind them. The "buttons" are anywhere in this man where I can insert myself into his particular mourning process.

With respect to timing, I want to return to a portion of the same session: "I am there with my client while he screams at his father and pounds his fists on pillows. I watch the movements of his hands change pace. He slows. The clenched fists open. His eyes become moist. The open hands begin to gently caress the pillow and sounds of deep sobbing emerge from his belly." I know from previous experience that we can't love someone fully while hoarding angry feelings; the anger needs to be expressed. At that point the person naturally enters a stage of softness, of tenderness with the loved one.

The rhythm of ambivalence needs to be cultivated in the therapy situation. Knowing this basic dynamic and keeping my eyes open, I see the transition from his rage to his tenderness. All I need to do is recognize it, follow it, and reinforce it. "Put into words what your hands are saying to the pillow," I whisper at the moment his hands begin to move tenderly over its surface. "I love you daddy . . . I'm gonna miss you so much," he responds.

With respect to shifting gears, it should be remembered that human beings are very complex and tricky mechanisms; yet the metaphor must be taken with a grain of salt. In the above incident, the patient shifted gears for himself, moving naturally from rage to tenderness. Ideally, we set a scene in such a manner that the atmosphere itself coaxes the person to do the shifting out of his internal rhythm, his inner sense of rightness. Later in the session, I am more directive in my request or proposal. Once he has "buried" his father, I encourage him to move on to a stage of self-affirmation, building on his own words. I can see that he has finished the burial and that his energy is finished for that task. If anything else should be done within our time limitations, it should be done now. My sense of the aesthetic enters here, too—my fantasy that a death, if it is to be significant, should somehow end with an experience of ascendance, of celebration. And what person can resist celebrating himself?

Not all sessions have purity of direction, nor are they filled with enormous energy and drama. When a theme is clearly established, it is easy to "push" the client in a given direction. But even pushing must have an aesthetic integrity. There is a difference between pushing and pushing around, between encouraging and intimidating, between confronting and belittling. The expert safecracker does not bring a crowbar for his work. He brings sensitive fingertips and a keen ear. Only at the right moment does he attempt to pull the door open. But the safecracker analogy fails in one important respect. It does not communicate the therapist's love for his client, although I suspect that if you asked the expert thief, he would confess he loves the safe he works on.

In summary, the creative therapist is able to integrate two modes of consciousness, two modes of being in the world:

grabbing hold of	*and*	hanging loose
being active	*and*	living in passive, receptive wonderment
analyzing particulars	*and*	seeing the whole, the gestalt

being in control	*and*	flowing in the process
being certain	*and*	allowing oneself to experience confusion
being serious	*and*	playing, having a sense of humor
being curious	*and*	allowing oneself to float in dullness
experiencing wants sequentially	*and*	seeing the whole simultaneously
naming things	*and*	experiencing spatial imagery
being intellectual	*and*	attending to intuitions

Robert Ornstein and other physiological researchers have found that the first mode (left side) is associated with the left cerebral hemisphere of the brain and the second mode with

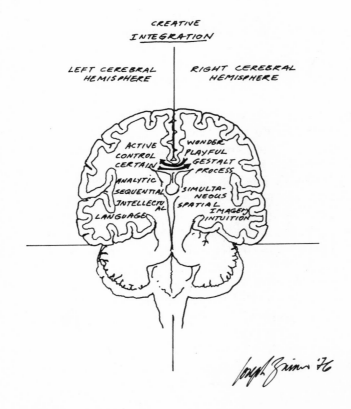

the right hemisphere.* Although all of us use our whole brains all the time, the creative person seems to have a special talent for dipping into his intuitive, image-filled right hemisphere while harnessing and illuminating his experience with his left brain.

✿ ✿ ✿ ✿ ✿

While completing this chapter, I took a short trip to Martha's Vineyard. On my way home, while sitting in the noisy rear entrails of the ferry boat, I jotted down the following images of the creative therapist:

No longer man or woman
        A sage
A parent—no, more grandparent,
        without worry—
A presence of fullness
The silent, silken ocean in midsummer
A child with sparkling eyes
        witnessing everything afresh
Bringing to crispness a vision
        a generosity which punctuates meanings—
A teacher, kindling the fires of flat lives
A healer, seeing the body pushing on itself
A priest, touching faces with blessed hands
A troublemaker, shaping lives with loving
        simplicity
An unpretentious craftsman, molding
        the medium briskly
An artist weary of lying to self
        not willing to pay in generous
        slices of mediocrity
        preferring the thinness of pointed
                brilliance.

---

*Ornstein, R. E. *The Psychology of Consciousness*. San Francisco: W. H. Freeman, 1972.

BLOCKS TO CREATIVITY

I want to address myself to the therapist's blockages in his attitude about being creative. He is stuck in two ways. First, his professional stance and theoretical orientation formalize his work and stiffen his approach. His predecessors taught him how to be formal, dignified and fixed in his approach to dealing with clients and helping people "adjust to reality." Second, like many other people, the therapist is stuck with some misunderstandings about creativity. If his background is scientific or research oriented, he faces the crazy notion that science and art do not mix: Scientists are hard-headed and disciplined; artists are soft and sloppy. If he is not hampered by the science versus art dichotomy, he may still be intimidated by the notion of "creativity" as a very special talent belonging only to those who have been blessed with the gift.

When we do make an effort to behave "creatively" in our work, we meet with enormous inner resistances. Ed and Sonia Nevis, colleagues at the Gestalt Institute of Cleveland, developed a program for diagnosing and working on one's blocks to creativity: "The blocks developed for this program were arrived at through a process of moving back and forth between reviews of the literature in this field, synthesizing out methodology and exercises that would tap central learning points. Out of this emerged the fourteen blocks which we finally formulated. We make no claim for their factorial independence; indeed, we readily admit to their interrelatedness. Nor do we say that these are the only blocks to creativity. However, they are all supported by the work of others in the areas of creative behavior, problem-solving and personality. Moreover, they make sense as practical handles for people to work with in analyzing their own behavior."*

The following represents each block to creativity and a shorthand statement of its definition. I have added some comments on its applicability to therapists.

---

*Nevis, E., Nevis, S. & Danzig, E. *Blocks to Creativity: Guide to Program.* Cleveland, O.: Danzig-Nevis International, Inc., 1970.

1. *Fear of Failure:* "Drawing back; not taking risks; settling for less in order to avoid the possible pain or shame of failing."

The therapist takes a safe stance. He may be apologetic and hesitant in his interactions and tend to engage in confluent conversation with his patients. He is generally perceived as supportive but not challenging or energizing.

2. *Reluctance to Play:* "Literal, overly serious problem-solving style; not 'playing around' with stuff. Fear of seeming foolish or silly by experimenting with the unusual."

Here we see the stern, serious therapist who has difficulty experiencing humor in his work. He has difficulty experimenting with new ways of experiencing his client. He can't laugh at himself.

3. *Resource Myopia:* "Failure to see one's own strength; lack of appreciation for resources in one's environment—people and things."

This therapist generally talks too much. He is mainly cognitive and fails to explore the client's relationship to the environment. When the client misses her child, he can't imagine having her stroke a soft pillow (with her eyes closed) to focus her experience on her physical awareness.

4. *Over-certainty:* "Rigidity of problem-solving responses; stereotyped reactions; persistence in behavior that is no longer functional; not checking out one's assumptions."

The "over-certain" therapist is generally sold on a particular school of therapy exclusively. He clings to specific techniques, e.g., talking to the empty chair or a particular brand of "body work." He has a tendency to resist reading about the work of others and incorporating it into his own style. He is often more interested in his particular way of working than in the creative needs of his clients.

5. *Frustration Avoidance;* "Giving up too soon when faced with obstacles; avoidance of the pain or discomfort that is often associated with change or novel solutions to problems."

Every therapist has his "blind spots," areas of his own difficulties. He "denies" or avoids frustration in the area of rage or sexuality if rage or sexuality throws off his own functioning. He unconsciously directs topics or themes to areas in which he has experience, where he feels he can do something constructive.

6. *Custom-bound:* "Over-emphasis on traditional ways of doing things; too much reverence for the past; tendency to conform when it is not necessary or useful."

Those of us who have been clients ourselves often imitate the model we learned from our therapist/teachers. We play the role of our ideal therapist models rather than being natural and comfortable with ourselves.

7. *Impoverished Fantasy Life:* "Mistrusting, ignoring, or demeaning the inner images and visualizations of self and others; over-valuing the so-called objective, real world; lack of 'imagination' in the sense of 'Let's pretend' or 'What if'."

Often this therapist is constricted in his own fantasy life. He has a tendency to tune in on the client's practical, situational sphere rather than on fantasy or dreams. He may neglect the latter in favor of "goal setting" and "making contracts."

8. *Fear of the Unknown:* "Avoidance of situations which lack clarity or which have unknown probability of succeeding; overweighting what is not known versus what is known; a need to know the future before going forward."

The therapist who experiments with his work takes a chance of getting into territory which is exciting, brand new. It is also frightening. If I learn to put someone into a hypnotic trance, I take a change of getting into difficulty bringing him out of it. If I touch my patient, I may need to deal with "transference-countertransference" issues. (In Gestalt, we may call it love or contact or sexuality.) We all have a tendency to stay in situations (intrapsychic or interpersonal) which feel clear and known to us.

9. *Need for Balance:* "Inability to tolerate disorder, confusion or ambiguity; dislike of complexity; excessive need for balance, order, symmetry."

Although it is important to define the issues—the themes in a particular therapy situation—it is also important not to "jump the gun" and fix one's perception of the person too

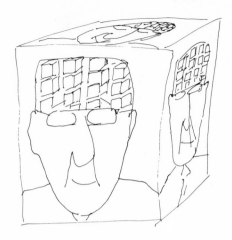

Over-certainty. . . custom-bound. . .fear of the unknown.

quickly. We may need to struggle with avenues which lead to cul-de-sacs or a morass of apparent irrelevancies. A theme emerging out of confusion may be stronger, closer to the client's existential struggle than one which is prematurely wrapped and tied.

10. *Reluctance to Exert Influence:* "Fear of seeming too aggressive or pushy in influencing others; hesitancy to stand up for what one believes; ineffective in making oneself heard."

Some of us get into soft roles—chicken-soup helpers, understanding parents, accepting, non-judging or noncommital spaces. Too often we may refuse to push, cajole, persuade, raise our voices—as if the loving parent or mature adult does not do these things. Such blocking takes away an important dimension of our influence.

11. *Reluctance to Let Go:* "Trying too hard to push through solutions to problems; inability to let things incubate, or let things happen naturally; lack of trust in human capacities."

We cannot push through a piece of learning. We can't chew the material and transfuse it into the client's arteries. We cannot make the learning take place in our time, at our pace, but in the timing and pacing which are congruent for the client. Often we must be satisfied with having planted a seed. Most importantly, we need to have faith in the process of our work, the fact that important changes will take place in small units if we just hang in there with the person.

12. *Impoverished Emotional Life:* "Failure to appreciate the motivational power of emotion; using energy in holding back spontaneous expressions; lack of awareness of the importance of feelings in achieving commitment to individual and group effort."

The emotionally blocked therapist becomes immobilized when his client cries or raises his voice. He has not learned methods of heightening the feelings, reveries, or strong sentiments which enhance and deepen the person's experience. He is not able to provide learning at a deep, emotional level. He will hesitate to explore feelings which are difficult for him.

13. *Unintegrated Yin-Yang:* "Not making sufficient use of contrasting ways of getting at the essence of things; polarizing things into opposites, rather than knowing how to integrate the best of both sides; lacking unified perception of the wholeness in the universe."

The therapist who blocks in the Yin-Yang is personally bipolar. He has a rigid self-concept and is therefore restricted in his evaluation of the behavior of others. He *knows* what is beautiful or ugly. He lacks aesthetic subtlety. He has difficulty seeing beauty in a Euclidian theorem, in the structure of a salt crystal, in a pile of spilled garbage or a rusted muffler on the side of the road. He consequently puts his client into a polarized position and is not able to help another person become more fully integrated.

14. *Sensory Dullness:* "Not adequately using one's primary senses as a way of knowing; making only partial contact with self and environment; atrophy of capacities to explore; poor sensitivity."

A therapist who is sensorially blocked is primarily verbal and verbally conceptual in his work. He is able to clarify issues and raise relevant questions—even of high order quality. He may ask, "What are the implications of this difficulty with your father on how you relate to your husband?" He understands human nature but is blocked in his sensory appreciation of his client's concrete, here-and-now humanness. He would have difficulty making observations like, "You look slumped over, as if carrying a huge weight on your shoulders," or "When I look at your chest I find myself holding my breath," or "Your voice is particularly tight and high-pitched today."

In the following foreshortened version of a therapy session, I am going to illustrate some of the blocks to creativity. Since this book addresses itself to therapists, the blocks will be discussed in the context of the therapist's interventions, rather than the client's behavior. I suggest that you begin by reading the interview in its entirety, without referring to my comments on the right-hand side of the page. Once you have an overview of the dynamics operating in this session and a sense of your own response to the interventions, read the interview again and include my comments. The reader should keep in mind that this session is not presented as a model of poor or excellent work. It is simply an effort to illustrate some of the Nevis blocks as applied to Gestalt therapy.

I would like you to read the action without burden of the background of the client. Briefly, this is the fifth session; the client, Pete, is a 35-year-old college professor who is struggling with his attachment to his mother and his competitive feelings with a younger brother. The therapist, Tom, is about the same age.

Pete: (Silent, looking pensive and tense)

Tom: I could say something to start off. I'm glad we're together again. I would really like to do something special for you—within my limitations, my abilities.

Fear of failure: Tom sounds like he is reassuring himself and Pete of the soundness of his work. He is also apologizing in advance for possible failure in the coming hour.

Pete: I have mixed feelings about you, Tom. I'm not quite sure you're the one who can help me. Both of us have a tendency to get into our heads. What I need is to do some work with my body, not to think so much all the time.

Tom: So, what do you feel now?

Custom-bound: Tom is in the habit of asking for feelings and has learned to stay in the "now." So he poses a familiar, safe question. He is not attending to the obvious—Pete's doubts about his ability to help him as well as interest in working on his body experience.

Pete: I feel pretty anxious right now. We have had some good sessions, but I'm not sure I can trust you to help me get into my feelings. At the same time, I do have some warm feelings about you, about your friendliness and caring.

Tom: I'm pleased about the warm feelings you have about me. I have had some experience doing bodywork. Do you want to get in touch with your body right now?

Emotional improverishment and sensory dullness: Tom is not able to linger with Pete's expression of warmth, and puts it aside. In addition, he does not hear salient points of Pete's statement—his concern with anxiety and the question of trust. Instead, he backtracks to the earlier request about body-work which only reinforces Pete's feeling of not being heard.

Pete: (Silence) I'm checking myself out physically. My breathing feels shallow. I need to breathe more . . . I feel more comfortable now. I'm leaning back now—back away from you and that feels even more comfortable.

Tom: Mmhm. Do you want to move away from me and be more comfortable that way? Are you willing to stay that way?

Pete: I'm not quite sure. I am still feeling ambivalent about you.

Tom: I see you breathing more heavily.

Sensory dullness: Once again Tom is blocking his auditory input. Although his visual observation is correct, he does not tap into the ambivalence theme which is now repeating itself. He might propose a simple experiment: "Pete, how far would you like to move away from me to feel more comfortable. Stand up and try out different distances and tell me how each feels to you." This would help Pete concretize his own sense of boundaries in relation to Tom.

Pete: Yeah, now I'm giving myself air.

Tom: You seem relieved.

Pete: (Silent, pensive)

Tom: (Looking somewhat distressed and uncomfortable) Are you going to say something? You look like you're tasting something. As if you're tasting the way you feel about me.

Pete: I was wetting my lips. They are dry.

Tom: That's disappointing. I had wished you would offer some metaphor about the way I taste to you.

Pete: I'm sorry I'm not living up to your expectations.

Tom: (After a period of silence) I don't know what to say to you; where to go from here; what I can do for you. I'm feeling tense.

Pete: Perhaps you're experiencing the tension I feel right now.

Tom: Where do you feel your tension? In what way do you experience it?

Pete: I am reflecting a bit on that . . . I think it is mainly in my throat.

Tom: Is there something that you are holding onto in your throat that you want to share with me?

Pete: Yeah . . . that's it . . . I wanna talk about my mother, except I'm not sure I'm ready to deal with that right now.

Tom: Yeah, I know how you feel. Heavy things are not al-

Impoverished fantasy: Tom's response is correct as such, but

ways easily available. Suppose you have a choice now.
You could either try to talk
about your mother or get into
your physical experience.

lacks imagination in engaging
Pete's difficulty talking about
his mother. He might suggest
the following: "I would like to
help you with that. Would you
be willing to try this experiment? Close your eyes and visualize your mother. Take your
time . . . can you see her? Okay,
now talk to her about your feelings without actually saying it
out loud. That way you can feel
some privacy. When you feel
like it, you might tell me what
it felt like to talk to her." If Pete
were willing to do this, he
could get started sharing some
feelings about his mother without having to reveal specific
content.

Pete: Boy! Now I feel like
you're pushing me. Pushing
me to do something right
away.
Tom: I had no intention of
doing that. I was merely offering a choice for you to
have a place to go at this
point. You can go back to
your body and just tell me
what you feel in your body
right now.

Once again, Tom is appropriate
and reasonable in his response.
He reassures Pete of his intentions and gives him something
to focus on. However, blockage
in fantasy and in listening to
Pete's language keeps Tom
from responding creatively to
Pete's verbal offering—the
twice-repeated, juicy word is
"pushing." He could fantasize
pushing Tom physically. His
unintegrated Yin-Yang keeps
Tom from flipping the fantasy
around and imagining Pete
pushing him. After all, Pete is
already behaving assertively

and is "pushing" against Tom's responses. An experiment could emerge in which they would physically push against each other and experience the sort of brotherly contact that results in greater trust for the client.

Pete: I'm feeling blank. I'm feeling no sensations in my body right now.

Tom: Do you need to do something about that right now? Do you want to tell me what the blankness is like for you?

Pete: Blankness is blankness. You know, Tom, what I'm feeling increasingly is that before I can get into some heavy work I must first make some contact with you, have you be more real with me.

Tom: Well, Pete, I'm trying to be as real with you as I can. It seems to me that you raised several important issues: one about being in your head, another about a difficult feeling with your mother, and yet another about feeling out of contact with me.

Custom-bound, need for balance, and emotional impoverishment: Tom is again faithfully reviewing Pete's issues without responding to Pete's feelings or his own. His own emotional impoverishment interrupts his natural curiosity. He might say, "Your demand for contact scares me a bit," or "What sort of contact would you like to have with me?" or "How can I become more real to you—is there something you would like to know about me?"

Pete: Now I feel more distance between us again. Somehow you sound so academic to me.

Tom: Well, I'm really trying to follow you, Pete, to stay in touch with what's important to you. I don't experience myself being academic with you.

Pete: Boy! Now I'm really getting pissed with you. You sound so objective and therapeutic. Why don't you listen to me, damn it! What I need from you right now is some sense of your humanness.

Tom: It's exciting to see you get that worked up. I haven't seen you this angry yet. I'm a little scared and excited at the same time.

Pete: That's a relief! It's a relief to know you can be scared—that you can feel some of the tension and scariness that I often feel.

Tom: Maybe we could both stop talking and think of some way of making contact physically with each other.

(After a long pause Tom extends his hands to Pete. Pete grasps them warmly and looks visibly moved by the experience.)

Reluctance to play: Tom is being too defensive and reassuring to play with the possibilities for experimentation with Pete's language. The word "academic" is Pete's. Tom could help Pete get in touch with his portion of having that quality by suggesting: "Pete, could you imitate how I sound to you?" After Pete imitates the therapist, he could ask, "Does any of that sound like you?" Even if projection were not the issue here, the contact between the two would be enhanced.

Pete: This is nice . . .

Tom: I like the strength I feel in your hands, firm and strong . . .

Pete: You feel more real to me. (They unclasp their hands. There is a long, peaceful silence while the two men lean back in their chairs comfortably.)

Tom: Maybe this is a good time to stop.

Pete: Yeah.

Tom: See you Thursday, Pete.

A FINAL WORD ON IMPECCABILITY AND POWER

As a social being, the therapist/artist is always reponding to his social and personal culture. His challenge is to convert his need to please, or to explain, or to be praised into an internal energy system which feeds his uncompromising artistic standards. I call this stance "impeccability."

Only the artist can know deeply within himself and judge his honesty. He knows when he is performing. He knows when he merely wants to make others laugh or cry or be impressed. The moment he loses touch with his honesty, he loses his impeccable, uncompromising center. For example, as I write I am sometimes enamored by the words themselves and how they sound to you, the reader. Sometimes my writing becomes more dramatic and perhaps romantically sentimental, rather than truly accurate. I suspect myself. One must always suspect oneself without making oneself sick.* I strive for impeccability, purity of motives, and an appreciation of the process of the work itself.

Another way of referring to impeccability is to think of discipline. One must develop a method of work which has structure and continuity. One must trust one's process. One

*Castaneda, C. *The Teachings of Don Juan.* New York: Ballatine Books, 1968.

must be willing to be the master and pupil in one body. One must be critical in a loving way, rather than in a punitive way.

A wise man once told me that what is taken as psychotherapeutic magic by the innocent witness is only the outcome of many years of struggle and error on the part of the experienced therapist. The concert pianist practices five hours a day for a lifetime. He makes awful mistakes. He struggles with his conscience, his values. He is purified by his suffering, his self-criticism, and by interspersed successful outcomes in tiny dosages. Then he performs on stage and people say that God is in his hands, that he makes miracles.

The fact is that the creative person, or the creative therapist, is a disciplined craftsman whose "gift" is a reaching out toward his most profound personal potential. It is this practicing with love and stretching beyond himself without stereotypic, shallow self-seeking and righteousness that has the makings of a creative person. I don't mean to sound glib, puritanical or evangelistic. The reality for me is that deep down I am a pleasure seeker and that making something new with other people and with our mutual lives gives me great pleasure and joy.

It is during this process of transcending my own heaviness or dullness or stereotypes that I feel pure, good, beautiful, powerful, holy, rich, magical. This feeling, when it is there, is not mine alone—it saturates the space around me and is exuded by the other person or persons who share in it.

And it is not clear if God is in our hands and hearts, whether we are in his lap, or if this is the way artists create God. It does not matter. During those rare moments of creativeness, when an ordinary person has something in common with the making of the universe, he feels a sense of transcendence, of moving beyond his daily life. What could be a greater reward?*

---

*For further reading on transcendence in creativity, I suggest: *The Teachings of Don Juan* by Carlos Castaneda (New York: Ballantine Books, 1968); *The Act of Creation* by Arthur Koestler (New York: Dell Books, 1964); *The Farther Reaches of Human Nature* by Abraham Maslow (New York: Viking Press, 1971).

Chapter **4**

Roots and
Assumptions

One of the demands the creative process makes of the therapist is for structure and organization in his work. Structure evolves out of the intrinsic nature and content of the situation, guided by the theoretical constructs floating in the therapist's head. These constructs or "cognitive maps" create order and lend direction to the complex mass of information which evolves during the course of a human encounter.

Cognitive maps are not static, nor are they always clearly evident to all parties involved. They are not framed and hanging on the walls of the consultation room. More often, cognitive maps or theoretical constructs are silent partners supporting the elegance of the work's ongoing process. A therapy session, like a work of art, is sloppy without structure and direction. It may be colorful and exciting, but without organization its gains are difficult for the client to assimilate and "take home."

THE LIVELY MOMENT:
PHENOMENOLOGICAL HERE AND NOW

In a Harvard talk many years ago, E. E. Cummings said to

his audience: "You haven't the least or feeblest conception of being here and now, and alone, and yourself. Why (you ask) should anyone want to be here, when (simply by pressing a button) anyone can be in fifty places at once? How could anyone want to be now, when anyone can go whening all over creation at the twist of a knob? . . . As for being yourself—why on earth should you be yourself; when instead of being your-self you can be a hundred, or a thousand, or a hundred thou-sand other people? The very thought of being oneself in an epoch of interchangeable selves must appear supremely ridic-ulous." Cummings wisely cautioned his listeners: ". . . re-member one thing only: that it's you—nobody else—who de-termine your destiny and decide your fate. Nobody else can be alive for you nor can you be alive for anyone else."*

The term phenomenological implies that process which one experiences as uniquely one's own; adding the dimensions of here and now gives these personal phenomena existential im-mediacy: I am this person, Joseph, sitting on this bed, propped up on two pillows, feeling the support thereof, in-tently scribbling notes on a small pad held in my left hand against my right knee . . . I feel a kind of clarity in my head and the light here is very crisp, the sort of light I experience in the late summer afternoon when my vision seems to outline all the intricacies of the world around me. These ongoing phenomena (and more) constitute my world. When I die, when my awareness permanently ceases, the whole Josephian world will be forever finished. And phenomenologically, *the* world will come to an end.

Carl Rogers pointed out that the phenomenological world is the experienced world.** I am what I experience myself to be in this moment and if you ask what I feel right now and I say, "Nothing," you can safely assume that in this moment I live in a world colored by "nothing," that I feel "nothing" inside me, or that what I do experience I interpret to have a value of

---

*Cummings, E. E. *Six Nonlectures.* New York: Antheneum, 1971.

**Rogers, C. *On Becoming a Person* (Boston: Houghton Mifflin, 1961); *Counseling and Psychotherapy* (New York: Houghton Mifflin, 1942); "A Process Conception of Psychotherapy" (*American Psychologist*, 1958, *13*, 142–149).

"nothing" in my communication with you. Instead of respectfully understanding the "nothing" of another person's experience, some therapists tyrannically press him for more, as if he
never responded to the question. In existential therapeutic
circles, the "here and now" seems to be changing from that
which compels my experience in this moment, to a twentieth
century reverse puritanism that implies immediate satisfaction of needs: a system of situation ethics with little insight
into human blockages, resistances, or levels of awareness.

Inexperienced "Gestalt" therapists with meager theoretical
backgrounds have used the term "here and now" as a kind of
slogan, a demand for extracting the other person's immediate
experience. The client does not always have a conscious
choice to share himself, to hand what he feels to others on a
golden platter using a few briskly descriptive words. Consequently, Gestalt therapy has been associated with tough con-
frontations: The person must tell all, express everything.
These matters need clarification.

Sensation

Experiencing the here and now begins with sensation. In an
organism with a small cerebral cortex, the sensory moment-to-
moment fluctuation is primal; the cognitive process does not
become elaborated. Not so in an adult human being. Sensory
experience is automatically named and cognitively elaborated, even embellished: I see a light. It is a yellow light. It
streams directly downward and upward from a table lamp
with a matted glass base shaped like a holiday whisky decan-
ter; the lamp has an off-white paper shade. It is ugly. I don't
like it. I want to get rid of it.

Generally speaking, we forget that our language has sensorial roots, that our words stem from concrete experiences. We
treat words as if they themselves were the experience.The pedantic (or casual) manipulation of concepts and abstractions

can remove us from the immediate impact of our reality.* To be sensorially in contact is difficult in an increasingly automated world in which we are constantly distracted by static.

Exploring myself is an active process of directing my attention in a simple, naive fashion: Now I sit bent over the pad. My weight rests on my behind and my right calf on the edge of the bed. My left hand is holding on to the pad with thumb on top. My red, white and blue watch strap jumps into my eyes as I glance at it—it cuts across my wrist, dividing it in half. I feel my heart pounding with excitement as if I have discovered something important. Now I want to lean back. I have tingles in my toes. I feel alive. My sensory exploration enlivens me in this moment.

Time

Reality always exists in the present. Even in terms of my most profound and clear awareness, memory, and anticipation, I have no way of living my own yesterdays and tomorrows. I am anchored to this moment—anchored with this body that is now resting on a chair, with the sound of windows rattling in the wind, with the visual experience of this page I am writing on, with the pulsing of my heart. Images of yesterdays are tinted by this nowness; they are like postcards pasted in an album, an audio-visual reference library in my head, mere aboutnesses. As E. E. Cummings put it, ". . . anyone can go whening all over creation . . ."

The whens of our lives are devoid of a pulse, of a liveliness, especially when we try to verbalize them. We can pump life into the whens by re-enacting them as if they are taking place now, and thus the memory comes to life as it is acted out muscularly and brought into the present. We can even enliven

---

*This is not an attack on the use of concepts, as without concepts this book could not be written, we could not record our history, we could not have mathematics or literature or a theory of relativity. Without concepts we are not human beings. But with concepts alone, without basic sensory exploration (and conative evaluation), we are rendered to a position of computer print-outs.

Reality always exists in the present.

a fantasy, dream or anticipation in the same way. But these re-enactments become present events and are not to be confused with the actual events that took place or are about to happen. The re-enactment is inseparably fused with this me that sits in this room writing and knowing myself now.*

Harvey is a young therapist working on his doctorate. I have been seeing him in individual psychotherapy as part of his postgraduate training at the Gestalt Institute. This is part of session # 8, emphasizing Harvey's present experience.

> *Harvey:* I've been working on this paper for months. People who read it don't give me what I want. Either they approve wholeheartedly but don't follow up with some personal discussion, or they don't like it. Here, too, I find myself abandoned . . .

---

*For further reading in this area, I suggest *Gestalt Therapy Verbatim* by Fritz Perls (Moab, Utah: Real People Press, 1961) and *Gestalt Therapy* by Fritz Perls, R. F. Hefferline and P. Goodman (New York: Julian Press, 1951).

He continues talking. He is not looking at me; his gaze is pointed down. He seems slightly uncomfortable, without ease. He is sipping hurriedly from a plastic cup of coffee. I am sitting with him, my eyes half closed. I begin to feel a little tired and sleepy. I am looking, listening. His voice is in the distance.

> *Harvey:* . . . I am glad you are interested in my writing. I am a bit surprised. The paper is about Adler. It is quite complex . . . theoretical. I see various levels of order in Adler . . .

His words melt into each other and go on for what seems like ten minutes.

> *Joseph:* And what are you feeling now?
> *Harvey:* I am feeling kind of revved up.
> *Joseph:* Your words were beginning to melt into each other for me just then. I wonder what you feel.
> *Harvey:* I find myself not looking directly at you.
> *Joseph:* Yes, I've been feeling lonely and a bit more tired. You are looking at me now. Right now.
> *Harvey:* (Looking down again) I feel scared a bit. I feel like you're gonna take it all in and then you'll shoot me down. Shoot me down like that professor did.
> *Joseph:* I feel badly for you. It must be a strain to keep looking out for a killer.
> *Harvey:* Yes, that prof really got to me. Last year . . . (he goes on for a while, telling of his prof's criticisms)

Harvey has left again; his eyes are on the floor. Once again I am alone. I look out the window at the large clump of oak trees. It is winter; the trees look stark against the gray sky. I find myself meditating on Harvey's words as if their sound were a mantra, a song, the surf. I find comfort in his voice.

> *Joseph:* And what is going on for you right now?
> *Harvey:* You know, when you commented before that I

have a good theoretical mind, I felt like I shouldn't go on talking 'cause I would sound like I am bragging or something. Then you might be critical of my bragging.

Joseph: Look at me, Harvey. What do you experience?

Harvey: I see a man. (Long pause) I see *you.* You look soft.

Joseph: Harvey, there is more color in your face. Especially around your eyes and nose. You look sad.

Harvey: You look like a kind person. (Tears begin to stream down his face) I can't imagine that you would want to hurt me . . .

Joseph: Don't leave me with your eyes again. Keep staying with me.

Harvey: My father was a cold man. He never saw me. My father never said "Yes," or "It's OK." My father talked about me while I was there as if I was an object. He never embraced me. Not even with his eyes the way you seem to now. How nice. I feel bathed in your looking . . . (His tears stop; his face is flushed)

Joseph: You are nice to look at. If you were my son, I would be proud of you. (Pause) What are you feeling now?

Harvey: Strange. I just learned something. It was I who wanted to shoot *you* down. I've been acting like my father with you. I've been looking coldly at you. I know because looking at you right now allows me to feel your easiness and acceptance.

Joseph: I am pleased.

Harvey's experience of himself and of me became clarified each time I pressed and encouraged him to attend to his present experience. No amount of discussion about the professor or his father would have brought him to his senses, to the obvious observation he finally makes about himself. And the discovery is his own; no one makes it for him.

Space

Spatially, my experience, my reality takes place here, where I am. The range of my "here" is determined by the space I occupy and by the range of my senses. I make the thing sensed come dynamically into me. If I am clearly in touch with something in space, the distance between me and my object-choice is experientially foreshortened; it is as if the object is "on top of me." The dynamic point at which this sensation relates to the object is the contact boundary.*

An object that has a negative valence for me may be spatially pushed away and even visually contracted—the other person complains, "There is such distance between us." A psychotic girl who became very threatened by a therapy group complained that everyone looked "very tiny and far away"; she left the room to experience a safe distance and finally withdrew from the workshop altogether—a position of optimum safety for her.**

The here and now represents a highly personal sensorially-anchored experience at this moment in time and at this place where I am.

Process

Within the realm of psychology, phenomenology is the uninterpreted study of the ongoing, ever-changing nature of human experience. Our personal reality is not static; it is never experienced segmentally or as a discrete point in time. I am constantly in process: My experience has a continuous, ongoing, ever-changing quality; my propensity is to go on, to continue. This is the characteristic of all living things: They are

---

*Perls, F. Hefferline, R. F. & Goodman, P. *Gestalt Therapy.* New York: Julian Press, 1951.
**For a richer understanding of psychosis from this theoretical vantage point, read *The Phenomenological Approach to Psychiatry* by J. H. Van den Berg (Springfield, Ill.: Charles C Thomas, 1955).

in process. Life knows only itself; life is inclined to perpetuate itself.

The ordinary state of affairs for the normal person is to move fluidly from a state of need arousal to need satisfaction, from tension to relaxation, from figural attention to homogenized disinterest. Moreover, the well-functioning person "lives comfortably in the changing flow of his experiencing."* The person is the ongoing process; he does not experience himself as a static object.

It is under circumstances of disturbance, of conditioned inhibition, of pathology that one interrupts one's flow, segments one's behavior, freezes one's fluidity. In this case, the individual's psychological life is in a state of incongruence, where there is a considerable discrepancy between behavior and awareness.**

Ownership

Reality as I experience it is *my* actuality. No one else can experience my inner life for me. The sensitive person may express what he experiences when he is with me, and this experience of his may touch something close to me. But if he were to make an interpretation of the "real" meaning of my statement or behavior, he would lose the purity of my experience. He would remove himself from me by utilizing what Fritz Perls calls the "computing function."+

Interpretations aside, the significant point is that I am the sole owner of my experiential life. The old song, "You made me love you; I didn't want to do it!" is out of line with my view. No one makes me do what I do; no one else can be held responsible for my behavior. The existential philosophical view stresses this point strongly. This is no coincidence, since

---

*Rogers, C. "A Process Conception of Psychotherapy." *American Psychologist*, 1958, 13, 142–149.
**For further reading I suggest the article, "A Process Conception of Psychotherapy" by Carl Rogers (*American Psychologist*, 1958, 13, 142–149.)
+Personal communication.

phenomenology is the basic method used by the existential philosopher. Phenomenology is a language of understanding the human predicament, as mathematics is a language of understanding the physical world.

The experiential here and now, therefore, does not exist in a vacuum; rather, it is owned by a self, a person, a me. It is for this reason that the Gestalt therapist repeatedly asks his client to "take ownership" of his statement or observation.

Content Validity

The content of my experiencing is as valid a datum for me as another person's experiencing is for him. There are no "good" or "bad" awarenesses. If I report my experience—"I've had a bad day today"—how can someone disagree with me?

The content of my experience is also in constant flux, in process. If I manage not to interrupt myself, dull and uninteresting content may develop into material which is colorful, rich, exotic. The accompanying experience moves from lifelessness and boredom to excitement and exhilaration.

To stay with my internal process is an act of faith: I assume that my experience will lead toward completion and culminate in something more satisfying and fulfilling than that with which I started. The longer I can stay with my ongoing awareness, the greater the possibility of heightening, expanding, deepening my awareness. It is important that I not jump the gun prematurely into complex abstracting. I must allow the concrete, pre-verbal, elemental experience to come to me. In such instances I may surprise myself with an inner revelation.

The most profound discoveries or learnings take place when the person is self-directed (rather than directed by others), when he supports himself, and when his total sensory-motor organism participates in the process. This kind of learning can come only from a personal framework which carries a respectfulness for one's uniqueness and integrity.

Here and Now Therapies

Because phenomenological matters constitute the raw data of experience, it stands to reason that all personality theorists begin their deliberations from an experiential base. Freud gathered free associations and based his findings on the unconscious from the content, structure and process of these associations. However, Freud interpreted the content of experience. He sought underlying essences of motivation and not the topography of experience in its own right.

Interest in the latter originated primarily in existential philosophy, which was variously concerned with the ontological nature of man and his condition of being thrown alone into the world, unsupported by preconceived essences.* Phenomenology was originally a branch of philosophy and dealt with the problems of developing a faithful, uninterpreted description of the changing nature of human experience. Phenomenology is the language of existential thinking in general.

Briefly, such are the philosophic/theoretical roots of our current concern with the here and now. On the broadest level, such modern psychotherapies as existential analysis, ontoanalysis, client-centered counseling, and Gestalt therapy are all related to existentialism.** Although the methods of these therapies differ, they share a primary interest in the person: how he unfolds himself in the immediacy of the therapeutic encounter.

Daseinsanalyse means the analysis of the state of being here; however, this expression does not necessarily cover a concrete and behaviorally extensive working relationship in the here and now of the therapeutic situation. Daseinsanalyse appears to be an attempt to interpret the person's state of being in the world at a grand level. Its methodology is still tied to psychoanalysis, with an emphasis on the cognitive and

*As seen in the works of Dostoyevsky, Berdyaev, Jaspers, Buber, Kierkegaard, Tillich, Binswanger, Boss, Sartre, and many others.
**A few names associated with these therapies are: *Existential and Ontoanalysis*—R. May, T. Hora, E. W. Straus, Bugental, A. VanKaam, B. Elkin, V. Frankl, M. Boss, P. Schilder; *Client-Centered Counseling*—C. Rogers, E. Gendlin, V. S. Berg; *Gestalt Therapy*—F. & L. Perls, E. & M. Polster, J. Simkin, S. Nevis, P. Goodman.

discursive rather than the experimental and behavioral. They do a lot of talking and very little doing.

The purest form of "here and now" therapy is Rogerian client-centered counseling.[+] Rogers works solely with the material presented to him by the client in the counseling situation, be it an individual or group encounter. He accepts precisely what the client shares with him and does not search for unconscious motives. He stays in the present, verbally working the material of the client. Even discussions of a historical nature appear to have this quality: "You feel now that your sister's bullying made you act in a more withdrawn manner in high school, is that right?" It must be very refreshing to be heard and accepted, to have another person help clarify exactly how one feels right now, what one needs to express.

Rogers' principal requirements for creative process are the therapist's empathy, genuineness, and unconditional regard for the client. No interpretive statements are heard from the counselor and when he ventures to move beyond the content of the client's expression, he takes ownership of his own experience: "When I look at you sitting like that, bent over, I feel (as you might) very sad and alone." This seemingly simple analysis of the person's experience is powerful in the hands of an acutely sensitive therapist. However, this therapy also fails to ask the person to modify his behavior during the therapy session. For Rogers, this effort would constitute manipulation of another human being, breaking faith with the notion that the person can make himself well.[*]

Gestalt therapy is a unique example of the integration of behavioristic and phenomenological approaches.[**] Heavily influenced by the organismic views of Kurt Goldstein[***] and Wilhelm Reich,[****] Gestalt therapy attempts to understand

[+]Rogers, C. *On Becoming a Person* (Boston: Houghton Mifflin, 1961); *Counseling and Psychotherapy* (New York: Houghton Mifflin, 1942); "A Process Conception of Psychotherapy" (*American Psychologist*, 1958, *13*, 142–149).

[*]Rogers admits that one reason he does not do experiments is that he feels uncomfortable with them and cannot use them as skillfully as certain other therapists can.

[**]Perls, F. *Ego, Hunger and Aggression*. San Francisco: Orbit Graphic Arts, 1966. Perls, F., Hefferline, R. F. & Goodman, P. *Gestalt Therapy*. New York: Julian Press, 1951.

[***]Goldstein, K. *The Organism*. Boston: Beacon Press, 1963.

[****]Reich, W. *Character Analysis*. New York: Orgone Press, 1949; *The Function of the Orgasm*. New York: Orgone Press, 1942.

the individual's being here at every level of functioning. The therapist begins by reporting his observations to his client: "When you begin to talk about your bully sister, your mouth tightens. Do you feel it?" Having made a faithful observation of the person's appearance, the therapist may become a more active teacher and suggest that the client experiment with his tightness: "Try to talk about your bully sister while tightening your mouth even more." The therapist uses the client's total organism to teach him something about his feelings. This is done without interpreting behavior. The therapist waits for the client's own revelation: "When I tighten my mouth, I also clench my teeth, and this reminds me of the time I bit my sister. . . ."

The Daseinsanalyse of Gestalt is always in the here and now of the therapy session and includes work with the client's full range of functions. All Gestalt experiments are anchored in the person's experiential life as he presents himself in the situation. Arbitrary exercises thrust on the person (or group), devoid of experiential roots, are not within the realm of phenomenology and of Gestalt therapy at its best, because they do not carry an experiential base, a living context for the client. It is within this living context that most lasting learnings take place.

The session with Harvey described earlier continues with the emphasis on doing, on acting out his dilemma.

> *Joseph:* Would you like to explore being like your father some more?
>
> *Harvey:* I don't like being like him. I always thought I was different. I suppose this may be useful.
>
> *Joseph:* So, behave like you are going to shoot me down the way he would.
>
> *Harvey:* I'll start with words: You are a fragile little man. I am stronger. I could wipe you out like this (clicks his fingers). And you are Jewish too. You are greedy and selfish (voice getting deeper). You will cheat me and other folks like me. . . .
>
> *Joseph:* What do you experience?

Harvey: Some parts are me and others are my father. Especially the Jewish stuff. . . I feel ashamed about that part.

Joseph: Would you share that with your father as if he were here with us now?

Harvey: Yes . . . Dad, I am physically strong like you and I like my voice, too. That's like you, too. And those parts I like.

Joseph: Stay with it.

Harvey: I like being physically strong. And if Joseph hit me, I could beat the shit out of him if I wished. But I am not like you with that Jewish shit. I am not willing to swallow that. You can keep your prejudices . . . stuff them! I am not going to carry that baggage for you.

Joseph: And what is useful for you right now with me? What does it feel like to shoot me down?

Harvey: When I get into that space in me, I feel more. I feel more present—like I am physically larger or something like that. Yes, the room seems a little smaller and you are not the giant I made you out to be. You are Joseph. Just that person. I trust you (looking directly into my eyes). I am not afraid of you, Joseph.

I have tried to help Harvey sift out actual differences between himself and his father, and begin to evaluate aspects of his father's character which he wants to keep or get rid of. Looking through the eyes of his father's strength is supportive. Looking through the eyes of prejudice gets Harvey in touch with his own real values. The experiment allowed him to see what parts of his father he still carries with him and to test out concretely what his internal world offers him and how he can begin to modify it.

Such are the workings of the here and now in Gestalt therapy. Now E.E. Cummings comes back to me. I would hope that I have, in part, remedied his complaint that, "You haven't the least or feeblest conception of being here and now, and alone, and yourself." He continues, ". . . remember one thing only: that it's you—nobody else—who determine your destiny and decide your fate. Nobody else can be alive for you; nor can you be alive for anybody else. Toms can be Dicks and Dicks can be Harrys, but none of them can ever be you. There's the artist's responsibility; and the most awful responsibility on earth. If you can take it, take it—and be. If you can't, cheer up and go about other people's business; and do (or undo) till you drop."*

THE SATISFACTION OF NEEDS:
AWARENESS-EXCITEMENT-CONTACT CYCLE

A psychophysiological cycle goes on in every person. It is related to the satisfaction of needs and is sometimes referred to as the cycle of organismic self-regulation.**

The cycle begins with sensation: I'm sitting here and as I am working, I am beginning to feel some contractions in my stomach. These contractions are accompanied by sensations of dryness in my mouth. As I go on working, the contractions increase and I feel slight nausea. I experience this conglomeration of sensations as "hunger."

Sensations become awareness. I am able to name and describe these sensory mechanisms. Unlike an infant, I do not feel at the mercy of sensations alone. I know what I can do about them. Awareness, therefore, allows me to understand what my body needs at this point in time. I know from previous experience of having neglected my hunger that the next sensation will be a vascular headache. Awareness is a blessing because it enables me to understand what is going on inside, and what I can do to make myself feel better.

As I become aware of my hunger, my body becomes mobilized. I'm feeling certain muscles in my legs warming up. I visualize going to the refrigerator and getting some cheese, bread and fruit. As I'm visualizing, I feel an increase in my

---

*Cummings, E.E. *Six Nonlectures.* New York: Antheneum, 1971.
**Harmon, R. L. "Goals of Gestalt Therapy." *Professional Psychology,* May 1974, 178–184.

respiration and a general mobilization of energy in my body. I am entering the stage of excitement or mobilization of energy. If I were not to have this energy, then I could not put down the tape recorder, get on my feet, go to the kitchen, and help myself to the food. We often take this energy for granted.

I get up and go to the kitchen. This process involves the muscles in my legs and arms; increased respiration and heart rate support my activity. This is the action stage.

The next point in the cycle is called contact. As I take the cheese and begin to chew it, I develop a sense of comfort in my stomach. I'm enjoying the taste of the food. Contact is the psychological process where I engage myself with this food. I'm aggressing the food. The rest of my digestive system comes into focus and transforms what was originally a piece of cheese, a differentiated part of the environment, into something which eventually becomes Joseph. The food and I become one.

As I continue eating and drinking, I become aware of a fullness in my stomach. Now I am satisfied. I feel full and a

GRETA WALDAS

Movement from sensation to contact to withdrawal, and back to sensation.

little dull. I enter a stage of withdrawal, of relaxation, recuperation, disinterest. All of us have experienced having eaten well in a good restaurant, and as we leave the place we glance at the leftovers and feel almost nauseated by the food that was so attractive only minutes before. Complete disinterest sets in once we have gorged ourselves.

As I enter this stage of withdrawal and satisfaction of my need, I become aware of the work I left behind. I am no longer distracted by hunger pains in my stomach, and I am able to focus once again on my awareness of the task at hand. The work emerges as the existing need, and my sensations, awareness, energy, and action are all there to help me carry it out. This movement from sensation to contact to withdrawal, and back to sensation is typical of every organism. In its healthy state, the cycle is smooth, uninterrupted and graceful.

FIGURE-GROUND

Another important concept of Gestalt theory is the figure-ground phenomenon described many years ago by Kohler, Koffka, and Wertheimer.* These Gestalt psychologists talked about figure and ground in relation to perceptual and cognitive phenomenon. Gestalt therapists are interested in figure-ground with respect to all functions of the organism.

Kohler, Koffka and Wertheimer discovered that as we experience the environment visually, we choose a particular focus of interest which stands out for us against a fuzzy background. That which stands out is called figure and the rest is ground; for example, as I am looking at my notes, I see a page which says "Energy" in large, green lettering. This page is figure for me right now. Visually, the ground is the rest of my desk, which appears to be cluttered with a number of things of secondary interest to me. These other things surrounding the page are the ground of my visual experience. If I move my head and look around, I see a beautiful vase. Now this vase

---

*Kohler, W. *Gestalt Psychology.* New York: Liveright Publishing Corp., 1947.

Koffka, K. *Principles of Gestalt Psychology.* New York: Harcourt, Brace & World, 1935.

Wertheimer, M. "Gestalt Therapy." *Social Research,* 1944, *11.*

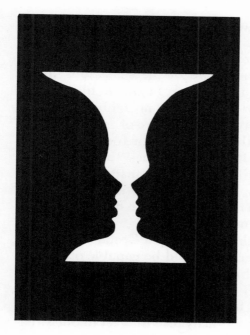

In this perceptual exercise, we may perceive either the vase or the faces as figure.

becomes the figure of my interest, and the page, which was figural, becomes ground.

The healthy individual is able to clearly experience and differentiate something in his foreground which interests and captivates him from that which is not interesting. He experiences the sharpness and clarity of the figure, with little interest in a homogenized ground. In disturbed individuals, there is confusion between figure and ground. There is a lack of purpose and focusing, so that as they look at a particular situation they are not able to pick out that which is central for them, that which has importance for them. From one moment to the next, they are unable to separate the important things for themselves from the unimportant things.

A FINAL INTEGRATION

The development of awareness can be likened to the emergence of a clear figure, and the stage of assimilation and withdrawal is akin to the destruction of the figure into a homogeneous ground. Thus, the sensation, awareness, contact cycle is the *process* by which a figure develops.

As I sit here and become aware of the sensations in my stomach, the figure, which is my work, begins to blur. As my awareness changes to food and I become mobilized to do something about feeding myself, the figure of my work gradually fades and I shift to the new figure of food. I abandon working at my desk and it, then, assumes the position of ground. In the healthy individual, this transition is smooth and flowing, not jarring or disturbing. One moves from one figural need to another emerging need as the first need disappears. It is the natural rhythm of life.

In terms of these models, the goal of Gestalt therapy is relatively simple: Every person should be capable of becoming fully aware of and acting upon his needs. He should be able to insert himself into the environment with all of his skills and resources to get for himself what he needs. As he satisfies himself, he will temporarily lose interest in one situation and move on to his next focus of attention. The satisfaction of needs, if it is to be healthy, usually occurs approximately at the time when they arise, although there are situations in which satisfaction must be postponed in favor of more pressing matters. Most of us learn to postpone the satisfaction of some needs for the sake of long-range goals.

Our interest in the satisfaction of needs does not imply a philosophy of hedonism. It merely states that if the individual is aware of what goes on inside of him and does something about it, he will feel better about himself than the person who does not possess the awareness or postpones satisfying himself.

The implications of this simple proposition are enormous. If I know what I want, I will not look to other people to tell me what I want, nor will I project my own needs on to others. Existentially, my awareness will make it possible for me to take responsibility for actions I take to get what satisfies me. When another person tells me something which angers me and I don't engage him with the feeling I have at the moment,

I will be left with a sense of being suspended. This will happen either because I am not aware of my anger at the time, or because expressing it feels too risky. Sharing the anger is better than not expressing it at all. Postponed expression is difficult to deal with because both parties have already grown stale to the original experience.

Gestalt therapy emphasizes not that we live for the moment, but that we live *in* the moment; not that we meet our needs immediately, but that we are present for ourselves in the environment.

Chapter 5

Goals and
Aspirations

Gestalt therapy is an existential encounter between people. It allows the person to reveal himself in the process of this encounter, rather than assuming an a priori monolithic view of humankind. It is for this reason that Gestalt therapy lends itself to creation; both emphasize the unfolding of something in pure, organic form. However, while Gestalt therapy does not seek to fit people into molds, to deny that goals are implicit in the therapy would be unrealistic. Through a creative involvement in the Gestalt process, it is my hope that a person:

—moves toward greater awareness of himself—his body, his feelings, his environment;

—learns to take ownership of his experiences, rather than projecting them on to others;

—learns to be aware of his needs and to develop skills to satisfy himself without violating others;

—moves toward a fuller contact with his sensations, learning to smell, taste, touch, hear and see—to savor all aspects of himself;

—moves toward the experience of his power and the ability to support himself, rather than relying on whining,

blaming or guilt-making in order to mobilize support
from the environment;

—becomes sensitive to his surroundings, yet at the same
time wears a coat of armour for situations which are
potentially destructive or poisonous;

—learns to take responsibility for his actions and their
consequences;

—feels comfortable with the awareness of his fantasy life
and its expression.

As work progresses, the person flows more comfortably in
the experience of his energy and uses it in a way which allows
him completeness of functioning. He acts without dissipating
his energy by learning to creatively integrate conflicting feelings within himself, rather than pushing against his own organism or polarizing his behavior. Such are some of the general goals of Gestalt therapy. This chapter will detail the
application of the concepts presented in the preceding chapter as a means to achieving these goals.

BRIDGING INTERRUPTIONS WITHIN THE
AWARENESS-EXCITEMENT-CONTACT CYCLE

The Gestalt therapist is particularly interested in bridging
blockages of the awareness-excitement-contact cycle within
the individual. Interruptions within this cycle may be related
to psychopathology as described in psychiatric nomenclature.

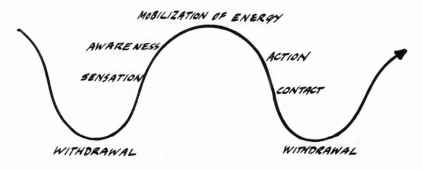

Those of us who are accustomed to formulating our thoughts into conventional psychopathological terms may find the forthcoming discussion useful in the integration of Gestalt theory and psychoanalytic thinking.

All interruptive states may also be discussed from the vantage point of defense mechanisms. For example, the person who blocks sensation from awareness resorts to the defense of repression. He does not allow the emergence of awareness from simple sensory data. The person who blocks between awareness and energy mobilization suffers from introjection; he has swallowed other people's ideas about what is right or wrong and is unable to locate his own energy. The individual who separates his action from his energy is a retroflector; he does to himself what he should be doing to the environment. For example, he devours his stomach (the result is an ulcer)— feeding on himself, rather than feeding on the energy available in his environment. The person who splits his action from his contactfulness suffers from insulation of affect and depersonalization; he's not able to relate his activity to his experience.

Interruption Between Withdrawal and Sensation

When a person is unable to swing back into sensory experience from a state of withdrawal, he may very well be somnifacient, semi-comatose in deep non-REM sleep, or in a hypnotic trance. Another way of looking at this is that the person may be in a dissociated state. Certain profound disorders may be identified in this way, such as undifferentiated schizophrenic states in which the person does not appear to be responding to sensory inputs from his body. The deeply withdrawn individual does not appear to hear or respond to other people. He either chooses not to or cannot take sensorial hints from his body, and may consequently overeat, starve or become incontinent.

Some years ago, when I was a college professor, I decided to demonstrate to my students how hypnosis works. I chose

Interruption between withdrawal and sensation.

an older, mature-looking person, and after some brief history taking, decided he was a suitable subject. Unfortunately, he neglected to tell me he had years of experience with various drugs and had experienced "flashbacks" from numerous encounters with LSD. After having put him into a fairly deep trance, I decided to bring him back. I had conditioned him to hear my voice at all times and to move out of the trance when I said, "Come back to us." But my order didn't seem to touch him; he seemed to remain in a dissociated state and quite comfortable to be away from the ongoing action.

At first I used my voice calmly, ordering him to listen to my words and confirm his auditory response by nodding. Slowly, I proceeded to check out his senses. I took his hand in mine and asked him to attend to the sensations in his hand and arm. Gradually, he began to use simple words like "nice" and "good." All this time his eyes remained closed. I then asked him to slowly open his eyes, look around, and tell me what he could see, beginning with his visual image of me. Later, I had him turn his head around and look at the other students. He began to recognize his friends and to return to the situation while still in a daze. Finally, I had him touch himself—his hands, chest, and face. I asked him to tell us his name and age, and to share his feelings about the experience. (It was at this point that he told us about his LSD trips.)

The bridging of withdrawal and sensation is a slow process. Often such states occur in severely depressed or conversion states. The creative therapist must find a way to insert himself into that part of the person's experience which is still alive, still perking. From there he teaches the client, through directing his awareness, to anchor himself in the environment. This may include the person's awareness of his body, its weight on the chair, its position in space, its minute sounds and movements.

Interruption Between Sensation and Awareness

When a person blocks at the boundary between sensation and awareness, he may experience some of his sensations but he does not understand what they mean. The signals from his body are strange and may even feel frightening.

For example, in an anxiety situation, hyperventilation and rapid heartbeat may be translated and experienced as a "heart attack," rather than an expression of distress. In schizoid and schizophrenic persons, certain sensations in the head, for example, may be misconstrued to mean that the head contains a neoplasm. One such client told me, "My head feels like an empty container filled with blood." Sensations in the lower abdomen and pelvis, which often have sexual connotations, are particularly frightening to some people and are experienced as anxiety, abdominal pain, cramps, lower backache and a variety of other experiential mistranslations. The conversion hysteric may experience anesthesias or temporary paralysis without consciously associating these blocked sensations and movements with sexuality.

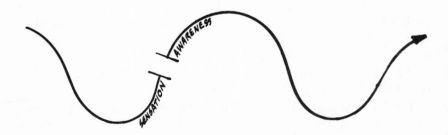

Interruption between sensation and awareness.

There are also many individuals who are simply impoverished in their awareness within a wide range of repression,
including misinterpretation of gas pains in the abdomen to
anxieties about various thoughts, fantasies and feeling states.
In this case, the client is asked to attend to his sensory
experience.

"John, what do you experience in your body right now?" I
ask a man who is blocking anger.

"I am feeling a tightness in my arms, especially my wrists,"
he answers.

"What might you do with your arms to express the tension?" At this point I am getting him to think about the tension in the most general terms—at the level of awareness most
comfortable for him.

Moving his arms up and down, John tells me that he could
swing or stretch them. At this moment he does not know what
his tightness "wants to do." I ask him to continue making
these movements: "Stay with the process of moving your arms
and let me know what you experience."

As John swings his arms up and down, the benign expression on his face slowly changes. He is beginning to look distressed. "I would like to hit something with my fists." There is
a slow transformation from the mere awareness of muscular
sensation to a more complex articulation of a feeling. Eventually, John is able to make a declarative statement about being
"pissed"—transforming the original sensory experience into a
clear awareness of his anger. As he is making hitting movements with his arms, I may ask him to visualize the object of
his anger. In this case, a man who disclaimed all feelings of
resentment was able to contact such feelings at the level of
muscular sensation.

Interruption Between Awareness and Mobilization of Energy

This type of interruption is common among many intellec-
tuals and obsessive-compulsive individuals who may understand themselves cortically, yet feel listless, depressed, and
unable to mobilize themselves for action.

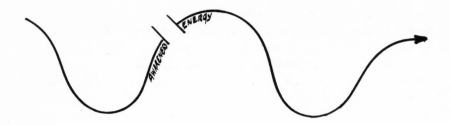

Interruption between awareness and mobilization of energy.

Many individuals, although they are aware of what they need to do, are not able to develop enough impetus to execute what they know is only right and fitting for themselves. The person says, "I know I should stop smoking, but I just haven't got the motivation," or "I am aware of wanting to disagree with my teacher, but I feel like I'm going to faint," or "I understand that it's okay to say 'no' to my parents, but when they get on the phone I start shaking and I just can't do it; I haven't got the push to do it; I haven't got the guts."

Energy is blocked most often by fear of excitement or strong emotions. These emotions include sexuality and anger, as well as expressions of self-righteousness, self-worth, assertiveness, tenderness, and love. Many individuals feel if they allow themselves to become angry, they will annihilate their environment; if they become sexual, they will be maniacal and perverse; if they express love, they will overwhelm and suffocate the other person; if they allow themselves to brag, they will be ridiculed and rejected.

The physiologic blockage accompanying fear of excitement is frequently in respiration. The individual unconsciously makes his breathing shallow, reducing oxygenation of his body and thereby robbing himself of energy. Neurotics and schizoid individuals are commonly shallow breathers. Alexander Lowen points out that the psychotic individual is fixed in an expiratory position, i.e., his chest stays deflated because he is afraid to take the external world into himself. This is one form of disrupting the flow between awareness and a self-supporting energy system. Lowen proposes that neurotics are fixed in the inspiratory position, that their chests are generally overly inflated because they don't exhale fully.*

This form of energy depletion does not allow healthy expression of one's feelings. I think of the multitude of depressed people who complain of fatigue, listlessness, lack of verve. Often, the depressed person retroflects his expression, fearful of expressing dissatisfaction or anger with "loved ones." Instead, he lets the criticism bounce off others and penetrate his own being, suffering his own criticisms, dissatisfactions and angers. Instead of tapping the world of its energy, he saps his own juices.

The retroflector turns against himself rather than turning against those who displease him. Another form of retroflection involves doing for oneself what is wished from others. Thus, he strokes himself instead of approaching a potential stroker; he masturbates in secrecy (and often in shame) instead of approaching a potential sexual partner. The price he pays—among other things—is that of using his own energy rather than being replenished by another person. His rewards are independence, self-reliance, doing better for himself than another can, privacy, and the development of his individual capacities and talents.**

When the murderously angry person overdoes his retroflecting, he kills himself (which in my view is superior to killing others).⁺ Unfortunately, too many people turn against themselves, robbing their lives of the energy needed to express their potency, creativity, innovation, and need for social change.

The retroflector usually suffers physical (muscular-skeletal) symptoms which show where the energy is frozen. Thus, you can expect dull chest pain in the person who interrupts energy by breathing very shallowly or by inflating the chest without adequate exhalation. Tension in the neck, shoulders and arms

---

*Lowen, A. *The Betrayal of the Body.* London: Collier Books, 1967
**It must be kept in mind that every interruption, every "defense," is also a system of saving the self, of supporting, buttressing and protecting oneself.
⁺My friend and colleague, Cynthia Harris, and I have often discussed this issue. Cynthia points out that retroflection is the mark of a civilized society. Imagine the chaos generated if everyone in New York City decided to undo their retroflections!

may reflect interruption of energy with respect to needs involving contact with others—needs to hold, hold on to, hit, aggress.

Much of my work involves finding the focus of interrupted energy and bringing the sensations to the person's awareness. Before he can free his energy, it helps to have a kind of cortical endgram that says, "If I begin to exhale more fully, I'll feel more energy and that will help me get rid of my depression." Once the awareness is integrated into the person, he can accept the notion of doing breathing exercises. If he knows, for example, that his voice will be stronger and more powerful when he fills his lungs with air before speaking, he will have good reason to attend to his breathing.

Bridging blockages between awareness and energy is crucial. Think of the hundreds of people who "learn" to understand themselves, their marriages, their families, the situation in the world by talking to friends and reading. This form of learning is limited; too often words beget more words. What Gestalt therapy offers is the notion of energizing the action systems which the words imply. As you are reading this page, begin to attend to your breathing. (Breathe fully but not rapidly, or else you will hyperventilate and faint.) Let the breathing affect your awareness. What processes in your body come into focus? Bladder tension? Lower bowel fullness? Dryness in your mouth? Dullness in your visual field? Tightness in your genitals, sphincter, chest, shoulders or lower back? Put the book down and continue breathing gently, focusing on the area that comes to your attention most fully. Let that area "warm up" with energy, as if your breathing infuses that part of your body with warmth, with a call to action. What sort of action or movement is implied?

These words alone are not going to change your behavior—only mobilization of your inner liveliness will do that. Yet thousands of counselors, social workers, therapists and analysts have not worked with their clients beyond verbal exchanges. The beauty of Gestalt work is that it bridges verbal proclamations with muscular expression, with activity. Here is where Gestalt enters the province of behaviorism, Reichian analysis, and bioenergetics. It invites the person to act out that which is partially formulated on the basis of historical understanding and conceptual insights.

"Acting out" in Gestalt therapy is not equivalent to "acting out" as described in psychoanalytic literature. For the analyst it connotes leaving the office and engaging in behavior which is not ego-integrated—an impulse driven by the essence of the neurosis itself. It is the bursting forth of a symptom, such as buying an expensive car while deep in debt or becoming promiscuous without understanding one's motives. Within the Gestalt process, acting out takes place as controlled experimentation, often within the therapist's office. The client acts out of the energy which has been contacted and directed to a system which is long overdue in its use. The client may raise his voice or pace the room or pound pillows. He may be moved to hold the therapist's hands or withdraw into a corner. He may allow himself to cry out for help or dance or act like a young child. He practices the use of energy which has been mobilized for the first time. In "homework" assignments, the person may be asked to experiment with contacting his awareness and extending it to concrete physical expression.

Interruption Between Mobilization of Energy and Action

In this form of blockage, a person is spinning his wheels,

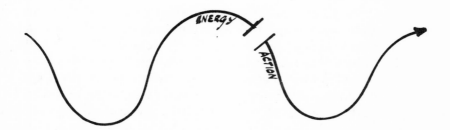

Interruption between mobilization of energy and action.

unable to act on his impulses. He may be mobilized, yet unable to use his energy in the service of activity which gets him what he wants. His chronic unexpressed mobilization may result in somatic symptoms, including hyperventilation, hypertension, and chronic muscular tension. Another category of dysfunction would include impotence, a situation in which the person may be in contact with his sexual energy but unable to achieve full erection or ejaculation. An extreme example of interruption between high energy and action is that of catatonic schizophrenic states, in which the individual may be rageful but appears listless and suffers from either complete muscular flaccidity or severe spasticity.

In most of these states, the task and goal of the therapist are to allow the patient, if only in the most minute and limited way, to express the energy which he experiences within himself. The person has good reason to hold himself in, so it is important that such expression take place at the level and dosage comfortable for him. The novice therapist must be familiar with basic pathology so that he does not push the client into action for which he is not ready. For example, the catatonic schizophrenic must learn the full scope of awareness and contact and its relation to the range of his energy; only then can complete expression take place. For such a person, small dosages of verbally expressed anger are a safe and appropriate goal. He needs to learn how to control, grade and modulate his rage, rather than to burst forth with it.

In most instances, the Gestalt therapist works with neurotics who are often unable to put the most basic feelings and energies into action. He invents experiments in which such action states can be explored in the relative safety of the consultation room. I see the average middle-class or upper-middle-class client belonging in this category. I know this is a dangerous oversimplification, but it's worth making for the sake of the point. The point is that most of these people wish away their lives with "if onlys": If only I could take a vacation in the islands; if only I could ask for a promotion; if only the kids would know how hard I work; if only I liked the notion of making money, etc., etc.

Very often, the person has the awareness of his wish and

even the energy. What happens? What does he *do* at the precious moment when the energy is there? Often he deflects the energy; he switches on the TV set, goes to the movies, or engages in bullshit about "how it would be" or "how it should be." He breaks the energy as it builds for fear of failure or ridicule, or the disappointment or disapproval of others. It is also true that often the person doesn't move beyond simple awareness of the wish and does not even recognize the availability of energy to do what needs to be done.

Most of my work is with college teachers, therapists, students, and professionals in general. They are often bright, gifted, intact, and at the same time, stuck. Unlike the lower-class folks who may learn to translate impulse into action too readily (another awful generalization), most people I work with get stuck in a morass of ideational self-deceptions and rationalizations.* My work, therefore, involves making some of their ideas believable, locating energy systems sitting behind these notions, and most importantly, putting the needs or convictions into action. You want to learn to swim? *How* do you experience the lack? *Where* is the energy behind this lack? What can you *do* with this energy to start swimming? You want to change the Republicans? What is it to you if they remain the same? Do you have energy to do something about it? What could you do tomorrow morning?

My clients are the silent majority—except they are not really silent. They bitch and moan and their preference is for me to stroke them and say, "Now, now, things will get better." No such thing—if you are not willing to get off your ideational ass and translate thoughts into even the most humble, minute (but for you, significant) behaviors, then we are not engaged in Gestalt therapy!

---

*The lower-class, culturally deprived person living in the ghetto is, in a way, the polar opposite of those I am talking about. He needs to learn to be more fully aware of experience, and even to gargle it intellectually; he could use some of the intellectual rumination of the middle-class persons. If he is in a bar drinking and someone calls his sister a whore, it may help him to stay with his awareness for a moment or two before pulling his Saturday night special and shooting. In Gestalt therapy, this man would visualize his feelings in the bar. He may become aware of the fright that was bypassed, or the feeling of guilt or humiliation. All those thoughts/feelings are jumped over into impulsive behavior. The outcome is that even the expression which takes place is not integrated into himself.

Interruption Between Action and Contact

Interruption between action and contact.

This is a person who is often clinically "hysteric." His feeling is diffused; he talks a lot and does a hell of a lot, but he cannot assimilate his experience. He is not in contact with his work and is not nourished by his energy output or the consequences of his behavioral generosity. His energy is diffused throughout the boundaries of his body, rather than focused in a specific system and supporting a particular function. He is not able to act pointedly; he is all over the place; he is distracted. When he eats, he cannot taste the food. When he makes love, he has only vague genital sensations. When he runs, he is not aware of the contraction and relaxation of muscle groups. When he plays tennis, he swings hard, not watching the ball carefully.

These dysfunctions give him a sense of inner unreality. He often feels out of contact with his environment and sometimes experiences a shallowness or an emptiness in his inner life which may be physically translated into a feeling of emptiness in his chest cavity or abdomen. He may attempt to compensate for his sense of emptiness by overindulging in sexual activity, eating, or the use of drugs. Accentuated sensation gives him a sense of contact with himself, however limited; at these moments homogenized states of consciousness are transformed into clear figures of self-awareness.

The so-called hysteric needs help in becoming fully aware of small bits of behavior and their consequences. The therapist's goal is to help the client localize his inner energy, attend to it, and keep it from bursting forth prematurely. For example, he may be asked to walk around the room and allow himself the full awareness of his activity, without rushing or becoming distracted. Controlled experiments may also be executed with reference to sexual activity or the expression of anger. The person can thus constantly focus on that which nourishes him and learn to clearly verbalize how and in what way he is in contact with his sexuality or anger.

Interruptions Between Contact and Withdrawal, Withdrawal and Sensation: Disturbances in Rhythm

There is rhythm between contact and withdrawal. One learns how to pay attention to one's needs, how to go about satisfying them, then to withdraw and rest. Being constantly mobilized is also a kind of sickness, a sickness of not having peace. Many people have a stereotyped view of happiness or self-actualization. They want to be "up" or "high" and not "down." They conceptualize the down as a sickness or a state of uselessness, rather than a part of the cycle in their daily lives.

One example of an actual cycle is that of wakefulness and

Disturbances in rhythm.

sleepiness. Physiological psychologists have discovered that all of us have wakefulness cycles, that within a 24-hour period we move from mental and physical dullness to mental and physical sharpness repeatedly. We are excited and later we feel quiet; we talk and then we are silent; we work and then we rest. Sometimes we feel accepting and at other times we push away; sometimes we are jolly and later we are sad; we gravitate toward others and at other times we need solitude.

Our culture reflects a prejudice against experiencing this natural rhythm. It is more acceptable to be verbal than silent. Consistent productivity is favored over "laziness." Confluence is preferred to confrontation. Being jolly is reinforced and sadness discouraged. Socializing is preferred over solitude.* Being satisfied with oneself is often seen as more desirable than being dissatisfied. To be fully in control is preferred to shyness or embarrassment. Certainty is superior to confusion. Energy is preferred to tiredness. These Western cultural preferences are rejections of a life which has rhythm, variability of movement, and continuity.

The individual who interrupts contact and withdrawal is not able to let go at the height or culmination of his experience. He hangs on to the experience beyond the point of its optimum return and may use the defense of denial to shut out sensations of fatigue, heaviness or dullness. At the contact boundary, where the action takes place with respect to the world, he becomes confused. He does not know if he has had enough stimulation or if, indeed, the stimulation has taken place. If he is holding another person's hand, he may not sense the other's need to let go of his clasp. He may approach the other person too closely or rapidly, not sensing where the other experiences contact comfort and where the contact needs to be stopped. He also has difficulty with contact dosage, not knowing how much to give or get, and has a tendency not to hear the messages of others. As a result, he may find that he is rejected and feel confused about distances between him-

---

*For many, solitude connotes loneliness. For creative, healthy individuals, solitude is a state in which one feels grounded, solid, comfortable, and self-supportive while being alone. Some people don't see it that way; they see aloneness as a lack.

self and others. Thus, he may maintain too "wide" a distance from others, not enjoying nourishment when it is available.

He has a dosage problem with himself as well. He may overwork because he has interrupted his own sense of well-being, or if he is stuck between withdrawal and sensation, he has difficulty getting back into alertness and action. He may not be familiar with sensations which connote fatigue and sleepiness. At the level of neurosis, the person drives himself or slumps into a depression or vacillates between the two. The manic-depressive person is merely an exaggerated form of this difficulty, partially supported by physiological factors. At the basis of fears of aloneness or inactivity is the fear of ultimate stillness—death. The person who fights giving up the day and stays up till four o'clock in the morning may be frightened of the daily rhythm of living and dying.

One purpose of the therapeutic experience is to become open to the variety of rhythms in our lives. It exposes us to the richness of silence and the need for rest. When a client falls silent and feels anxious, I encourage him to attend to the quality and sensations of being there without words. Words fill the lacuna of anxiety; anxiety raises specific issues not faced before, and provides the fuel for problem-solving.

I would prefer to live a life in which I can be with others when I choose and enjoy my solitude when it comes upon me. I would much rather give myself permission to be dissatisfied or critical of myself than to exaggerate parts of my life which are good and right. I would like to teach my clients to stay with the sweetness, freshness and purity of their shyness and embarrassment, and let those states radiate into newly found awareness. Childlike qualities and playfulness are as significant in the rhythm of life as "adult seriousness." It is important to appreciate my confusion and to stay with it until clarity is born.

To everything there is a season, and a time to every purpose under heaven: a time to be born, and a time to die. A time to plant and a time to pluck up that which is planted. A time to kill, and a time to heal. A time to break down,

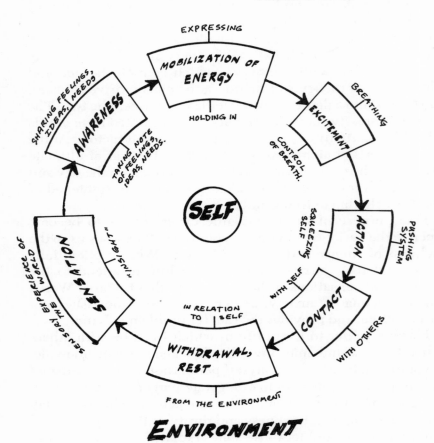

SELF, ENVIRONMENT, &
THE AWARENESS-EXCITEMENT-
CONTACT CYCLE~

and a time to build up. A time to weep, and a time to laugh. A time to mourn, and a time to dance. A time to cast away stones, and a time to gather stones together. A time to embrace, and a time to refrain from embracing. A time to get, and a time to lose. A time to keep, and a time to cast away. A time to rend, and a time to sew. A time to keep silence, and a time to speak. A time to love, and a time to hate. A time of war, and a time of peace.*

The Case of Carol

Carol begins her work in the group by indicating that she has very little to say. There's a long silence; Carol looks pensive and stares at the floor. After some minutes, she tells the group she has difficulty expressing herself because she has feelings of incompetence. Some discussion ensues about competence: She does not feel the word is quite right to describe her experience; it has implications of professional inferiority and that is not precisely what she means. I suggest the word "inadequate" and she is satisfied.

Carol's sensory experience seems obscured. My hunch is that whatever richness of sensation there is does not emerge into her awareness due to anxiety about sharing it with the group. My co-therapist suggests that perhaps Carol tell us something about her sense of inadequacy in everyday life situations. I modify that request by asking her to tell individual group members how she feels inferior to them.

After some careful consideration, Carol turns to me and tells me ways in which she feels inadequate, and also ways in which she feels equal to me. Then she turns to another member and shares another piece of her sense of inadequacy.

After a few statements to group members, there is a long pause and I am aware of how carefully Carol is considering everything she has to say. Her voice is monotonous and her breathing extremely shallow. She expresses very little feeling

---

*Ecclesiastes 3:1-9, *The Oxford Annotated Bible, with the Apocrypha.* Oxford, Eng.: Oxford University Press, Inc., RSV. 1965.

and seems to have no energy. Her statements are made slowly and with excruciating caution.

From the quality of her language, I suspect her level of awareness has been activated and is quite rich. Yet it remains hidden from the group, serving as a self-protective stance. She is holding on to herself, to her ideas; she bloats herself with thoughts. Her energy is retroflected, turned inward; she is working against herself, her awareness and her potential to contact others. The result is half-assed output with constant blocking at every level in the awareness-contact cycle. Consequently, much of the energy is coming from myself, my co-leader, and other group members.

I suspect her narcissistic orientation allows her to imagine herself as superior to others in reaction to her own self-doubts. I say to her, "Carol, underneath your feelings of inadequacy are delusions of grandeur, and I suspect that what you're actually thinking are the many ways in which you are superior, or at least equal, to any of us."

"Yes," she says, "I was just having great difficulty finding other people to whom I'm clearly inferior."

"Well, then," I say, "lean into the feelings of your grandeur and tell as many people as you can the ways in which you are superior to them."

Carol seems challenged by this task and her energy level rises. She turns to one person after another, sharing—at first in a negative way and then in a more declarative, positive style— how she is better than the other person.

Yet there are still heavy pauses between her statements—a kind of deadly, ominous silence in the room. I say to her, "For a person who needs to be superior, you must feel like the words you choose should be perfect to describe the person accurately. And if you choose ordinary words, then you will be either inferior or equal to us. You burden yourself by having to invent precision in your language."

Margaret suggests to Carol that she look the people over and describe what goes on in her mind during her decision-making process. Carol's eyes liven up at this possibility and after some initial nervousness, she begins: "I'm looking at you,

John, and I cannot think of any way in which I am superior, so I am now shifting my gaze to Mary and I think I can think of something to say to you, Mary, but I feel protective of you. . . ."

In the process of describing her internal experience of the people in the group, Carol begins to lubricate herself. I can sense her increasing involvement in the process. Her energy flows more fully as the process continues, until she begins to support herself in her own expression.

Although Carol is now able to be verbally fluid, her face and manner continue to be flat. Her eyes, however, are very expressive. I encourage her to express her feelings toward the people in the group in a more concrete, physical manner. My co-therapist suggests that Carol begin by making eyes at people. In the process, Carol stands up for the first time. She approaches people and gazes, stares, blinks or playfully winks at them.

As she continues relating to people in this way, there is great animation and liveliness in the room. At one point she approaches Harriet and gazes at her very steadily and fully. Having previously told Harriet that she feels more grounded than Harriet appears to be, Carol now seems to have a spell-binding effect on her. Harriet begins to weep and they embrace. There is a great deal of warmth and intensity of feeling between them as Harriet shares the sense of peacefulness she experiences with Carol.

At this point, Carol is encouraged to attend to her breathing and to look at people as if she were breathing through her eyes. This instruction further facilitates her movement toward completion of her experience. She becomes active, playful and intensely physical with people, actually wrestling with some group members. Her contactfulness is evident in both her glowing appearance and her authentic relationship to the group.

Finally, Carol sits down. Her face is open, her breathing free. The group proceeds to give her feedback and some of the learning which is initially fleeting and tentative becomes more fully assimilated. Before the end of the session, Carol says, "I am learning that the world is more pliable than I imagined it to be. I am also learning not to be so introspective and stingy when there is so much richness around me and such opportunities to express myself."

This woman had sat through most of the workshop without getting even minimally involved. She felt quite threatened, and the possibility of getting anything done was fairly remote unless the therapists worked with expressive behavior directly related to her own output, i.e., the use of her lively eyes. Obstacles and resistances were converted into interactive events of some meaning to both her and the rest of the group. Carol progressed from her intense thoughtfulness, which was taxing, heavy, and lacking vitality, to verbal interaction, to physical interaction and active relation to other people in the group. By the end of the session her behavior was self-initiated and supportive. The gradual mobilization of her energy was vital. At each stage of the sensation-awareness-contact cycle, more energy became available so that she could support the kind of activity required to experience completion, withdrawal and rest.

THE DISCOVERY OF NEW CONCEPTS

Let us say I have an experience, Experience A. This Experience A leads me to believe certain things about myself—Concept A_1. The learned belief is that I am physically inferior. This belief is of no use to me, especially since by most criteria I am quite "normal." Yet I carry around the concept of my physical inferiority and it limits me in performing certain functions: I may not be willing to lift heavy objects or to engage in some other physical activities which I construe as too dangerous or strenuous.

In my therapy I share my concept of frailness with Erving Polster. In the course of our work, he stimulates me to dance, show my gracefulness and physical strength. I even learn how to stand on my head. Out of these experiments, I am compelled to think differently of my body. I move from Experi-

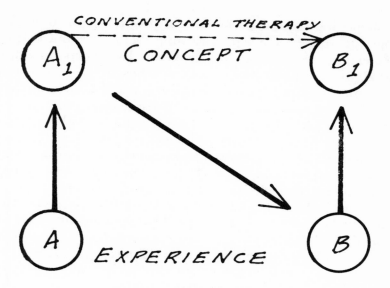

CONVENTIONAL THERAPY

CONCEPT

EXPERIENCE

The discovery of new concepts.

ence A and Concept A₁ (frailness) to Experience B, which is a new physical experience of myself. The next step is that out of this new experience, I evolve a new concept, B₁, which is a novel statement about myself. The new statement may be something like, "I may be thin, but I am strong," or "My body may look frail to others, but I am graceful," or "I may look fragile, but I am nimble and quick."

Gestalt therapy may be conceived of as the development of new concepts of ourselves by inventing new experiences of ourselves in the therapeutic situation. Such a transition is more powerful in terms of learning than a transition from Concept A to Concept B. In other words, if I am talking with someone and I say, "I am physically sickly," and he says, "That's not how you look to me," and I respond, "I suppose you're right; I don't really look sickly," the assimilation of the new concept is much more difficult than when the concept comes out of a concrete experience in the therapy situation.

I associate psychoanalysis with a lateral learning in which one moves from Concept A to Concept B to Concept C, without acquiring basic experiental and physiological underpinnings for the new concept. Learning that moves out of concrete experience, such as that generated by an experiment, is like zigzag learning. The person reaches down to concrete experience and develops ideas about himself which are supported by these behaviors and facilitative of new ones.

Let's go back to Carol's case. She began her work with two primary self-concepts: inability to express herself and a sense of inadequacy. During her work she engaged in a progression of expressive experiments with group members. She had an opportunity to concretely compare herself to others by generating data as well as engaging in physical encounters. Her conceptual understanding of herself began to change. She developed a new view of herself as someone who could move in a more pliable world, experience its richness, and express her inner life. As a result, her orientation to herself and others moved from a kind of retroflective "stinginess" to a more realistically balanced appreciation of herself and her environment. These learnings were behaviorally based—embedded in her voice, her eyes, her movements, her total organism. My feeling is that this organismic learning has longer staying power than a cognitive learning experience in which one "computes out" one concept and "computes in" a substitute concept of the self.

THE EXPANSION OF EXPERIENTIAL RANGE

Another purpose of psychotherapy is to acquire a broad range of internal experience of the self. Not only can one know both sides of a particular phenomenon, but one can also experience all the intermediate points within that phenomenon. Gestalt therapy conceives of "symptoms" not as discrete items, but as the narrowing of a range within a certain set of functions. A person's response to a situation may become so narrow that it cripples him in terms of fluidity and flexibility of functioning.

Let us say that a person is either hysterical or compulsive in

RANGE:

STRETCHING THE SELF

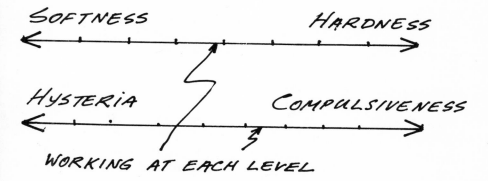

SOFTNESS   HARDNESS

HYSTERIA   COMPULSIVENESS

WORKING AT EACH LEVEL

relation to the environment. If he responds hysterically, his reaction time is very fast and his experience widespread, like a flash flood. He has enormous difficulty assimilating the experience, much less learning something from it. His learning potential is like water running through a pipe without any place to cling.

In the compulsive mode, the individual is so reluctant to respond and so slow and deeply self-searching in relation to the stimulus, that he is not able to function flexibly or quickly enough to nourish himself.

Carol falls on the compulsive extreme in this particular polarization. There is nothing wrong with compulsiveness when it fits a particular task. But when it immobilizes one's expression, as it did in Carol's case, then the person can use a bit of "hysteric" expressiveness. The object was not to help Carol become a thoughtless act-outer, but to help her discover where she can function fluidly and creatively between her compulsiveness and hysteria. In the group she was able to play with her behavioral range enough to learn that expressive generosity which is thoughtful and does not violate her integrity is most satisfying. Gestalt therapy helps us find these in-between behaviors so that we can use the full potential of the experiential range within ourselves.

META-NEEDS AND META-THERAPY GOALS

Abraham Maslow talked about a range of human needs, including "meta-needs." By meta-needs he meant needs which are no longer reducible to a smaller component.*Meta-needs would involve the need for purity, justice, beauty, truth. If you ask a lawyer why he practices law, and he tells you, "Because I love justice," and you ask him, "Why do you love justice?" and he says, "Because I love justice," he is telling you that justice is an aspiration for him which is no longer explainable beyond what it is. It is like Jehovah saying, "I am who am," meaning, "I am the absolute which is no longer reducible. My own validity is what it is."

Maslow then went on to conjecture that whenever meta-needs are frustrated, "meta-illness" results. If a person lives in an ugly environment and has a need for beauty, he will suffer symptoms stemming from the ugliness of the environment. If he is living in a totalitarian state and is not able to tolerate the lack of freedom or truth or free movement, he begins to suffer the pain related to that state of frustration. These needs are so powerful that he may decide to climb over the wall to freedom, even if his chances of survival are small. He would rather die than be suppressed.

Symptoms resulting from frustration of ordinary human needs, such as physiological comfort, security, safety, love, belonging and recognition, result in neuroses, psychoses and

*Maslow, A. *Toward A Psychology of Being* [2nd Ed.] Van Nostrand, New York, 1958.

other disorders described in psychoanalytic literature. On the other hand, the frustration of meta-needs, although it may result in pathology that mimics the aforementioned, requires a different kind of healing experience. Whereas most therapies are designed to cure the "common" pathologies resulting from frustration of lower-level needs, these therapies do not address themselves to the frustration of meta-needs and to meta-sicknesses in our society, sufferings of the spirit, of the highest human potentialities.

When we teach techniques for curing symptoms, such as in Wolpian desensitization or conditioning therapy, we teach how to eradicate symptoms rather than how to deal with the deepest levels of the human spirit. I would hope that most therapists are fairly equipped to deal with the usual symptomatology, but I suspect that most of us are not equipped to deal with meta-sicknesses. It is for this reason that many Eastern schools of thought or combinations of Eastern schools and Western psychotherapy have become so popular in America in recent years. As our welfare system grows and more people survive physically, we become aware of people who suffer from soul sickness, a sickness of the spirit. This kind of deprivation requires a curative methodology which is transpersonal and more profound in its orientation. An example of such a method of therapy is found in the Arica school.

The Gestalt therapist who himself is able to grow and move beyond a level of technical competence toward personal expansiveness, depth and spirituality is more capable of working with meta-sickness than one who has merely learned the technical aspects of adjusting individuals to their existing environment. The latter—the "grease and oil" therapists—maintain society at the level of adjustment; they give society the lubricant by which it can function from day to day, by which people can live their lives and adjust to their daily demands.

As I experience my own growth, I aspire more to reach the person at the level which is most relevant for him. Occasionally it is also important to inspire people, to model the full range of humanness which jolts them into goals they never understood, much less considered.

Generally speaking, Gestalt methods are oriented to behavioral change rather than intellectual insight alone. We have learned over the years that a person may "understand" himself in great depth, yet continue behaving in the same dysfunctional ways. Gestalt therapy bridges the gap between cognitive therapies and behavior modification. We expose the person to experiential insights. Such are some of the goals. These goals by no means summarize the system, nor do they give credit to its respect for subtlety, individual styles, and complexity of human functioning.

Sometimes I feel that we are too ambitious in our goals and aspirations, that we "shoot for the stars" before we achieve ways of having simple and concrete support experiences within ourselves and with loved ones. We must learn how to chew, taste and smell saltine crackers before we can enjoy gourmet food. We must acquire internal richness before being able to distill a range of life experiences into personal essences. And later, we must learn to see the cosmic irony in these essences—that becoming fixed in any system, including the one in this book, is to imprison ourselves.

Chapter 6

The Experiment

Gestalt therapy is an integrated version of phenomenology and behaviorism.* Our orientation is similar to phenomenology because we respect the individual's internal experience: Therapeutic work is rooted in the client's own perspective. At the same time, we modify concrete behavior in a graded and carefully timed manner. Thus, a unique quality of Gestalt therapy is its emphasis on modifying a person's behavior in the therapy situation itself. This systematic behavior modification, when it grows out of the experience of the client, is called an experiment.

The experiment is the cornerstone of experiential learning. It transforms talking about into doing, stale reminiscing and theorizing into being fully here with all one's imagination, energy, and excitement. For example, by acting out an old, unfinished situation, the client is able to comprehend it in its richest context and to complete the experience using the resources of his present wisdom and understanding of life.

Experiments can involve every sphere of human function-

*Kepner, E. and Brien, L. "Gestalt Therapy: A Behavioristic Phenomenology." In J. Fagan and I. L. Shepherd, *Gestalt Therapy Now.* Palo Alto, Cal.: Science and Behavior Books, Inc., 1970.

Watt, T. W. (ed.) *Behaviorism and Phenomenology.* Chicago: The University of Chicago Press, 1964.

ing; however, most experiments have one quality in common —they ask the client to express something behaviorally, rather than to merely cognize an experience internally. There are some experiments which do include the active involvement of cognitive processes, such as visualization, fantasy, and guided dreams. These experiments may not rely on the use of skeletal muscles—at least that is how it looks on the surface. However, as I carefully watch a client imagine a scene in his life, I often note changes in breathing, posture, muscle tonus and facial expression. The absence of gross body movement does not imply lack of body involvement; every experiment has a strong behavioral component in it.

The nature of the experiment depends on the individual's problems, what the person experiences in the here and now, as well as the repertoire of life experiences which both client and therapist bring to the session. Experiments may include verbalization at a new and novel level for the client. I may ask the person to focus his fantasy on his childhood, make up a "memory" of it, and share it verbally. An experiment may include moving parts of the body or concentrating on aspects of one's physical functioning, such as breathing or muscle tension. I may ask a client to talk to imaginary forces within himself, to address people in his life, to sing, or dance, to jump or change his voice, to pound pillows, to assume attitudes of gruffness, hardness, softness, anger, sweetness, sentimentality.

The experiment asks the person to actively explore himself. The client becomes the chief manager of his learning experience. He helps set up the way in which a problem is approached and acts upon his own judgment in carrying out his plan. He progresses with the encouragement, prodding and imaginative suggestions of the therapist, who acts as the consultant and director of the creation of a scenario for which the client provides the content and feeling. Everything comes to life in the here and now of the therapy hour. This process transforms dreams, fantasies, memories, reminiscences and hopes into lively, ongoing, dynamic happenings between therapist and client.

At a certain point in this self-generated event, the client experiences an Aha! He says, "Now I understand how I am," or "Yes, that's how I feel," or "Now I know what I need to do, how I need to act to get what I want in this situation." He is his own teacher. His own Aha! cannot be superseded by another person's experience, suggestions, or interpretations. His discovery stands solidly on its own feet. The consultation room becomes a lively laboratory, a microcosm in which the person explores himself at a realistic level without fear of rejection or criticism.

The creative experiment, if it works well, helps the person leap forward into new expression, or at least it pushes the person into the boundaries, the edges where his growth needs to take place. The long-range purposes of the experiment are to increase the client's range of awareness and self-under-

At a certain point, the client experiences an Aha! He says, "Now I know what I need to do!"

standing, to expand his freedom to act effectively within his environment, and to broaden his repertoire of behaviors in a variety of life situations. More specifically, the goals of creative experimentation within the therapeutic setting are:

—to expand the person's repertoire of behavior;
—to create conditions under which the person can see his life as his *own creation* (take ownership of therapy);
—to stimulate the person's experiential learning and the evolution of new self-concepts from behavioral creations;
—to complete unfinished situations and overcome blockages in the awareness/excitement/contact cycle;
—to integrate cortical understandings with motoric expressions;
—to discover polarizations which are not in awareness;
—to stimulate the integration of conflictual forces in the personality;
—to dislodge and reintegrate introjects and generally place "misplaced" feelings, ideas, and actions where they belong in the personality;
—to stimulate circumstances under which the person can feel and act stronger, more competent, more self-supported, more explorative and actively responsible to himself.

An experiment is not a monolithic event which solves a central problem and neatly wraps it in the elegant structure of the session. An experiment is a tool, a way of working with a person experientially. Experiments may often be used to sharpen questions, not just answer them:

Client: I don't know what I want to work on today.
Joseph: Would you like to play with the notion of "not knowing" to see if there is something in it for you?
Client: Yeah, never thought of that. I often put myself down for not knowing something in advance . . .

Here, instead of pursuing what is to be worked on, the experiment explores the client's attitude about the *manner* in which he experiences his way of approaching problems.

> *Joseph:* Good, get into a state of not knowing; look around the room and start telling me what you see and experience from the point of view of a "not knower."

Here, the experiment is searching for a more central theme for the client.

> *Client:* I am looking at the abstract painting. I don't understand what it means. My father is a painter, as you know, and I always felt inadequate in my understanding of abstract art.

In this way, the therapy session may become a series of small experiential situations which are organically intertwined with each other, each event serving a particular function for the client and holding in it a potential surprise, a discovery totally unexpected by both client and therapist. Unlike a rigidly structured scientific procedure, the Gestalt experiment is a way of thinking out loud, a concretization of one's imagination, a creative adventure.

THE EVOLUTION OF AN EXPERIMENT

An experiment takes place in a field of psychological energy between two or more people. We call one person a therapist or counselor, and another a patient or client. These names do not account for the complex transactions by which two people create a drama within a particular space and time sequence, a drama which often changes their lives. As in the case of observing lovers, one cannot always tell who gave and who received; one cannot generalize that this person created and the other followed instructions.

The making of the experiment is a complex dance, a cooperative journey. The therapist is often the guide, frequently pointing out important sights. He gets his hands dirty in exploring the road. The client is hardly a passive follower. He is often aware which directions in the road will move him closer to his own self-actualization. To make things more complex, the "client" may be a whole group of people, or the therapist and client may be the same person, as in the case of one's working on oneself in a time of crisis.

The process by which an experiment is developed is complex and difficult to describe. As with any other creation, it is tempting to say, "It just happened," or "The work evolved that way," or "Watch what I am doing and find out for yourself." At the same time, I know that the development of my work does have a lawful sequence, a sense of order. Although the sequence, content, and form change over time, I want to present a general cognitive map with which you can identify.

An experiment generally evolves in the following sequence:

> —laying the groundwork;*
> —negotiating consensus between therapist and client;
> —grading the work in terms of experienced difficulty for the client;
> —surfacing the client's awareness;
> —locating the client's energy;
> —focusing awareness and energy toward the development of a theme;
> —generating self-support for both client and therapist;
> —choosing a particular experiment;
> —enacting the experiment;
> —debriefing the client—insight and completion.

As I think about these developmental levels of the experiment, I realize that the sequence may be arbitrary. For exam-

*The notions of groundwork, consensus and grading have been brilliantly formulated in the teachings of Dr. Sonia Nevis, Gestalt Institute of Cleveland.

ple, preparatory groundwork may actually follow consensus, or work around location of energy may evolve immediately in the natural course of events between people. I prefer to look at these variables as cells which float in and out of the organic process as the experiment evolves over time.

Groundwork

Before something can grow on your earth, you must understand the earth's configuration, be willing to clear it of its rocks, and till it well. And so it is with the creation of an experiment in the therapy session.

First and foremost, one must be willing to explore the other person's perspective: What sort of background is the other person communicating out of? Is it an aspect of his childhood? Is it filled with complaints? Is it related to current relationships with other people? Is it filled with bodily aches and pains or other physical discomforts? Is it judgmental or hysterically scattered or frozen by obsessive perfectionism?

Taking in the other person's experience requires the development of rapport in the beginning of each and every session —a warming-up process of re-establishing contact again and again. In the beginning of the session it is important not to interrupt the person, but to allow him to develop the feelings and ideas which spontaneously arise in him, in order to fully understand what is in his mind. The client will often allow himself to be interrupted and even diverted to an area of interest for the therapist, and if an experiment develops out of such an interruption, it will have little relevance or investment for the client.

As the person is encouraged to spontaneously communicate his feelings and experience in the here and now, a number of strands of communication are established and gradually distilled by the therapist into a unifying theme which he can then pursue in the form of an experiment. However, it is important that initially one of these strands be developed further in order to lay the groundwork for the unifying theme.

I will use an example. In one of my last workshops, I talked to a young therapist, whom I'll call Dick. He spoke of how he always felt in the "one-down" position in relation to "well-known therapists." As he spoke, it became obvious that he needed to deal with his feelings of lack of worth in relation to accomplished individuals, as well as feelings related to people in authority, including his own father. However, what was foreground for me as he spoke was not so much the content, but the speed with which Dick spoke to me.

As he talked, imagery floated through me. I saw him dressed in a long-distance runner's outfit. He was running very fast through the countryside. Somewhere on the side of the road were his mother and father, his priest, and some important teachers in his life. It was summer and the landscape was bright and colorful. But Dick was so intent on his speed and on getting to his goal of greatness that his vision blurred and he couldn't see anything on the side of the road. He couldn't see his father clearly enough to understand his father's messages. Is the old man pleased or is he critical or is he crying with joy for his boy?

I asked Dick about his hurried speech. At first he was stunned, not being fully aware of what I meant. Then, after some consideration, he said, "Because I'm afraid that what I have to say will not be of interest to you. I wanted to get it over with."

The groundwork with Dick involved asking him to speak more slowly, not only to create general temporal space between his words, but also to articulate each word more carefully and deliberately. In this way, Dick was able to establish a timing in his verbalization and behavior which would eventually be useful in gaining the greatest benefit from experiments related to his feelings of inadequacy and lack of power. Although this phase of work would seem tangential, a very important warming-up process took place. I was preparing him to more fully and expansively assimilate future stimuli and responses associated with his own power and grandness.

For every learning process, there is a matter of preparation and timing. If one cannot take the time to establish the field within which the experiment can be done properly, the client will not learn very much nor will he remember the substantive outcomes of the experience. Even when the experiment may be very powerful to the watching outsider, the person himself may have difficulty assimilating its meaning and implications.

Another important aspect of groundwork is the therapist's curiosity. He must be respectfully interested in another human being—have a sense of wonder about the nature of another life. Such interest yields the richness of the background against which the other person expresses his feelings. The resulting experimental work often has historic roots without which it is in danger of being a shallow and stereotyped act.

Consensus

The process of negotiating with the client in designing an experiment and the client's willingness to participate in it is called consensus. The client needs to know that I am there for him—that he is not alone.

Consensus is the cornerstone of the work of some of my colleagues. They need clear agreement, a mini-contract, with the client to execute a particular task; at every critical stage of the work, the therapist makes it clear to the client that he can either agree to try something new or agree not to do so.

The manner in which consensus takes place is a matter of personal style. If I have a good relationship with the person I'm working with, I don't feel the need for repetitive verbal requests for agreement. At times, such transactions can deflect from the fluidity of the process in the therapeutic encounter. I prepare my client to say what he needs to and express what he experiences from moment to moment. There are exceptions, of course, and people leave the office feeling as if they've been had by me, and then they need to tell me their resentments at the next session.

Generally, consensus is something I assume, unless the cli-

ent protests or in some other nonverbal way resists my suggestions. Then I try to invent experiments flowing out of the
content of the resistance. Clear agreement from the client is
particularly important when I work with a group in a strange
city for a weekend or some other short period. In this case, I
don't know the other person very well, not having had an
ongoing relationship with him. Therefore, it is essential that
little is taken for granted in this new relationship. The client
should be forewarned from one experiment to the next that he
has a choice to refuse and that he need only try out behaviors
which feel congruent, safe, and comfortable for him. Consensus also applies to the group as a whole, its expectations, and
its community standards.

Grading

By grading I mean helping the client execute an experiment
at the level at which he is ready to do so in a given therapy
hour. If he is not able to participate in a particular exploration
because it is too difficult, the therapist should be ready to
scale down the task so that the client may have a better chance
of succeeding in his efforts.

Let us say I ask a shy woman who feels inferior in her
femininity to walk across the room as if she were a very sensual person. This would appear to be a relatively simple request for someone who has had experience in experimenting
with new behavior as a way of changing one's self-perception.
But if this woman has never participated in the kind of
"theatrical act" I am after, then she needs preparation for it.
In this case, if the experiment is too difficult, I might scale
down my request by asking the woman to use her voice as if it
were the voice of a sexy girl. The use of her voice may be
much easier for her in this context than the use of her total
body.

My colleague, Sonia Nevis, speaks of grading up or grading
down. One grades the experiment up when it is below the
client's level of functioning—when the experiment is simply

too easy for the client, will not be challenging, and will not earn him a new experience. One grades the experiment down when it is too difficult for the client, as in the case I just described.

The grading up or grading down of experiments requires a certain sophistication of understanding human functioning, as well as a creative imagination, because the process does not necessarily involve the same system of functioning. For instance, if I wanted a client to experiment with a new way of moving his body, yet he found it too difficult, I might suggest an initial experiment in the verbal sphere, i.e., ask him to talk in a way that reflected the new movement, or ask him to begin by simply imagining a situation in which he would express himself in that way.

Let's return to the shy woman and call her Sadie. Sadie is 35 years old. She lives alone. She has a degree in chemistry and is working as a lab technician in a large company. She is shy around other people. Many years ago, while in college, she was in love with a young man, but the relationship ended when he started dating one of Sadie's friends. She was broken-hearted and blamed herself for the failure of the relationship.

Sadie is not deeply disturbed. She is able to do a good job at work and survive fairly well in the world. However, she has always felt closer to things than to people: "I feel a sense of closeness and understanding with the materials in the lab. I also like to decorate, but I feel uncomfortable with people, especially men. I feel graceless and awkward. I have closed off my sensual feelings from everyone. I sublimate to my work." Sadie is a bright woman. She is able to verbalize her feelings adequately, but feels stuck in her expressive abilities. She has recently joined a Gestalt group without prior experience in group psychotherapy. Although she has some intellectual insight into her sexual-expressive difficulties and their origins, she has great difficulty relating her knowledge to actual situations.

As I talk with Sadie in the group, I begin to formulate a range of experiments which may be useful for the exploration of her social-sexual behavior. I think of the simple act of walking across the room and feeling sensual as one walks. I have a fantasy of the variety of walkers I see at the local shopping mall. Some people, I think to myself, really luxuriate in their bodies when they move through space. Sadie looks stiff and wooden when she walks into the room. I think to myself, it would be nice to get her out of her words and into some concrete actions.

> *Joseph:* Sadie, how would it be for you to walk across the room as if you were feeling really sensuous?
> *Sadie:* That's kind of scary to me. I don't want to do that. I feel a little shaky in my voice just telling you that.

(Inside my head) Boy, I really overstepped in suggesting that experiment. She seems to be comfortable and more in contact with her voice.

> *Joseph:* How do you feel about your voice now?
> *Sadie:* It's kind of pitched high and jittery. (Pause) I used to sing as a kid. I like my voice ordinarily.

(Inside my head) I'll go with her voice and work into her sexual feelings later.

> *Joseph:* Would it be more comfortable experimenting with your voice?
> *Sadie:* I guess.
> *Joseph:* Okay, then how about telling me what you feel in your voice now.

(Inside my head) I'm going to start exactly where she's at.

> *Sadie:* It's a bit less jittery now. Seems like my voice is getting a little deeper as I am talking to you.
> *Joseph:* Sounds very different now, almost a bit hoarse.
> *Member of Group:* Sadie, you are blushing around your neck as you talk with Joseph. You look pretty with that color in your face, too.

Sadie: Really?

Joseph: Sadie, are you aware of your face?

Sadie: (To group) I am feeling shy and excited all at once.

Joseph: I experience the sensuousness of your voice now.

Sadie: Yes, I feel that a little.

Joseph: Could you continue talking with us with that sensuous quality in your voice?

Sadie: Yeah, sure. (After a pause she turns to another member of the group.) You know, John, I have always found you good looking. (Everyone laughs. There is excitement in the room.)

(Inside my head) She is looking good now. Her breathing is less shallow and she seems to be pumping a lot of energy into herself. She is excited about herself, about her voice, and the group is with her. If there is time, I'd like her to get into her sensuous feelings with more of her body, like that walk I was thinking about, or maybe looking at people seductively. No, I think the simple walk would be easier and more fully involving of her body. I think she has the energy now to make that jump. I'll let her continue working with her voice for a while with each person in the group, before we jump into the next stage too fast. She might as well have a chance to assimilate the experience of her sensual voice first—no use rushing something good.

The grading up which has taken place moved from Sadie's awareness of jitteriness in her voice, to a sense of depth and hoarseness, to a feeling of sensuousness, to making contact with John. It is nice to watch Sadie changing right before our eyes.

The diagram which follows illustrates how grading up of experiments may be executed with Sadie in future sessions. This is only one possible avenue, one in which there is a leap from voice to larger movement. A more naturalistic approach may involve expanding Sadie's awareness of how her voice relates to her breathing. I might ask her to speak to each person in the group as sensuously as she can and give feedback about how she supports herself physically in propelling her

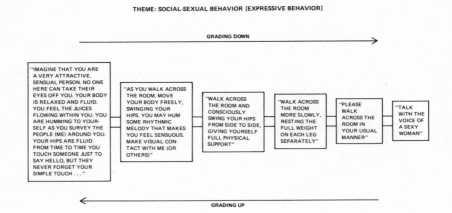

THEME: SOCIAL-SEXUAL BEHAVIOR [EXPRESSIVE BEHAVIOR]

voice. She may wind up singing a beautiful love song for us—a more profound and moving experience than what she started with—and that would be plenty upgrading right there!

The upgrading in terms of larger physical movement may be left for a later session or completely abandoned if it doesn't fit Sadie's experience the next time in the group. Yet, it remains a cognitive map inside of me. Together with the ongoing cues I get from Sadie, these images comprise a variety of potential experimental situations to be explored in the future. In the meantime, I have the satisfaction of having stayed with Sadie's experience of her voice and having upgraded that area of expression to a level of significance for her.

Awareness

My receptivity and appreciation of the content and quality of the client's awareness figure heavily in the development of an experiment. Sensation is generally the unspoken preparation to awareness and one's awareness is constantly accompanied by a rich variety of sensory inputs. When I attend to the person's sensation and awareness in addition to a variety of moment-to-moment physical observations of his behavior, I get a fairly clear, or perhaps perplexing, picture of what is going on for that person.

If a client is telling a story of woe and has a pasted-on smile on his face, the confusing message I get must have some confusing counterpart inside him. The experiment may thus develop as an attempt to clarify that sort of confusion. For example, I may say to that person, "Would you continue telling me about your mother's illness and try to smile and laugh as you tell it?" If the person is willing to exaggerate this sort of contradictory behavior, he may find enlightenment in a very sudden way: The hysterical laugh may break through to genuine weeping.

The client's sensation and awareness, together with my own ongoing observations of the action, become the basic building blocks for construction of the experiment.

From here on, I will discuss the development of the experiment in the context of work I did with myself a few years ago when my brother underwent a major operation.

> I am sitting here in a waiting room of a hospital, waiting to find out the disposition of my brother. Ted has just undergone cardiac surgery. As I am dictating into my tape recorder, I am aware that my voice is low and deep. I have a slightly nauseous feeling in my belly. I am feeling heavy and somewhat sad. I have a slight pain in my back. I am sitting hunched over. I feel very much alone. I think to myself, no one is here with me to comfort me or share my feelings about my brother. I bear the full burden of responsibility in this particular venture. This is my awareness.

> Now, as I am talking, my awareness begins to change and is more focused on my breathing. The miniature tape machine is leaning against my chest; I am visualizing my brother and his difficulty with his breathing; there are so many tubes attached to him, including one thick tube that goes down his trachea. (This I visualize from my previous visit with Ted.)

Energy

Now I am focusing on my breathing and my energy is mainly in my chest. Earlier, my energy seemed blocked in my throat and my voice was rather deadly. Now, I am feeling a slight enlivening in my voice.

When I work with a client, I attend to where his organism is activated, where he is "perking." Once we have located his source of self-support, he can then literally lend his excitement to our encounter. An experiment will have a tendency to drag if the only source of energy is that of the therapist.

One can think of energy as a general "charge" exuded from the person's surface; for example, a severely depressed person has a low energy level emanating from his total being. Or one can think of energy in a more localized sense, looking for excitement or frozenness in the person's face, arms, neck, shoulders, chest, belly, pelvis, buttocks, legs. The presence of energy may be detected in the form of movement, level of breathing, color of skin, relative position of various body parts, and posture.

Ideally, the person wants to work on an area of his life in which he has invested energy or where he feels a dramatic lack of excitement. Thus, the person is aware that he is working out of some charge within himself or for the very reason that the charge is absent.

Focus

Now I see an experiment at this moment as a problem-solving scheme. My problem right now is that I need some form of support. If I were my own therapist, I'd create experiments related to my self-support.

In order to develop an experiment, I must find a psychological "place" or event which needs to be followed or tracked. In a sense, when I locate the person's energy and move my attention there, I am focusing my work on the area in which a potential experiment may take place. During the course of a therapy session, the focus may change several times, depending, of course, on the client's quality of experience and its direction. Nevertheless, the focus must be there at all times, because without it the work becomes dissipated, loses a sense of purpose for the client, and diminishes the possibility for a solid learning experience for him.

Preparatory Self-Support

> One set of experiments may deal with my physical position. I may ask myself to sit up, which I will do now, in a position of optimum physical support. I place my feet firmly on the ground. I start breathing more deeply. This set of physical changes allows me to be more fully and clearly supported in a physiological sense.
>
> As I am following my own instructions, I begin to feel energy spreading into my legs and up into my head, and as I am looking at my notes, they appear more sharp and well-defined. I feel a sense of being present—here in this room—more than I had before.

Have you ever watched how a concert pianist carefully adjusts his bench before beginning to play? Or how a violinist plants his feet on the ground while performing? Or have you noticed how a brick layer positions himself in relation to the bricks and mortar, and the pace he sets during his work? They are all establishing conditions, both in their bodies and in the environment, which will optimally support their particular activities.

When I work with a client, I attend to my physical position and breathing, as well as to potential distractions which may take my attention away from the work at hand. I also make an effort to teach my client to support his own activity, so that everything emanating from him is "well-grounded," fully supported in his organism. His words (or mine), for example, must not be like a flock of birds flying around the room making noise. Ideally, they must be well-chosen, well-paced, and well-supported by full breathing so that both of us can respectfully listen to them and be nourished by them.

Development of Theme

> As I continue sitting here, feeling physically supported, I become aware of my aloneness again. This theme involves people who are absent from this room: my mother and father, my wife, my children, my brother's wife, my brother's children.

Whereas "focus" defines the process and direction of a therapy session, the theme is related to its content. The therapist is presented with a mass of varied content which he must distill, condense, summarize, name, unify. The distilled name of the client's concern is called a theme. As in the case of focusing, the theme of an experiment does not remain static. Themes are woven into one another to create a rich experiential fabric in a given (existential) situation.

Themes may exist in different units or sizes, both in the therapy session and in a person's lifetime. We may return to each theme again and again, but approach it at different levels of sophistication. Thus, my aloneness in the waiting room is initially related to a need for social support in that situation, while the notion of aloneness may have a more profound scope in light of facing my own ultimate death.

A good experiment is built on a given theme. It is intended to either explore it more fully, analyze its peculiar qualities, or direct it to a possible solution. At the end, the client, having tilled the soil of a portion of his existence, should be able to articulate how he understands or perceives it at a new level. He can then proceed to further exploration of the "fit" between this particular experience and the rest of his experiential life.

Choice of Experiment

An experiment might involve asking myself to imagine these people sitting around me. What would I say to them? "Look, people, you should be here, I need you. I need your support. I need to tell you what my brother looked like when I just saw him. I need for you to share your own experiences of having been in surgery. I need to discuss with you the possibility that Ted may die. We need to be together at this time of crisis, to hold each other's hands, maybe to cry together."

As I am saying this, I am feeling slightly dizzy. I don't know whether this is excitement or a slight sense of fear. I would need help to modify this experiment in order to carry it through to some sense of completion. Right now, I feel that at least I have called out.

Acting as my own therapist, I ask myself to speak for the people who are not here with me. As my brother's wife, Helen, I say, "Look, the man didn't want me to come. He didn't want me to come back to the hospital until surgery was completed, so I'm staying away. I'm fulfilling his wishes."

And then I (Joseph) answer her, "You are a respectful person. Still, I feel that you should not take him literally. You know that he needs you and you know that you and I need each other to support each other and be nice to each other."

This dialogue has helped me clarify cognitively, at least, the issues involved in my aloneness in this waiting room, so that I can have some sense of peace about the meaning of my being here by myself.

Another part of me comes into focus now—the feeling that I really like how I am taking care of myself and what I am doing with myself in this state of aloneness. The fact is, I enjoy my solitude most of the time. Good company.

Interesting ideas. Fun writing or reading by the fire. I love painting and listening to music. Solitude is often sweet—even now, at this moment, I feel good about myself. I feel supported in my solitude. I realize that when I don't manage to support myself in my aloneness (as I felt before), I experience anxiety or boredom or loneliness. If I had a colleague with me, I might be able to take this theme further, to a place which I can't see.

Another experiment might involve two internal forces within me. One would be the sickening feeling in my belly, which I identify as my fear of dying. The other would be the force of breathing in my chest, which feels like the breath of life. I might engage in an internal dialogue between my fear of dying and my breath of life.

A new series of thoughts comes to mind related to several unfinished situations in my life which involved the death of loved ones during my youth. As my own therapist, I suggest to myself that I act out the situations in which I escaped with my life and others were killed.

The Experiment

I move from chair to chair in this empty room, playing three parts: first, I am my own therapist; I am also the person presenting an unfinished situation—the client; later, I act out a dialogue with Aunt Paula in which I am both myself and my aunt.

Therapist: What is your memory?
Client. There are a number of them related to this theme of death and dying. One stands out indelibly. I will never forget . . .
Therapist: Tell it in the present as if it is happening now.
Client: It is wartime. The town is burning. The Germans have already entered it partially. Most people who are still alive are huddled in basements. Uncle

Wolf, a physician, has arranged to have his clinic ambulance evacuate us out of town, together with his staff. The rendezvous is completed as my parents, my brother, and I are hurriedly picked up on a street corner. We are packed into the rear of a small, green, square truck. It is filled with medics from the clinic. I am sitting at the rear, looking out the back panel door windows. The next stop is another rendezvous with my mother's only sister, Paula, her husband and her baby. The truck stops at the appropriate street. We wait. Maybe 15 seconds later the truck begins to roll away. In the distance I see Aunt Paula running after the truck. I am dumb. I am paralyzed. I am still. I am frozen. I may be yelling. I don't think I am yelling . . . I don't remember exactly.

Therapist: Yell out to her, Joseph.

Client: "Aunt Paula is there! Stop the truck! Stop! Stop now!" No one seems to hear me! The truck keeps moving faster and faster. Aunt Paula is still running, holding the baby in her left arm and waving with her right hand to us. Her husband is running just behind her waving his arms. His mouth is open. He must be yelling, but I can't hear because the doors are locked.

Therapist: Joseph, yell out to the driver, to your parents.

Client: "Stop this fucking truck! Stop it, you frightened bastards. The street is empty; there are no Germans to be seen. Stop it—we can crowd them in! They will fit." (I am crying—I am wailing.) "Let's save them!" I love my Aunt Paula. I want them here with me!" The truck is far from them now. They are just dots at the end of the street. They were all killed shortly after we left.

Therapist: Bring your Aunt Paula back now, Joseph. Bring her back and tell her your feelings.

Client: Aunt Paula, I am sorry. I was only 7 years old. I never forgave myself for your death and Uncle Meyer's and the baby's. I am sorry.

Therapist: What does she say?

Paula: My little Joseph. I always loved you so. You were my favorite nephew. You could not do anything. I forgive you if you need forgiveness. I forgive you a thousand times. Please let me rest in peace now. Let go of me and let go of this nightmare of yours—this private nightmare. Live happily. Bury me in peace. Rejoice in your life, in your family, in your work.

Client: (Crying) I am weeping for you, for all of us—for the difficulties, for the tragedies. Before I say good-bye, I just want you to know that I named one of my daughters after you—Karen Paula—she is very lovely . . . Goodbye. (To Therapist) This scene is so alive for me. I've been struggling with this guilt for 34 years. (To Paula) Paula, you would have been proud of me if you were alive now. I know it. Your love was not wasted. Your purity is here inside of me.
(Long silence)

Therapist: What do you feel now?

Client: I am glad I made it. I am glad to be alive. I wish I could dance now—like Zorba on the beach. I am still a bit heavy inside. It's so hard to part with my sense of tragedy.

Therapist: Can you part with your sadness for now?

Client: Goodbye sadness. I need to rest now.

This was a powerful, releasing experience for me. I allowed myself to regurgitate and ventilate, to emotionally relive and spit out the deepest and most painful experience of my life. I surprised myself with the aliveness of those old events as they unfolded in my work. I felt that I partially resolved a very difficult unfinished situation. At the end I felt drained and relieved at the same time.

The experimental work with myself yielded a process of natural, uncontrived grading from material which was fairly easy to handle (ego-syntonic) toward content which had deep historic roots with painful feelings attached to them (ego-alien). The following diagram illustrates this process of natural, unplanned grading; at each stage I gave myself the dosage of difficulty I could handle at that moment.

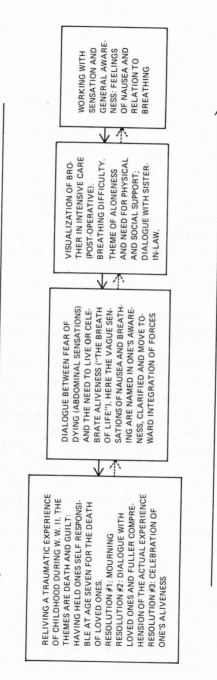

EGO SYNTONIC VS. EGO ALIEN GRADATIONS IN AUTHOR'S EXPERIMENTS WITH HIMSELF

GRADING UP: INTRODUCING EGO ALIEN MATERIAL

GRADING DOWN: LESSENING ANXIETY WITH MORE EGO SYNTONIC CONTENT

RELIVING A TRAUMATIC EXPERIENCE OF CHILDHOOD DURING W. W. II. THE THEMES ARE DEATH AND GUILT: HAVING HELD ONES SELF RESPONSIBLE AT AGE SEVEN FOR THE DEATH OF LOVED ONES. RESOLUTION #1: MOURNING RESOLUTION #2: DIALOGUE WITH LOVED ONES AND FULLER COMPREHENSION OF THE ACTUAL EXPERIENCE RESOLUTION #3: CELEBRATION OF ONE'S ALIVENESS

DIALOGUE BETWEEN FEAR OF DYING (ABDOMINAL SENSATIONS) AND THE NEED TO LIVE OR CELEBRATE ALIVENESS ("THE BREATH OF LIFE"). HERE THE VAGUE SENSATIONS OF NAUSEA AND BREATHING ARE NAMED IN ONE'S AWARENESS, CLARIFIED AND MOVE TOWARD INTEGRATION OF FORCES

VISUALIZATION OF BROTHER IN INTENSIVE CARE (POST-OPERATIVE). BREATHING DIFFICULTY. THEME OF ALONENESS AND NEED FOR PHYSICAL AND SOCIAL SUPPORT; DIALOGUE WITH SISTERIN-LAW.

WORKING WITH SENSATION AND GENERAL AWARENESS: FEELINGS OF NAUSEA AND RELATION TO BREATHING

Insight and Completion

Suddenly the theme made full circle for me. My story dealt with aloneness, death and guilt: I felt alone and privately guilty about Paula's death. In my childish omnipotence, I felt solely responsible for saving Paula's life. I also felt guilty about my own good fortune. Being alone in the waiting room while my brother was on the brink of death brought back similar feelings and fed this old theme.

But now I am an adult. I know that if Ted doesn't survive, I will feel very sad and very sorry, but I will not hold myself responsible. I say to myself, "The surgery was your decision, Ted, and you had a hell of a lot of courage. I am glad you made it. I am also glad for myself, for being in good physical shape, being alive."

This is the learning I experienced after the series of experiments. The sensitive reader will no doubt have a number of important insights which emerged for him about me, but which I am not consciously in contact with at this moment.

There is a lesson to be learned here: Never assume that your client, having completed an experience, learned from it what you did. Ask him what he learned. Although his verbalization may not match his organismic experience, nevertheless, he is still sharing his present learnings. Very often these learnings will sound incredibly simplistic and limited in contrast to the depth of your understanding of the action. Much of the learning is difficult to express in words and needs incubation inside the client's organism over time. One day it will appear as a phenomenally "brand new" insight for him, while the therapist has been in touch with that particular phenomenon for months.

When I started working on myself I had no idea of the possible outcome of the experiments. I relied basically on my awareness, imagination, and most importantly, a faith in my inner process. The faith says: "Stay with it and trust your feelings, hunches and intuitions as you go on. Nothing terrible will happen that you cannot handle, because if you truly cannot handle an area you will simply avoid seeing it anyway.

Besides, chances are that something good will happen at the end if you stay with yourself long enough to reach partial completion of the work."

TWO CLASSIC EXPERIMENTS

Certain Gestalt experiments have become classics. The *reenactment* experiment allows the person to "relive" an unfinished life situation so that it may be modified in the liveliness of the here and now, as well as by the renewed competence of the client. *Enactment* can be used in working on a dream or fantasy; here, the person is asked to act out his dream and its significant components. Later, he may engage in dialogues between parts of the dream to get in touch with polarized aspects of his character. The *empty chair* and *around the world* experiments, described below, are ways of working with the integration of opposing forces within the personality.

The experiments described here are reflections of my own style as it interfaces with the people I work with. "Classic" experiments are useful only when they are tailor-made to particular situations with specific clients, and yield only mediocre results when misused as rigid formulas. Experiments are tools, and as such, they are meant to be constantly modified rather than exhibited as "professional trophies."

Around the World

A man who is alert and interesting with me complains that he is dull and boring to others. In what I call the "around the world" experiment, I ask Mort to "lean into" being dull and boring with me, to become that part of himself as fully as he can.

We begin by accepting Mort's experience as valid—the theme of dullness is real for him. I then move with him into his boredom and dullness, giving him permission to explore the qualities he fears. My feeling is that, if he can relate fully to his actual dullness, Mort will eventually come around to the opposite polarity, his brightness. Hence, going around the world.

Mort starts talking slowly and heavily, sharing some information about molecular research in his laboratory. I encourage him to become as dull as he can be, and at first the content of his sharing is rather flat and ordinary. But the more he tries to exaggerate his dullness, the more colorful his language becomes.

As he talks, I ask him to attend to his energy and its location, and to focus on talking out of this source of enlivenment. The energy, Mort says, "is stuck in my middle." He complains of discomfort in his chest. As he attends to his shortness of breath, his voice gains strength and rhythm, and his breathing becomes somewhat fuller.

Later, Mort spontaneously moves out of his chair and paces as he continues explaining problems in his research. I let the time pass and don't push. The man captivates me with his increased involvement. I ask him, "What is happening with your feelings now?"

> *Mort:* I don't feel dull right now. I am really into this thing with you.
>
> *Joseph:* Did you feel that way at the start? (Getting him to express the awareness of contrast)
>
> *Mort:* No, I felt like I was dragging and kind of heavy in my chest. Now the heaviness is leaving me.
>
> *Joseph:* How did you experience a change as you talked? (Asking him to think about changes in his body which he associates with involvement)
>
> *Mort:* I am not exactly sure, Joseph, but I feel like I let myself breathe more and then I felt warmth in my chest and belly. After that I felt more flow in my speech also. I am still feeling my flow.
>
> *Joseph:* So, how do you make yourself dull to others, Mort? Have you any thoughts about that? (Pushing for clarity of awareness about ways he creates his own dullness)

Mort: I don't give myself a chance to get excited. I sit there expecting to be dull and I clamp down on my breath. I deaden all of me, damn it! You know, when I got up and started pacing, that's when I really felt alive. Damn it, Joseph, I think I can solve this problem in the lab, too.

Joseph: Before you get to that, Mort, tell me first what you can do the next time you fear becoming dull with others. (Making him focus on one problem at a time, and making sure he knows exactly what he learned and how he can use this learning in the future)

Mort: Well, first I just have to give myself a chance to develop my ideas, to give myself a little time. I always rush. You really let me take my time. Also, I should pay attention to my breathing and where I am feeling the energy inside me. I can't be exciting right off the bat. It seems like I have to start out slow and build up to where I am more flowing in my language and movement.

Joseph: Yes, that makes a lot of sense to me, too. Perhaps you can experiment with this process during the week. Whenever you start feeling dull, take your time and get into your breathing, your excitement, and stay with it without giving up prematurely. Okay, see you next Tuesday. (Confirming the validity of his learnings, giving "positive reinforcement," and asking him to do some homework, i.e., to continue using the changed behavior in the outside world)

This little experiment was significant for Mort. Most important, he took ownership of the learning experience. In teaching me about his experience, he became his own teacher. His whole being was involved and he was able to achieve some sense of completion. For me, this process is more dynamic and effective than a client's response to my interpretations about his behavior. The learning "sticks to the ribs" because the person makes his own discoveries.

The Empty Chair

There are certain recurring themes in our lives, themes related to conflicting voices within us or to our clashes with environmental pressures. The empty chair experiment gives the person an opportunity to take ownership of opposing forces within himself and to integrate them creatively. The empty chair allows the person to come into dialogue with a polarity within himself.

In another form, the empty chair becomes a person from one's past whom one has unfinished business with. For example, Dorothy complains of feeling guilty. When questioned, she speaks of the "things my mother taught me." I ask Dorothy to imagine that her mother is sitting in the empty chair. I ask her to share her guilt feelings with her mother, thereby helping her to contact her mother's opinions, attitudes and beliefs which she had swallowed whole. In the process, Dorothy begins freeing the energy which was bound up with her internalized mother.

Too often we feel "manipulated," "forced," "pushed," "intimidated." We project, give away, relinquish our own power to the environment. In this case, the empty chair becomes the power with which the person talks, and later, takes back for himself. Thus, the empty chair is used frequently because it is an effective device for reclaiming what one has unwittingly disowned and for learning to nourish oneself with something which originally seemed difficult, painful, repugnant.

When Dorothy comes in complaining of anger with her church, her parents, or her husband, the empty chair experiment may help her take ownership of her own rigid morality (attributed to the church), or her own reluctance to leave home (attributed to her parents), or her anger and insensitivity (projected to her husband). Without denying the validity of Dorothy's world view, the empty chair experiment can also allow her to separate her own rigidity from that of the church, her own reluctance to leave home from the unspoken signals coming from her parents, or her own insensitivity from the anger and insensitivity of her husband.

If Dorothy has little awareness of how the church has influenced her values, a dialogue with the church in the empty chair is designed to bring this institutional influence to her attention. Telling stories about the church without a sense of purpose hardly gets anywhere, dissipates energy, and rarely creates behavioral change.

The experiment helps Dorothy switch from telling about her church experiences to engaging herself directly with its image; from talking to me—where there is an unspoken promise of forthcoming advice or explanation—to directing that energy to the source of her experienced dismay and anxiety. This arrangement frees me from being fixed by her gaze and gives me the freedom to observe her work, formulate its meaning, plan future strategy, and give her the feedback she needs to crystallize her own insights.

Dorothy is addressing herself to "the church" in the chair, a world reality which she brings into the room. But there is another level of work in the same experiment, perhaps a bit deeper: At a certain point of development, Dorothy sees her inner acceptance of some doctrinal values and rejection of others. At this point the experiment takes another turn:

Joseph: Dorothy, do you ever think of the church as a part of your inner life?

Dorothy: What do you mean?

Joseph: Well, is there a part inside of you which criticizes you relentlessly?

Dorothy: Yes, especially when I tell myself that sex is bad, that I shouldn't enjoy myself.

Joseph: Suppose we give that part of you a name, like Ms. Dorothy Church, and let you talk to it—perhaps something new would happen.

Dorothy: Let's see if I've got this straight—in this chair I'm Dorothy Jones who wants to enjoy herself, and in the other chair I am Dorothy Church who makes me feel guilty all the time.

Joseph: Yes, that's right. And when you work I want you to consciously address her by her name each time you shift chairs. (The use of her own name helps her emphasize ownership of attitudes attributed to the church.)

Dorothy: Dorothy Church, I hate you; you make me sick.

Joseph: You make yourself sick. (Pause) Try speaking for Ms. Church. (Here, I accent the matter of responsibility—she, not the church, is responsible for her feeling sick.)

Dorothy: (Shifting chairs) I am going to make you feel sick. (Turning to Joseph) You know, I often feel nauseous. (Looking back at the empty chair) I am going to make you sick every time you get interested in a man.

Joseph: Please shift chairs. (The physical movement from one place to another reinforces differentiation—and later integration—of polarized aspects of Dorothy's character.)

Dorothy: Dorothy Church, I am angry with you.

Joseph: Dorothy, are you angry with yourself? (Once again, I help her look at herself—help her locate internal feelings rather than projecting blame.)

Dorothy looks as though she hasn't heard my last statement. I assume she is not ready to process her work yet. She continues working, using the different names. Slowly she begins to recognize that besides having to deal with the church out there, she is fighting with a woman within herself: Ms. Church is sadistically critical, a guilt-maker. She rarely approves of Dorothy's behavior. Part of this character is the internalized mother church as Dorothy experienced it through the eyes of a young child, ready to eat whatever was fed to her. At this point I consider working on the expression of her anger more directly. I choose not to pursue this avenue because I feel at this point in her work, a fuller expression of feeling would be too frightening for her. She looks like she is handling all she can. My judgment is that she is working at her capacity level.

Here is another stage of the encounter:

Joseph: You say part of it is the mother church. Is there another part?

Dorothy: The way I am talking in this chair reminds me also of how mother used to talk to me.

We spend more time talking of her internalized mother and letting Dorothy express some anger with both church and mother. Slowly it dawns on her that the focus of her work must be on the internalization of values, rather than on projecting blame. Somewhere along the way, Dorothy may realize that she must learn to integrate her relentless critic with her need to live her life fully and freely—that she can't extricate the critic and bury it, but must tame it to become more responsive to her legitimate needs, the needs of a mature woman.

The level and emphasis of the experiment change as Dorothy works first on her relationship with the church qua church, and then on her dialogue with Dorothy Church, the parts of the church she introjected as a child. Still later, Dorothy works on her mother as an introjected critic. Finally, she works on integrating her self-criticism with her expressive self, her need for guiding values with her active partaking of life.

At this stage of work, Dorothy can appreciate the actual doctrinal problems of the church without torturing herself. She can begin to look at her mother as an old lady who comes from a little town in Ireland and who needs love—another human being living out her life and struggling with her own problems. She feels softer inside herself and begins to experience an inner comfort with herself.

ELEGANCE OF EXPERIMENTS

Developing an experiment is like developing a work of art—both the process and the outcome can have elegance. An elegant process is one which is well-paced, such that each part of the work is easily observed and assimilated by the client. I associate elegance with a clarity and lucidity of purpose: The client has some sense of the relevance of the work to his problem or dilemma, and the therapist has clarity about the purpose of the experiment or what he is searching for. I associate timing with elegance of work: Each aspect of the experiment is presented at a point of developmental readiness for the therapist, and most importantly, for the client.

Elegant experiments have grace and fluidity of transition from one aspect or dimension of the client's experiencing to another. The work is smooth and flowing and unhurried. I experience elegance in my work when I am able to focus on and track another person's experience from moment to moment without becoming unduly distracted by irrelevant details. I know I am not doing well when, in the midst of an important theme for the client, I ask a question about some detail because my personal interests intervene. For example, a client tells me of how he has been self-destructive and just smashed up his brand new car. I ask, "What kind of car was it?", forgetting to focus on his feeling destructive or mournful. It is important to keep in mind, however, that one should be respectful and attentive to one's own ongoing imagery. It is out of the raw material of such imagery that creative experiments are often born.

A creative experiment emerges out of a range of images such that the chosen action fits the experience of the client—it addresses itself to the nucleus of the problem, rather than to a tangential phenomenon associated with it. To go back to Dick, who complains about his one-down position in relation to others (see p. 130), I chose to work with the speed of his language only to prepare him more fully for the larger theme. Had I been absorbed with the speed alone, I would have made a crucial tactical error in my work with him. However, one must always be prepared for creative surprises. For example, as Dick is slowing down his speech he suddenly remembers that he always had to rush himself when talking to his father, otherwise his father would suddenly walk out of the room. Here we see how the natural development of the experiment moves from the periphery to the central theme.

An elegant experiment or, more accurately, series of experiments, is like a symphony. There is a beginning movement in which information is introduced and a general theme emerges. The second movement has a searching quality in which many details are filled in and the person's understanding of the theme is enriched. The third movement may uncover an important developmental dynamic of the larger theme, and the fourth ends in a sense of resolution and integration, as well as celebration of the self.

In Dick's case, the first movement dealt with the information of his one-down position. The second movement dealt with how he downs himself and prevents assimilation by speeding up his experience. The third movement comprehensively stated his relationship with a critical, real-life father. In this movement he gained a clearer understanding of the modeling which his father provided for him and how he swallowed his father's disapproval. Also, he began to recognize his own internal tyrant who constantly put him down, and to take ownership of the internal dialogue between his hurried, helpless little boy and his internal tyrant. In the last movement, Dick flows into his sense of self-praise, grandeur, and self-celebration. He is like Zorba the Greek, taking his time to enjoy his substance and freedom.

In an elegant experiment, the therapist is open to a range of emerging feelings—from heaviness to lightness, from sobriety to humor, from softness to hardness, from celebration to mourning, from profundity to child-like simplicity. He has a sense of what is aesthetically workable: where humor works and where it falls flat: where irony provides richness and where it is abrasive, jarring and inappropriate; where he needs to be a hard taskmaster-teacher and where he can be a loving grandparent or mother. He has a sense of how dramatization expands the action and clarifies issues, and where it feels shallow and contrived.

As I am writing this, I am aware how often I fall behind my own goals for elegance. However, I am also in touch with the special times when, in the course of my work, the symphony appears inside of me in its total structure and is merely refined in the transaction between myself and my client.

Chapter **7**

Groups As
Creative Communities

At its best, a group is not only a small, cohesive community in which people feel received, accepted, and confronted, but it is also a place and an atmosphere where people can become creative together. An ideal group is a place for testing one's growth boundaries, a community in which members can develop at the highest levels of human potential.

In this context, a group may be defined as a *learning community,* i.e., people who have gathered with a trained leader to solve personal and interpersonal problems. "Problems" may range from an individual's phobic symptoms to feelings of isolation and alienation among people. The group's goal may also be relatively well-defined, for example, women gathering to deal with questions of life crises or increasingly changing roles in their relationships. Learning implies changing behavior, not only for the sake of adaptation, of adjustment, but for a movement toward higher levels of awareness and self-actualization.

A group cannot be accounted for simply by adding together the individuals in it. Every group is a unique system, with its

Portions of this chapter come from a tape-recorded conservation with Richard Borofsky and Antra Kalnins on 15 August 1972, in Wellfleet, Massachusetts. I appreciate their help in formulating my ideas.

own special character and its own sense of power: a conglomeration of energies exuded by individual members and interrelated in a systematic pattern. It is a whole, an entity, a Gestalt whose nature is greater than the sum of its various parts.

This interrelationship may be scattered or deflected by collusions, internal conflicts, loyalties and various forms of
static. The Gestalt therapist learns a variety of methods for
harnessing the group's energy into an integrated system of
creative work, a system which is pointed and directional. This
cooperative effort requires the group's acceptance of and regard for its individual members, as well as the leader's special
skill in converting the group's talents and resistances into a
sense of a unified community.

As a catalyst, the Gestalt leader integrates scattered individual themes into spontaneous community creations. This process of transformation is quite complex, and includes proper
timing, fluidity of interaction and movement with the ongoing
process, mobilization of group energy, and continuous feedback between the group and the leader. The Gestalt leader,
therefore, needs to be continuously sensitive to the group's
emotional and aesthetic range.

Before describing what I consider to be a Gestalt group
process, I would like to compare it to several systems of group
therapy as a way of highlighting what I do.

GROUP PROCESS MODELS:
THEIR DESIGNS AND LIMITATIONS*

Carl Rogers: Unconditional Regard and Humility of Leadership

Traditionally, the group has been used as a whole in various
ways. Rogerian therapists stimulate the group in a non-direc-
tive manner as a vehicle for members to develop trust and find
ways of supporting each other. The group determines its own

---

*My focus is within the scope of existential therapies as described in Chapter 4,
"Roots and Assumptions," rather than psychoanalytically-oriented therapies.

destiny, clarifying and pursuing its own direction. The facilitator stays with the ongoingness of the situation, rather than inventing new events to be amplified, developed, clarified, and explored by the group.*

I envision Rogers' group as a circle of individuals, all of whom have equal power, with the therapist (indicated in the diagram by an X) as one of the participating members.

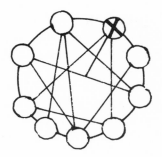

The Rogerian therapist attempts to give full power to the group and its process. Within the group he is self-disclosing and does not present himself as an expert or source of power. He considers himself a non-authoritarian facilitator who is merely "there"—with complete freedom to express his feelings, observations, or responses to the group—and a member of a community which runs itself, with its emphasis on the ongoing process and the development of feelings.

I see the client-centered therapist as a kind of mother figure who lends support, a form, and a "glue" to the cohesiveness of a loving, self-disclosing community. The community formulates its own problems and works as a unit to solve them. The process requires considerable time, perhaps a week, before the group can function as an integrated, cohesive, problem-solving community, yet this approach is potentially powerful if the process reaches a point of resolution.

Sometimes I experience this system as one in which the

---

*Rogers, C. *Carl Rogers on Encounter Groups.* New York: Harper and Row, 1970.

therapist claims to have no authority and presents a kind of unreal humility. Yet, no matter what he calls himself or how he presents himself, the facilitator carries enormous power in the group. For example, if he were to leave the group in the middle of a session, his absence would have great impact on the group—much more so than the absence of any other member.

There seems to be an "enforced naïveté" of the group leader concerning the power dynamics operating in the group; a discrepancy may exist between group members' expectations of the leader as an active expert-guide and his presentation of self. A result of this discrepancy may be that issues of power and leadership are not dealt with openly within the group, but exist underground with the potential to distort and confound the working of "above-ground" issues.

Old Gestalt: The Broken Wagon Wheel

During the years I knew him, Fritz Perls taught Gestalt therapy by demonstration with one member of a group. The other group members surrounded him, observed, and were often delighted with the skill and artistry of Fritz's work with the individual member. No effort was made, nor was there any intention to involve the group in this process; Fritz felt that people can learn by observing, and may even have growthful experiences simply by witnessing his work. He was not interested in the group process as such, but in demonstrating methods of working with individuals in front of groups.

A number of Perls' disciples took this individually-oriented style literally and evolved a model of group therapy in which people take turns "working" with the master in the center, while the rest of the group observes. James Simkin's work, exemplifying this model, is powerful, concentrated, and elegant. In his groups, people commit themselves to work a particular issue, and then he engages them one by one in the center of the group. While the client may be asked to address himself to the group in an individual experiment, group members themselves are not required to participate actively in the experiment.

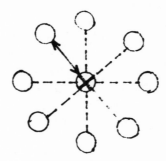

The above diagram depicts this system as a broken wagon wheel. It is broken because there is little interconnectedness between the members, but rather a vicarious connection to the action in the center. The broken wheel does not turn. It is not a community in the full sense of the word. People experience vicarious therapeutic contact with the therapist and the person in the "hot seat," but they have little kinship with one another other than their shared anxiety of moving into the center.

The potency of the system is that the therapist and the client experience a kind of community support; they seem to be surrounded by a circle of energy which says "yes" to the ongoing struggle of the person's work. This energy is clearly felt in the center and is visibly supported by occasional laughter and statements of appreciation. The weakness of the system is that it does not use the ideas, feelings, and talents of group members in the service of a creative process for the sake of the whole group. Another disadvantage of this model is that the therapist does all the work, and does not allow the group to support him or take charge of its own unfolding situation.

A final limitation is one which I attribute to the central value operating in groups led by Perls and his closest disciples: that of taking responsibility for one's self. This is reflected in the Gestalt Prayer: "I am I and you are you and if perchance we meet, it is wonderful; if not, it can't be helped." This outlook is not adequate to deal with the notion of social responsibility, of people taking care of each other in group therapy or any other community setting.

Psychodrama: A Revolutionary Movement

Another major way in which group therapy has existed is in psychodrama, where members of the group are used as characters in the drama of a particular individual who acts as the protagonist. The protagonist continues to be the focus of therapeutic attention in the group from beginning to end. Hence, a limitation of psychodrama is its focus on one individual and a commitment to a formal structure and to the integrity of the drama as drama, often to the neglect of the ongoing process in the situation and the unfolding self-awareness of group participants.

It is important to point out, however, that psychodrama was a truly revolutionary movement for its time. We use the phrase "here and now" as if the notion were just born. J. L. Moreno talked about the "now and here" in the 1920's and was a forerunner in his emphasis on creative problem-solving in a community through the medium of drama.* It is this emphasis on innovative acting out which buttressed the Zeitgeist of the 1950's and laid the ground for the popularity of the Gestalt approach to groups.

PRINCIPLES OF GESTALT GROUP PROCESS

Gestalt group process, as it has been developed at our Institute in Cleveland, operates according to four basic principles: 1) the primacy of present ongoing group experience; 2) the process of developing group awareness; 3) the importance of active contact between participants; and 4) the use of interac-

---

*Moreno, J. L. *Who Shall Survive? Foundations of Sociometry, Group Psychotherapy and Sociodrama* (Beacon, N.Y.: Beacon House, Inc., 1953) and *Psychodrama: Foundations of Psychotherapy, Volume 2* (Beacon, N.Y.: Beacon House, 1959).

tional experiments stimulated by an actively involved leader.

Primacy of the present experience means that the focus of attention is on the moment-to-moment experience of the individual. On the group level, this principle implies that no matter what happens in the group, it is relevant and needs to be clarified, emphasized, and creatively focused toward resolution. No behavior in the group should be dismissed. All group action is potentially relevant and generally reflects concerns that need to be attended to by its members.

Every individual theme is also a social-interactional theme. If, for example, one person is behaving like a beggar, there is always someone who refuses to give to him, just as there is always another person who gives too much. And this is where we create a society; this is where the group unfolds itself. No individual theme is isolated from a communal theme. The existence of the beggar may imply the existence of someone who is mean or stingy, or it may point to someone who is generous. When the group beggar behaves as if he has nothing in relation to others who may know about their emotional richness, we would not only explore the experience of the individual who feels like a beggar, but also what this sense of himself implies about other people in the group—the social Gestalt which emerges in the situation.

Let's take another instance: the so-called Oedipal situation. If a man is unduly attached to his mother and presents this problem in the group, it is obvious that there is a possibility of dealing with a mother figure selected from the group. But this man also had a father and he might have brothers and sisters and he also lived in a certain community. His love affair with mother did not take place in a vacuum; it happened in a social system. The group as a microcosm of society has the capability of not only recreating this system, but modifying it in a thousand different ways to allow a vision of how a community can be reinvented and how problems can be solved in a myriad of ways.

Awareness in Gestalt therapy simply means that an individual is attending to his experience. At the level of group process, this takes the form of shared concerns and themes. Although not everyone may be preoccupied with certain themes, they may dominate the group at a given moment. It is as if the theme hangs in the air above the group; it cannot be easily dismissed. This group awareness, these group concerns, are more than the sum of the individual awarenesses and must be dealt with by everyone. The strategy for dealing with group awareness is to first heighten or make explicit what the concern is and then to translate the awareness of that concern into excitement, then into action and interaction between group members.

Another principle in Gestalt therapy is that growth takes place at the boundary between the individual and the environment. In other words, it is the encounter between what is me and what is not me which forces me to invent new responses for dealing with the environment and moves me toward change. The environment has an impact on me. And through this balance of assimilation and accommodation to a changing environment, I grow. Gestalt group work emphasizes heightening the encounter and contact between individuals.

At the level of group process, contact is experienced as a sense of one's own uniqueness, a sense of the difference between each of the members of the group and also of similarities. It is an experience of commonality, community, as well as individuality. Each person, whatever he is doing, is encouraged to be aware of himself as a member of a society and his role in the group as it changes from moment to moment.

This is different from a "broken wheel" group where people retire into a kind of blank anonymity. In such a group, a withdrawn person does not think of himself as anything in relation to others. In a real community, a silent member learns to become aware of the role he is playing at any given moment. His suffering, as he experiences it, has a social significance. It has a dynamic value, a presence in the group. It is a force in the group, even though he may originally have experienced his silence as not having any social value or significance. People become aware of the roles which they are taking and realize that their roles exist and are defined by the fact that other people are accommodating them: For a person to be silent, someone else has to talk. And so we bring in all sides and forces of the group's life.

The social environment in its global sense is always accommodating. If I ask a policeman for directions, he either has to give me directions or tell me he is too busy. But even if he tells me he is busy, he is accommodating his response to my request. And so in our methodology we are shaping the group as a microcosm of our actual social environment. We want to give the person an opportunity to discover himself and understand himself in this social reality. We also want to teach him the power of modifying the behavior of others in a relatively safe and flexible experimental situation.

In Rogers' system, the therapist abdicates his authority and, in some subtle ways, denies his power, his skill, and his capacity to make an impact on the group. In the Simkin model, the therapist takes authoritarian control of the action. In the Gestalt process group, the therapist is clearly an authority, yet he has fluid movement within the group. He may choose to be in the center and active in stimulating individual work with group members; or he may choose to recede, to withdraw from the center and participate in the group as one of its members. His presence is always felt, and his power is clearly experienced. He coaxes and stimulates the group to be behaviorally experimental, to be intentional in modifying its own process.

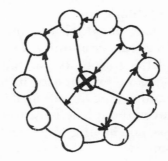

An overriding assumption, one which stands above the Gestalt principles, is that everything is possible in the group; that it has its own intrinsic life, its own energy, its special potentialities, and its own promise of experimenting with and fulfilling the vicissitudes of its individual lives. This creativity helps individuals deal with difficulties they are experiencing; it is also used to solve the problems of the community as a whole.

Ground Rules for Participants in Gestalt Groups

To promote the group's awareness, excitement and contact, Gestalt group leaders make an effort to communicate basic rules of thumb to participants. Some leaders are explicit about these rules at the very beginning, while others introduce them to the group when it seems appropriate to the group's process. Here are some of these ground rules:

—Take ownership of your language and behavior. "If you mean 'I,' say 'I' rather than 'you' or 'it' or the various other words which we often use to avoid explicit ownership of what we are saying, and which contribute to discussions being impersonal and general."*

—Give priority to what you are experiencing here and now. Share your present, ongoing feelings, thoughts, sentiments.

—Attend to the manner in which you listen to others. Jackson asks his students: "Are you listening to the person who is talking or are you tuning out, just waiting for your chance to jump in?"**

—When you ask a question you are often taking a safe way out of making a statement. Unless you are actually interested in information, e.g., "How old are you?", put your question in the form of a statement. Example:

---

*Jackson, C. W. Lecture, Gestalt Institute of Cleveland, Ohio, 1973.
**Ibid.

"Are you concerned about the welfare of people in this group?" is a cop-out for saying, "I feel you don't give a damn about me."

—Make an effort to talk directly to another person, rather than into a space in the middle of the room; you'll have greater impact on others.

—Listen to other people's feelings and acknowledge them. Avoid interpreting the "real" meaning of that person's statement; also, avoid searching for the causes of the other person's present feelings, e.g., "You feel anxious because . . ."

—Attend to your own physical experience as well as the changing postures or gestures of others. For example, if you are beginning to feel uncomfortable and head-achey while someone has been rambling, share your experience with that person.

—"Assume confidentiality of what others say unless there is some explicit agreement to do otherwise."*

—"Experiment with taking risks as you participate in the discussion."** The group is a humanistic laboratory in which you can test the influence of behaviors you have found heretofore unacceptable. There is a possibility you will turn people off; even so, how you react to such responses may be important to your own growth. For example, you may fantasize: "If I express my anger I will destroy someone." After expressing yourself in anger, you may find the other person is deeply moved or frightened, but still alive and breathing.

—Learn to "bracket off" or compartmentalize feelings or expressions which will definitely interrupt an important ongoing event in the group. If you don't do that for yourself, others will do it for you when they feel interrupted.

—Respect the psychological space of others as you would want to be respected yourself. If someone is withdrawn

---

*Nevis, E. "Ways of Heightening Contact." Lecture, Gestalt Institute of Cleveland, Ohio, 1975.
**Jackson, C. W. Lecture, Gestalt Institute of Cleveland, Ohio, 1973.

and depressed, respect his wish to be "left alone" for a while. Although we encourage people to change, we don't rape them into new behavior.

It must be kept in mind that these rules are not applied in a rigid, authoritarian atmosphere. Such intimidation kills the seeds of potential self-revelation and the development of a creative group process. Ideas meant to facilitate mobilization of energy and contact can be communicated in a way which stifles excitement and creates fearful mistrust. Here is where the leader's style of communication is significant.

THE GROUP EXPERIMENT

The Gestalt system is an integration of Rogers' experiential purity on the one hand, and Simkin's clearly structured approach on the other. Group action always begins with the ongoing experience of its members, rather than with a predetermined interaction between two people or an arbitrary exercise.

A group *exercise* is a learning device prepared for a group before it meets. Generally, it is not related to a natural unfolding of the group process. For example, a leader starts a session by asking people to break into pairs and talk to each other for 20 minutes. After the pairs return, they are asked to introduce each other to the group. Here, in passing, I would like to mention so-called sensitivity groups which consist of a collection of prefabricated, preplanned exercises which the leader simply distributes to the group in serial order, without attending to the group process whatsoever.

In contrast, a group *experiment* is a creative happening which grows out of the group's experience. The happening is not predetermined and its outcome cannot be predicted; it is a creation of the total group. The following is an example of such a happening.

Several group members become critical of the leaders. Each person seems to have a special style of dealing with the problem: Some are vocal and articulate, others are non-committal, and so on. The leaders ask the group if this situation is reminiscent of some experience in their past. Someone tells a story of a family in which the parents are having a good time with each other, but don't include the kids. Everyone seems to identify with the analogy and the leaders encourage each person to envision himself as a member of the present family. As the drama unfolds, the group develops insights into its relation to the leaders, e.g., how the children and parents collude to create dissatisfaction and rebelliousness. Each person has an opportunity to explore his place within the drama, and the experiment helps the group discover a new context for examining its own problems without insulating itself from the leaders.

Action in the group may begin with a statement by one of the group members or a conversation between several people. This interaction might include verbal interventions by the therapist, other group members in question, or the group as a total entity. The experiment always grows out of the data which are already there, the here and now existence of the group, then amplifies the particular situation and propels it forward. At its highest level, the experiment introduces the group to a novel problem-solving creation in which each member learns something special about himself.

Experiments may develop out of an individual member's experience, such as a fantasy or dream, or they may develop from a dilemma in which the group finds itself. The whole group may experiment with situations that exist in daily life: family conflicts, problems between lovers, situations of loss and grief, people's nightmares, problems concerning education, hopes, daydreams, aspirations, and unfinished life traumas. The imaginative group invents experiments for itself which are tailor-made for the situation at hand. In this way, the experiment not only gears itself to the theme of the group, but respects the capacity of its participants to carry out what the inventor proposes.

In this kind of experience, energy flows not only between the therapist and group members, but in various combinations and permutations of people with one another. The group uses its ongoing and ever-developing energy. When people don't sit on their energy, they are constantly enlivened and always have a sense that they have a choice to jump into the action and modify developing events. An individual's energy can be directed "out" toward the group in an attempt to change his environment, and group energy can also be directed "in" toward the individual as a catalyst and support for his learning about self. For example, a group may help an individual create new characterizations of himself by asking him to flip around his behavior in the opposite way to which he is accustomed.

Genuine group experimentation involves testing and expanding the therapist's role as well. He, too, may find himself in a position of changing his customary behavior in the group—it is not always the leader who invents the experiments. His most important job is to create an atmosphere or format in which the group's own creativity and inventiveness emerge. The group may come up with a theme that is significant and heavy, for example, grief. The therapist's ability to orchestrate this theme requires that he draw on a number of inner resources:

—his clinical understanding of grief and similar states;
—his ability to visualize a "real" situation which can be worked through within the group without forcing the action;
—his capacity to energize the group, stoke its fire, so that the action may develop toward resolution;
—his sensitivity to the emotional capacity of the group— dosage of intensity, craziness, physical encounter, and exertion;
—his sense of playfulness, humor, and flexibility, and his willingness to bend to the will of the group's imagery;
—his sense of timing—when to stop a situation which appears imminently dangerous to group members— and of resolution, so that no one is left hanging in pain at the end of the session.

At the same time that he considers the dynamic qualities of individual members and the group as a whole, the therapist is an improvisor, a director for setting the lighting, the music, and the arrangement of the drama itself.

It is especially the use of metaphor which allows people to come together and move in a novel direction. Metaphor is a way of connecting things that are not usually connected. The "family" metaphor of my earlier example gave the group a new common bond and called forth a rich store of memories and sentiments which gave new meaning and vitality to the present situation. Individuals can become connected through exploring a metaphor because the new image appeals to them all in different ways. Everyone's experience of family is similar yet significantly different in its detail of events and feelings.

The key is choosing a metaphor or image which is moderately novel—different enough so that people become excited to explore new ways of relating to each other without feeling threatened. At the same time, the metaphor should not be so far out of the reach of people's imagination that they are not able to identify and work with it. For example, it is easier to work with the notion of family than with an image of clusters of bacteria.

Group Experiments Flowing Out of Individual Experiences

A dream is reported by a group member. It is first worked through on an individual level, and then developed into a group experiment, such that each individual may reap fruit from the original imagery of the dreamer. My assumption is that all of us share archetypal themes. Images within the dream or fantasy are, therefore, selectively appealing to various group members, and may be used to enhance understanding of themselves within the group process.

The individual dream can be used, therefore, to benefit the whole group. Once the individual has played out his own dream and come in touch with himself in it, the whole group can take parts in the drama and actively participate in it. Thus, if the dream contains a rundown house, a crippled boy, his parents, and a station wagon, members of the group can pick roles which seem relevant to their own lives. One person may choose to be the crippled boy, telling the group how he feels impotent with strong women, and that this role would help him deal with his problem. Another person may choose the role of the domineering mother, and still another of the rundown house, and so on. The dreamer helps the group understand his characters, and the therapist facilitates the production of the dream as a dramatic experience for the whole group.

In my paper on dream work as theater,* I give an example of a vignette from the above dream, played by only two of the characters, neither of whom told the original dream. Part of the originally reported dream by a man in the group was, "I see my mother approaching, and I feel strangely uncomfortable in my chest . . ." The "crippled boy" is acted by John, a 40-year-old man. He has a sad face and curved-in shoulders and appears to be breathing shallowly; it is not surprising when he suggests that he play a son suffering from emphysema. Myra, a middle-aged woman who pouts a lot, volunteers to play the "domineering mother," and several members of the group smile and nod approvingly.

The vignette begins with introductions à la Perls. The man speaks first: "I am a crippled boy and I can't breathe, and this is my existence." The woman answers, "I am a domineering mother. I keep my boy crippled, and this is my existence." Myra's face flushes and tears well up in her eyes. She tells the group about her relationship with an older son. They go on . . .

> *Boy:* All my life I have needed you to take care of me, but now I'm beginning to feel your suffocation . . . I mean my suffocation. I feel that you are choking me to death.
> *Mother:* When you were very young, you were sickly and

---

*Zinker, J. C. "Dream Work as Theatre," *Voices,* Summer 1971.

I have tried to protect you from unnecessary discomfort . . .

Boy: (Interrupting) Yes, and by the time I was seven, I was afraid to go to school by myself and I would vomit when I got there.

Joseph: John, how do you feel in your stomach right now?

Boy: All right, but I still feel like she is choking me.

Joseph: (To Mother) Myra, put your hands on his neck and squeeze a bit . . . let him get in touch with the suffocation.

Mother: (Follows directions) I only want to take care of you . . .

Boy: (Tearing her hands away and coughing) Then get off my back! Let me live! (He looks as though he has suddenly taken his first full breath this evening.)

Member of the Group: She doesn't hear you.

Boy: (Hollering loudly) Get off my back; let me breathe; let me live my own life! (Panting deeply)

Another Group Member: I want to play alter-ego for Myra. (To Boy) If I let you be, let you go, will you hate me all my life?

Mother: (Completing statement) . . . If I could only feel that you will love me when you leave, it wouldn't be so difficult . . .

Boy: I need you to help me leave and I will always love you, but differently—as a man, a strong man, not a cripple.

The pair embrace spontaneously and Myra cries because she realizes she will have to have a talk with her son who flunked out of college and came home six months ago.

Individual experiences in the group may be generated into group experiments which can involve most members of the group, not just the leading characters. For example, in the above case, members of the group may choose to play alteregos for the different characters. The alter-ego expresses a force, a motive or sentiment which the "actor" overlooks but which another member in the group knows from his own experience.

This technique involves various members' getting up during the acting-out of the dream, moving toward the person who speaks, and speaking for part of his experience which may not be in his awareness. When the boy says, "All my life I have needed you to take care of me, but now I'm beginning to feel your suffocation," someone may move in and say, "Yet I don't know what I would have done without you looking out for me all the time." After this statement is made, the boy character is asked to repeat that line in order to get in touch with a polar force within himself. In the case of the mother, when she tells her son, "When you were very young, you were sickly and I have tried to protect you from unnecessary discomfort," another person in the group may reflect the mother's repressed feelings of anger: "Every time you became ill I would get more and more angry, and I really did want to choke you. I did want to get rid of you. You crippled my life in many ways, and I'm still angry with you for that!" Once again, the mother may choose to speak these lines. The action becomes more complex, yet more enlightening both to the mother and the "alter-ego" in the group who is working on his own anger in his family situation.

Other significant relatives and friends may be introduced into the drama to give it greater realism, and to allow the symbolic expression of other forces and conflicts in people's lives. One can have loving aunts, alcoholic uncles, accepting teachers, and other characters who are relevant to the dreamer or to others in the group. Thus, every person in the group can explore unfinished situations in his life.

The dreamer, the original creator of the drama, is not lost in the process; he can watch the drama, nightmare, or fulfillment of a wish take concrete shape before his eyes. He can move in and change the action. He can take over one of the roles and demonstrate it in detail. He can experiment with different outcomes: the crippled boy transformed into superman or a sadistic torturer or a self-righteous rabbi. Thus, the dreamer taps into a range of inner forces within himself and tests them out in the supportive arena of the group. He can experience or merely observe how certain behaviors affect others and the price he may have to pay for such behaviors.

The acting out of a dream may also be modified by the group to work its own issues. This is perfectly acceptable, especially after the individual dreamer and his primary characters have come to an understanding of the original theme and its relevance to their own lives.

Everyone becomes involved. People exchange roles, play alter-egos for each other, and try out different interpretations of the dream's content. Everyone is enlivened in the process of understanding a new part of himself. Each person in the group becomes an active creator of the life of a character, shaping it, moving in and out of it, experimenting with behaviors more freely within the make-believe context of the production. Finally, the group as a community takes ownership of the dream by spontaneously introducing variations in its process and modifying the outcome of the action.

Emerging Group Issues and the Development of Experiments

The therapist's development of an experiment is related to the situation in which the group finds itself. Here are some examples of such situations:

—dissatisfaction with leader;
—lack of energy in the group;
—lack of intimacy or cohesiveness in the group;
—difficulty beginning;
—getting stuck with ending the group experience;
—saying goodbye to someone who is leaving the group;
—anger within the group around a particular issue;
—development of group confluence;
—boredom within the group and a lack of stimulation;
—competitiveness and power struggles;
—passive-aggressive tendencies within the group;

—stereotyped advice-giving by group members;

—unresolved difficulty between two or more group members;

—the group reaches an impasse in dealing with a particular theme;

—group members engage in bullshitting without contact;

—death of a group member or group member's significant other;

—two people in the group fall in love.

These are only a few of many group issues which have their own integrity and may not involve simply one person presenting a problem. The creative therapist may, of course, work with just the experiential level of a particular theme. He may be there to lubricate, to encourage and clarify the issues involved by simply making clear and pointed observations of the ongoing process. On the other hand, he may wish to amplify and expand the process by developing situational experiments which have a problem-solving quality as their goal.

Let's take one situation in the group and then amplify it into an experiment which may be invented by the leader or by several other participants. The situation may be dissatisfaction with a group member: People are complaining that Mark has been overly tired, has often withdrawn into the background, and sometimes fallen asleep. The group feels he has not had enough energy, and when the energy has been there it has not been present for others. This is a serious problem within the group. It is easy for Mark to become defensive and get into issues of leaving the group. But before such drastic measures are taken, the group should have an opportunity to experience its imagination and problem-solving abilities.

Because Mark's behavior splits the group into factions, someone expresses the feeling that they are in a courtroom. The image is immediately attractive to the group because many of the statements are accusatory and judgmental. Slowly the courtroom image develops into an experiment. Beverly suggests that Mark be "put on trial." The idea of a courtroom and trial gives the group a sense of being able to stand above itself and look at the situation with some sense of perspective, a sense of humor about its own experience, as well as its perception of Mark as a real human being. It is a group dramatization with an uncertain outcome.

Mark asks the most vocal accusers of his poor presence to be the chief prosecutors in the courtroom. Several people sympathetic to Mark volunteer to be his lawyers and defendants. Other members point out that there are certain aggressive individuals in the group who support and collusively encourage Mark's withdrawal, and they should be on trial also. Melissa objects: "We've got to keep this thing clear; let's have a trial for one person only—Mark. He is our focus, our problem." The group agrees.

There is, of course, a matter of a jury, which consists of members of the group who are uncommitted on the issues and feel open about examining it. Several hours are spent in the production of the courtroom drama, and all the characters express themselves with renewed vigor. Although outcomes of such experiments are never fully predictable, they are frequently creative resolutions of conflicts within the group. Here are portions of the unfolding experiment:

> *Prosecutor:* Your honor, this man has made a mockery of group therapy! (In the background someone says, "That's right!" Another person laughs.)
>
> *Judge:* Order in the court. (Aside) Here is my chance to exercise some power in this group. Now I can be as opinionated as I want.
>
> *Prosecutor:* Yes, and I can point my finger at this man, too. (Pointing at Mark) What does he do in this group? He yawns and he sleeps and he farts around. He hardly responds to other people and their needs. He acts depressed a lot and refuses to accept offerings of help from his colleagues. He is simply a weight on this group! (In the background, "Hear, hear . . .")
>
> *Defense Counsel:* Your honor, there are people in this group who help Mark withdraw and become listless. May I call John to the stand?

Judge: You may.

(John sits in front of the group facing it. The judge is in back of John.)

Defense Counsel: John, you have been present in this group for many weeks. You seem objective and level-headed. Could you tell the court how some people in this group help Mark to withdraw?

John: Well ma'am, I notice that when Martha becomes vocal about women's lib issues and starts arguing with Bill about his attitudes, Mark withdraws. I believe Mark associates Martha's assertiveness and aggressiveness with his wife . . . and gets anxious. (In the background, "And with his pushy Italian mother, too!")

Judge: Order! Strike that word "Italian" from the record, please. And I suggest you question Martha directly.

(Martha changes seats with John.)

Martha: Your honor, I am what I am. I have not willfully encouraged Mark to withdraw. However, now that I think about it, I remember all the times I have raised my voice and seen the painful expression on Mark's face . . . I would like to become perhaps more quietly present for other people so that Mark—whom I like very much—can get a chance to speak his mind.

(The whole group applauds and Martha looks a bit pained.)

Judge: Counsel for the Defense will join us now.

Defense Counsel: I would like to reiterate this notion of collusive behavior in this matter. We have been sitting on our asses and helping Mark stay in his corner. All of us, not just Martha. People jump in declaring that they want to work and don't attend to each other; we don't hear each other.

The discussion continues; various other witnesses are called. Everyone seems to articulate his relationship to Mark with great care. From time to time Mark takes the stand to respond to various comments. There are applause, boos, and occasional outbursts of laughter. The room is electrified with

energy. The court scene has mobilized Mark. Never before
has he been so active and involved.

Defense Counsel: Your honor, the defendant wishes to
  speak on his own behalf to the jury.
(Mark takes the stand. His face is red; his lower lip is
  trembling slightly.)
Mark: Ladies and gentlemen. All my life I have been
  pushed and prodded by my mother and my father. I
  was always told what to do. How to act correctly,
  how to be more aggressive and ambitious about my
  career. I wanted to be a baker but my mother and
  father insisted I join the family business: I was never
  accepted for what I was. Now I am an adult. Yet
  much of the time I feel I am running. At work I don't
  have a moment's peace . . . At home I am told about
  the bills before I can hang my coat in the closet . . .
  Your honor, this group is special for me. It is the only
  place in the world where I can be Mark, where I can
  rest and get away from the humdrum of daily life. I
  can speak or be silent. I can laugh or cry—as I am doing now. I can even take a short nap if I wish . . . And
  now, in this sanctuary, this oasis, I am being pushed,
  prodded and accused! I am being coaxed and intimidated into behaving in a socially acceptable way.
  Your honor, ladies and gentlemen, I ask that I be
  allowed to be Mark, plain old me. That I be allowed
  to develop and to change at *my* pace, in *my* way.
(There is a long silence in the room. Someone is sniffling.
  Martha puts her arms around Mark's shoulders and
  kisses him gently.)
Foreman of the Jury: Your honor, we find the defendant
  not guilty of being an inadequate group member. We
  wish to encourage him to be more open with us in the
  same way he was during this trial—because he was
  eloquent and beautiful and he was with us. He gave
  us much pleasure with his presence.

Mark became his own strong and vocal advocate. As he experienced his emerging power and energy, his role in the group was transformed. He was seen as a more vital member of the group who could contribute to its life and development. In addition, several relationships in the group became more clearly defined, while others were strengthened. The vehicle of the courtroom gave the group an opportunity to examine its own nature. Old collusions were dissolved and new loyalties established.

There are other group experiments which may be invented, depending on the situation in which the group is involved. I will mention some of the experiments I have experienced in the course of working with groups over the years. Most of these happenings are based on the group's metaphorical view of itself.

> The group is on a spaceship or some other vehicle, and it is on a long journey. (An example of this metaphor is cited later in the chapter.)

> The group reconstructs a traumatic memory of one of its members.

> The group creates the death, burial, and resurrection of one of its members who is concerned about his "deadness."

> The group experiences itself as a congregation and performs a meeting of prayer and blessing.

> The group is a primordial tribe celebrating something of great significance to itself.

> The group performs a birth rite, beginning with symbolic lovemaking of two members and participation of everyone in a delivery room.

> The group as an institution—jail, school, insane asylum, particular work situation, etc.

> The group as a house or a building or a castle, in which

each member plays a particular aspect of the structure, depending on the individual's life theme.

The group as a zoo, in which each person chooses to be a particular animal.

The group as one animal, with each person playing a part of the animal—its sphincter muscles, genitals, belly, fur, strong back, etc.

The group acts out a fantasy of a member's existential experience in it. For example, someone in the group may say, "We are all floating around in space." This metaphor would then be acted out in a total engagement.

These experiments are not prefabricated. They always grow out of particular issues in groups and are designed for those specific situations.

THE "MECHANICS" OF EXPERIMENTATION

While an experiment may be perceived or experienced as a "happening," it does not "just happen"; it requires insight and work on the part of the leader. Issues of preparation, timing, cohesiveness, and availability of energy must be dealt with throughout the experimental process.

Techniques and Creations

To speak of techniques is a limited way of presenting our methodology. So, rather than talking about specific techniques or gimmicks, we can talk about different vehicles which can be used. One vehicle we have is dream work as theater, which in a metaphorical way expresses the existence and experience of a group.

This process involves the use of metaphor, fantasy, role-playing, story-telling, and improvisation. Themes can be archetypal, such as good and evil, or life-themes of birth and death, of separation, of marriage, of mourning, of life emergencies, of basic relationships between mothers and sons, fathers and daughters.

If you are a group leader, ask the group what metaphor or analogy comes to mind when they think of themselves. Are they an animal or some other organism? Are they a situation, like a journey? What sort of vehicle are they? What is their destination? Who is the navigator? Allow the process to unfold. Allow group energy to grow. Stimulate people who hang back to play out their roles in the creation, or to play their own polarities.

The group can start from a metaphor or a dream or a group fantasy and end by creating among themselves an entire society. The group becomes a microcosm of all the polarities, all the experiences of humankind. The group has the power to not only reenact life as the members have experienced it, but to begin life anew, creating a society as no society has ever existed. And this kind of experimentation can be so moving and so fully involving that the process of living through the experience alone is aesthetically pleasing and clearly understood. One no longer has to say, "This was the meaning of this experience," or "These were the implications of this experience." No one needs to interpret the experience—its impact is self-evident.

Preparation and Grading

It is not enough to invent an idea for an experiment. One must consider whether the group is ready to carry out such an experiment, whether the experiment is too difficult, too easy, or too unimaginative for the group to grab it and make something of it. The whole process of preparation for the execution of an experiment is crucial and cannot be bypassed without creating difficulties.

The table describes the gradation of a particular experiment involving an issue of non-communication within the group.

Gradation of Group Experiments

Situation	Level 1	Level 2	Level 3	Level 4	Level 5
People don't seem to be hearing each other—especially certain pairings who wind up getting into fruitless arguments. Mary and John are into an argument again, and John is so discouraged that he looks like he is about to quit talking altogether. The other group members look frustrated and impatient.	"I wonder, John, if you are misunderstanding what Mary has to say to you." (Simple intervention)	"John, I wonder if you could tell Mary what you think you heard her say?" (Simple experiment)	"Mary, would you tell John what he stated accurately and also when his statements distorted what you had to say to him?"	"As the group seems to have hearing problems I would suggest the following experiment: Pick the person you feel the least contact with or umderstanding of; go off to a corner somewhere and repeat what John and Mary did, then switch so both of you get a chance to test out the other's attentiveness and capacity to hear you."	"Let's talk about your experience. Were there any specific areas in which listening became dull or difficult?"

182

The first column presents the particular situation between Mary and John. Then we have Levels 1, 2, 3, 4, and 5 of building an experiment toward increasing levels of group participation. Each level is intended to present palpable material which individual members are ready to execute. Level 1 may be a simple intervention, such as, "I wonder, John, if you are misunderstanding what Mary has to say to you." This level is not an experiment; it is a statement of the therapist's impression of what he feels is at issue between John and Mary. At this level, John and Mary may be ready to think about their communication problem and be prepared for the next level of behaviorally executing a simple experiment, as stated in Level 2 of the table.

The experiment is then built in graded steps, such that each step contributes to the solution of the problem, until it involves the total group. In this example, the table is oversimplified, for it cannot encompass the various convoluted interventions and interactions of group members. And while the experiment may be modified, depending on the specific responses of group members, at no point should it lose its fluid, organic quality fitted to the feeling of the group.

Energy and Timing

A group is like a love partner. One must attend to its feelings, its needs, and its available store of energy. The matter of adequate energy is exceedingly important. Look at the group. Watch their eyes, their physical positions, their breathing, their attentiveness to one another and to yourself. What do they look like? Do they seem to want a coffee break, or do they look like they need more stimulation? Every teacher learns when his lecture begins to dull others. If he doesn't learn these fundamental observations of group energy, he turns into a boring, self-centered performer who loses the group after two or three contacts.

The therapist is in a similar position. He needs to know what energy exists in the group and he should not hesitate to check out his hunches with the group. The therapist, for example, may be full of energy and then project it on the group without realizing that the rest of the people do not share his interest and excitement. There is no sin in having the wrong hunch, and it is very satisfying to get confirmation of a right one.

The matter of timing is difficult to describe. It takes a special sensitivity to know when something will work and when it won't. One must consider the lateness of the hour and the receptiveness and relationships of individual group members to one another at any given moment. Sometimes it is prudent simply to stop the action because a theme has been developed as adequately as the community can tolerate in a given period. At other times, one needs to test whether, at that very point, the group is ready for a creative leap. A brilliant, intuitive experiment attempted in the wrong time frame will be a flop. Its poor timing, however, should have no implication on its intrinsic value.

Group Cohesiveness

Creative experimentation requires a hard-working, cooperative body of people, with a leader who is respected, enjoyed, and experienced as a real human being. Without a minimum amount of cohesiveness, cooperation, and willingness to engage the therapist, the group's efforts to be creative will simply fall flat.

There are several cues indicative of a group's cohesiveness. One positive sign is that when someone speaks, others look like they are investing energy in listening and reinforcing the speaker's process. The timing of responses is also an index of cohesiveness, though a tricky one. An immediate response to someone's query may be a sign of real interest, but one must listen to the content of the response. Sometimes people listen for a cue in the other person's language which they can use, not so much to understand the other, but to tell their own story:

John: I am very anxious about my midterm exams; I hardly did any studying.

Bob: (Deflecting) I used to have the habit of leaving my work to the last minute. I remember in my senior year that I . . .

In some groups, cohesiveness is reflected in ease of physical contact between members; in others, physical contact is a way of deflecting from real intimacy. Visual contact also reflects on a group's unity, especially when it is examined as part of the group's total life. I have noticed that in some families people are literally not visible to each other. It is as if the person speaking is already "known" and need not be looked at: "That's the way John is; he will probably complain and whine now," or "Beverly is *always* depressed; she will look sad and start crying any moment," or "Joe is our big protestor; he will disagree with most anything." Stereotyping of roles and characterizations prevents the freshness of contact and thins the group's cohesiveness.

Cohesiveness of a group is sometimes related to its own sense of purpose. When people look disoriented, they may need to be asked about the lost looks on their faces. I always feel more comfortable when I know ahead of time what the general purpose of the group is, especially when the group's time is limited. I have learned my lesson well: Some time ago I was asked by the administrator of a psychiatric hospital in the Midwest to spend a day with a group of psychiatrists for the purpose of illustrating how a Gestalt therapist works. I agreed to do so and assumed that the group members were aware of this particular plan. After working with them for six painful, distressing hours, I discovered that no one in the group (the administrator was not there) ever heard of me or Gestalt therapy or the specific reason for my presence. After the air was cleared, we spent two very useful hours learning from each other and about Gestalt principles.

People in cohesive groups often express strong feelings of affiliation and affection. These may be reflected both in pleasurable responses to each other and in the freedom people feel to confront one another on important issues. Confrontation is not poisonous, but reflects people's individuality and mutual trust. The confluent yessing of each other, on the other hand, is a sign of superficial contact. Cohesiveness can also be determined by the degree of trust in a group, usually reflected in the revelation of emotionally sensitive issues.

Generally, the building of cohesiveness involves building adequate contact between group members and pointing out where the group is losing a sense of connectedness. Let's return to the earlier example with John and Bob:

> *Bob:* (Deflecting) I used to have the habit of . . . I remember in my senior year . . .
> *Joseph:* I think, Bob, that John is not interested in your senior year experience. He is trying to tell us about his anxiety.
> *Beverly:* Yeah, you took the issue away from him. I want to hear some more from you, John.
> *John:* I just feel like I am destroying myself by not working when it really counts. I have to make up my mind what I want out of school . . .

John's theme begins to develop with the support of the rest of the group. It is this sort of support which was lacking in the Belville group, discussed below.

THE EXISTENTIAL JOURNEY

The Belville group met with me during the course of several weekends. The dramatic thing about this group was that no matter how diligently we dealt with individual problems, some of which were quite serious, the atmosphere of the group did not change. The group continued in a spirit of suspiciousness, dissatisfaction, argumentativeness, and lack of community.

I came into this weekend workshop feeling uncertain about

how I was going to deal with the difficulties of the group. I
felt that we needed a vehicle through which each person
could safely express his sentiments about life in the group. I
thought that a fantasy would have the advantage of not sound-
ing like a direct confrontation or a bold challenge to fight and
argue unproductively. Once expressed, individual fantasies
could be combined with each other to tell a story about the
group's problems. Because a combination of abstract images
has a certain distance from a distasteful and threatening reality of group paranoia, I reasoned that these bright people
might be fascinated by weaving a story distant enough from
their community not to threaten them. The finished product
would present a symbolic statement of the group's life; hope-
fully, a translation of this abstract statement would reveal the
group's concrete difficulties and existential dilemmas.

And so I started the evening by asking each person in the
group to write out a fantasy or dream of what it was like for
him/her to be in this group. When read, the fantasies were a
succession of nightmares, horror stories filled with monsters,
flaming meteors, prehistoric animals, sea creatures—devour-
ing and destroying in landscapes of loneliness, barrenness
and isolation. Whatever was beautiful was also tentative, uncertain, and unsafe. This process took a full evening, and in
recounting these personal dreams there arose a sense of recognition, of shared difficulty.

The next morning we proceeded to move from individual
fantasies and dreams to building a group fantasy. My hope
was that the group dream eventually could be used as a vehicle for the group to examine itself more openly and thought-
fully. Mark started to construct the communal dream and Jack
was asked to write down the dream verbatim. Other people
contributed to the dream as they wanted to, drawing on their
personal dreams from the previous night. This is the dream
that was created by the group:

"Fasten your safety belts," says the stewardness, whose
name is Brenda. She has a magic wand like a watering

can, watering people. Weird humming comes over the intercom—music of the sphere. Mort is riding on Pegasus, riding and yelling, "Hey Silver," when suddenly a tiger comes out of the tank of the plane. "Where are the birds?" the tiger says, licking its chops. He has a road map and is asking for directions. Everybody on the plane is an animal. Sid is a laughing tiger, a cock-eyed tiger. Next to him is a guy who keeps stopping the action and taking pictures. Flashcube bulbs blind people temporarily. And someone says, "This is my existence." There is a hijacker in a long black robe. Songs come over the intercom like Waltzing Matilda. A guy comes out with a Tarot deck of cards and passes out a card to each person. Barbara takes the Fool. The pilot announces, "I will now read from Genesis. Prepare to meet your Creator. Life must go on." Gynecologists in back of the plane take off their smocks, revealing trench coats. They are spies from a small Baltic country. "You killed Howard Johnson," they yell. A chorus of voices repeats, "No." One person says, "No, it was cock-robin." The pilot says, "In twenty seconds you will wake up." The passengers yell, "No, no, I don't want to wake up!" "Prepare for landing." "I don't believe it!" Panic strikes—nobody knows each others' names. The pilot's door opens and Roger in a leotard and a cape with an S on the chest runs down the aisle: "I am going to sabotage this plane!" Everyone is feeling terrible, incomplete, fragmented, excited, and they still don't know each others' names. We need a navigator, otherwise we will crash. And then we wake up.

After the dream was created, Jack was asked to read it back to the group. Everyone was stunned. Florence remarked that the text of the dream had the enormity of a religious theme for a community. I reasoned that if the group could consider its statement in a spiritual atmosphere, one which implies love and mutual respect, their own messages to each other might continue to carry weight in the group. I then suggested that David, a minister, stand up and deliver the dream as a religious statement. I added that, when something significant was read, people who identified with the statement could say, "And this is my existence" or "This is how we are as a group of people—this is what we are like."

I was surprised to discover that, as each phrase was read, the entire group responded often. Here is a selected sample of the ritual as it emerged, with the "religious text" read by David and responses from the "congregation":

David: . . . Everyone on the plane is an animal.

Group: And this is our existence.

Florence: Yes, and I have been hoping for weeks that we could be human with each other.

David: . . . Sid is a laughing tiger, a cock-eyed tiger . . .

Sid: And this is my existence.

Barbara (Fool): Sid, I have been enjoying your careless easiness, but today I need your adult, your maturity. And this is my existence.

David: . . . There is a hijacker in a long black robe . . .

Group: And this is our existence.

Bob (Pilot) to Ted (Hijacker): Just for today, Ted, I wish you could let us fly straight without telling us your latest troubles and threatening to leave if we don't respond. And that's where *I* am.

Group: And this is our existence.

Ted: Fuck you! (Long silence) But you are right and that hurts.

(Long silence)

David: . . . Gynecologists in back of the plane take off their smocks revealing trench coats. They are spies from a small Baltic country. "You killed Howard Johnson," they yell. A chorus of voices repeats, "No." One person says, "No, it was cock-robin!"

Group: And this is our existence.

Brenda (Stewardess): It's time we realized that our gynecologists, Joseph and Myrna, want to deliver our babies. That they have no other motives . . .

Jerry: It's time to stop being so paranoid about our lead-

And this is our existence!

ers. It's time to be more trusting. I am willing to become more trusting. And this is my existence. (In the background: "Hear, hear.")

Bob (Pilot): We have been suspicious and untrusting, and at the same time, we are so clever in denying and intellectualizing our mistrust of each other. And that's how I really feel. I feel sick about us!

David: . . . Panic strikes—nobody knows each others' names . . .

Group: And this is our existence.

A Voice: I feel ashamed of us.

Jack: It is time to know each others' feelings and fears. It is time.

Another Voice: Amen!

David: The pilot's door opens and Roger in a leotard and cape with an S on the chest runs down the aisle: "I am going to sabotage this plane!"

Group: And this is our existence.

Mort: Isn't it enough to have a hijacker? Do we need a saboteur too? For God's sake! What we need is a brick layer, a builder! And that's my experience. We need Brenda, the Stewardess, with her magic watering can to make us grow up.

David: . . . and they still don't know each others' names.

Group: (In a loud chorus) And this *is* our existence!

David: . . . We need a navigator, otherwise we will crash.

Judy: Amen!

Voices: This is the end if we don't get . . .

Mort: . . . a wise navigator!

Voices: And this is our existence!

At the end of the service, there was a hushed movement in the group, a feeling of poignancy about the truth of its own revelation. And sadness, too, at hearing this statement they had created about themselves.

After several minutes of silence, the group spontaneously began to act out the fantasy they had created. People took seats as if in a plane and started conversations with each other about where they were going, their destination. Then Bob looked up and around the room, saying, "We don't have a navigator. We will crash without a navigator." And Jerry responded, "There is a baby here. Let him be the navigator. He has the purest motives here." (Judy had brought her infant who was less than a year old.)

Mort volunteered to sit next to the pilot as spokesperson for the "baby" navigator. He spoke in a very soft, tender, almost pleading voice: "What I need to land this plane is to be loved. I'm just a helpless baby and I feel alone. I need you to care for me. I need you to love me." And as he spoke tears came to his eyes and spontaneously several people went toward Mort and started comforting him. Just as spontaneously, the plane full of people began to cluster into small subgroups of individuals who moved closer and closer toward one another until they were talking quietly with their arms around each other, comforting each other, telling each other what they meant to one another and sharing openly how lost they felt.

The drama continued as the pilot announced, "Fasten your seat belts, there is enough love here to land the plane now." People held on to each other as if bracing for a rough landing. Their faces were flushed; some held each other and wept. The voice of the stewardness emerged next: "Ladies and gentlemen, we have just landed in the county of trust, the city of brotherly (pause) . . . and sisterly love. . . ." Someone responded, ". . . and as soon as you collect your baggage, we've got a lot of work to do!"

This was the culmination of that particular group experience. It not only revealed the existential condition of the group, but for the first time people began to support and trust each other, and to see the possibilities of doing constructive work with one another in the future. It was the first sense I had in the group that indeed we could truly learn together, that we could be a community.

I began by dealing with the primacy of the group's experience through asking individual members to express the problem metaphorically. I felt that the group was in trouble as far as trust was concerned, and that metaphor would give us freedom to tackle the problem openly and creatively. Individual as well as collective awareness was stimulated by sharing these initial fantasies, and this process was enhanced through the creation of a group fantasy. It was as if the total group were looking into a wall-to-wall mirror.

Contact was stimulated by identifying the group theme of alienation, and further enhanced as the group continued working with the dream, especially when it was transformed into a religious ritual. The group's increased engagement with itself as a community was evidenced by the members' feeling safe enough to participate in the experiment. The eloquent statement of a theme is, in such instances, a means of understanding the problem—even of finding a solution to it.

In many ways, the solution of the group's dilemma was implicit in the style, the mode with which it was elaborated: the medium became the massage. As the dream was played out, it was worked with a problem-solving intention. So when I asked David to read it to the group as a religious declaration, I was already saying, "Let's emphasize how upsetting this is to all of us; let's pray to it; let's make it so important that we can't escape ourselves." Or by asking for a navigator, the group was making an attempt to say, "Let's find a way of guiding ourselves so we can all land this crummy airplane in an area of the world where we can live together." The resolution not only came about by dramatizing and acting out, but also by the way in which the fantasy was concretely translated toward a new way of looking at each other.

The experiment made it clear that this dilemma was one which the group itself had created and that by creating this dream, the group took responsibility for its own problems. In an authoritarian system in which the therapist proposes a solution, that proposal is much less compelling than the creative outcry and invention of the total group. The group hypnotizes itself with its own creative power. That kind of self-examination is impossible to dismiss. If the entire group cries out, "We have to land in a safe spot to live together," no one can step out and say to the leader, "Oh, that's ridiculous; you are proposing simple-minded things," because the total group has already committed itself to that kind of declaration. Everyone has internalized the message in his own way. It is inescapable.

Chapter 8

Polarities and Conflicts

It seems to me that the sine qua non of man's knowledge, happiness, and existence is to be found in the idea of the reconciliation of differences. It matters little whether we talk about mental health and personality structure or whether we talk in the context of society. It matters little what the size of the society is. It makes little difference whether the society is a marriage, a small group, a large industrial organization, a community, a nation, or many nations; the basic issue is that of the reconciliation of the individual with the group, the organization, the integration of parts into a unified whole. These issues are all matters of totality, wholeness, completeness, unity, order, structure.*

Conflict may be healthy and creative or it may be confluent and non-productive. The latter form of conflict occurs when I don't understand myself and accuse you of something of which I am guilty, and involves at least two forms of defense —repression and projection. Healthy conflict occurs when

---

*Jones, Ronald C. (Untitled). In Brockman, J. & Rosenfeld, E. (eds.), *Real Time 1*. Garden City, NY: Anchor Press/Doubleday, 1973.

each of us is an integrated person with some self-awareness and a clear sense of differentiation. Conflict arises when there is a clear sense of disagreement about something which is a real issue between us; it is not a result of projecting stuff on each other which we are unable to confront within ourselves. Healthy conflict, if handled skillfully, results in good feelings between people; it is a "win-win" rather than a "win-lose" proposition.

I am fond of telling my friends that I like making trouble. For one thing, people who disagree rarely bore each other. For another, conflict provides the potential to differentiate ourselves from the boundaries of other personalities. Too often, people who have deep ties also tend to drown in each other's psychological boundaries; they even look alike. When two clearly differentiated boundaries rub against each other, the individuals experience an exhilarating sense of contact.

The same phenomenon holds true of intrapsychic or internal conflicts. When brought into awareness with clarity, conflicts tend to allow the person the sense of his internal differentiation, and at the level of creativity, hold the possibility for integrated behavior—behavior which is highly adaptive because it spans the full range of responses between formerly experienced polar extremes. The person is able to respond flexibly to a variety of situations out of that sort of range. In contrast, polar responses are generally restricted, unimaginative, and brittle in relation to daily life stresses.

Conflict which repeats itself stereotypically, without unique solutions or learnings, leads to confluence rather than contact between people. Thus, it is the potential for learning which holds creative promise for conflict.

POLARITIES: GROUNDWORK FOR UNDERSTANDING CONFLICT

A good theory of conflict covers both intrapersonal and interpersonal conflict. It begins with the individual as a conglomerate of polar forces, all of which intersect, but not necessarily at the center. In an oversimplified example, we might

say that a person has within him the characteristic of kindness
and also its polarity of cruelty, the characteristic of hardness
and its polarity, softness. Furthermore, a person possesses not
just one opposite, but several related opposites, creating
"multilarities."* For example, cruelty may not be the only
polarity of kindness; another may be insensitivity or callous-
ness toward another person's feelings. Diagramatically, such
a simple multilarity looks like this:

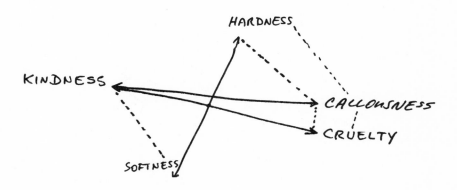

   Polarized conceptualizations and feelings are complex and
interlaced. They are, obviously, related to the individual's
particular background and perception of his inner reality.
One's inner reality consists of those polarities and characteristics which are ego-syntonic, or acceptable to one's conscious
self, and those which are ego-alien, or unacceptable to the
self. Often, the self-concept excludes painful awareness of the
polar forces inside of us. I would rather think of myself as
bright than dull, as graceful than clumsy, as soft rather than
hard, as kind rather than cruel.
   Theoretically, the healthy person is a complete circle, pos-
sessing thousands of integrated and interlaced polarities, all

---

*Multilarities is a term created by Erv Polster.

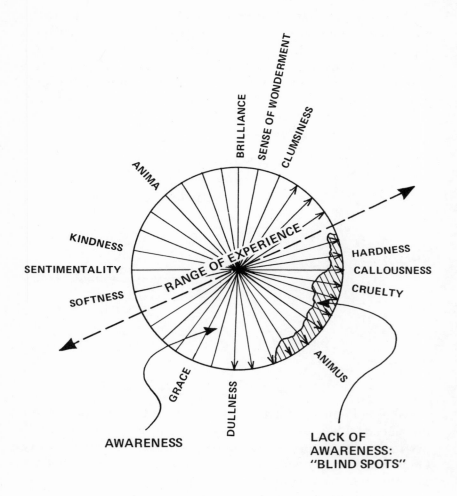

Healthy self-concept. Here the person is aware of many opposing forces within himself. He is willing to see himself in a multitude of "contradictory" ways. He experiences relationships between a variety of inner parts.

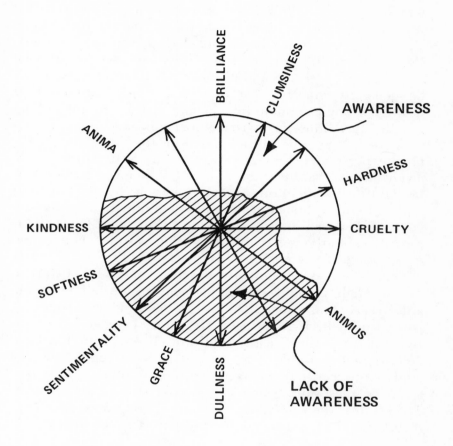

Pathological self-concept. The "disturbed" person sees himself in a unilateral stereotypic manner. He is always this and never that. His awareness of a multitude of inner forces and feelings is quite limited. He lacks fluidity and broadness of self perception. He is vulnerable to attack.

melted together. The healthy person is aware of most of the polarities within him, including those feelings and thoughts which society disallows, and is able to accept himself that way. He can say to himself: "Sometimes I am soft, but in situations where I am threatened, I really like my hardness. When I am in line and someone deliberately pushes in front of me, I don't feel soft, and it's okay not to be." A person may be generally graceful, yet clumsy in some situations. A healthy person can bump into a waiter in a restaurant and not have to say to himself, "What a clutz I am."

There still may be "blind spots" in the awareness of the healthy person. He may acknowledge his softness but not be aware of the hardness in himself. When his hardness is brought to his attention, he may experience pain, but he is willing to incorporate this new notion of himself into his self-concept. The healthy person may not always approve of all his polarities, but the fact that he is willing to suffer their awareness is a significant aspect of his inner strength.

There are massive holes in the awareness of a disturbed person. He has a rigid, stereotyped view of himself and is not able to accept many parts of himself: his stinginess, homosexuality, insensitivity, hardness. He denies his so-called negative polarities—those aspects of himself which he has been conditioned to think of as unacceptable or repulsive—and tends to project these characteristics on to others. Becoming aware of these unacceptable polarities makes him anxious. The result is the emergence of neurotic symptoms, with neurosis being the failure to control the emergence of anxiety.

INTRAPERSONAL CONFLICT

I view the self-concept as analogous to the dark and light sides of the moon. Intrapersonal conflict involves clashes between one's dark and light polarities. For example, when a woman says, "No," to her child, the light side of her moon says to her, "You're being reasonable; this is an unreasonable request, so it's okay to say no." At the same time, the dark side of her polarities (maybe something she has learned from her mother) says, "You're being cruel and unkind; you're not a good person to do that." So she starts torturing herself when she should have forgotten the whole thing. Although such situations usually involve other people, the conflict is brought on by what the person does to himself.

One aspect of the dark side of the moon is the conscience, or the superego. This dark aspect of the conscience is often a Hitler, an unreasonable, rigid, uncompromising conscience: "What do you mean you're going to bed at ten o'clock when you didn't answer those letters and you didn't return those phone calls?" Another way to define these two parts of the moon is to say that the nagging part of the moon is the sadist and the light part—that which takes all the crap and is unable to deal with it—is the masochist. It is almost as if there are two people in one.

One way to deal with a conflict like this is to clearly separate the "two" people. For instance, I might say to a client: "Put your sadist on this couch and your suffering victim on this chair, and let them talk to each other. Maybe they can work it out." In this process, the more "they" work it out, the more awareness the client develops about the dynamics and intercourse between his two parts. And the more he learns about the mysterious parts of himself, the healthier he becomes.

Essentially, that is what therapy intends to do—to remove that which is mysterious. When we are in the dark, we imagine devils and evil forces lurking "out there." When we turn on the light, we feel safe. This is what psychoanalytic theory is mainly about: the mechanics of pushing the painful polarities inside of us into our consciousness, and then dealing with what happens when they begin to bubble up and create anxiety. Freud made a successful effort to turn the lights on inside our psychological lives. Much of Gestalt therapy concretizes and operationalizes his ideas into more effective therapeutic interventions.

STRETCHING THE SELF-CONCEPT

My theory of polarities dictates that if I do not allow myself to be unkind, I will never be genuinely kind. If I am in touch with my own unkindness and stretch that part of myself, when my kindness emerges it will be richer, fuller, more complete. If I do not allow myself to be in touch with my femininity, then my masculinity will be exaggerated, even perverse— I will be a hard, tough guy. Many of my clients have said to me, "You're a man, but you're different; you're soft and that's nice." When one side of the polarity gets stretched, it is almost automatic that at some point the other side also stretches. I call this the "around the world" phenomenon: If you keep flying north long enough, you'll eventually be heading south.

In order to grow as a person and have more productive conflict experiences with others, I have to stretch my self-

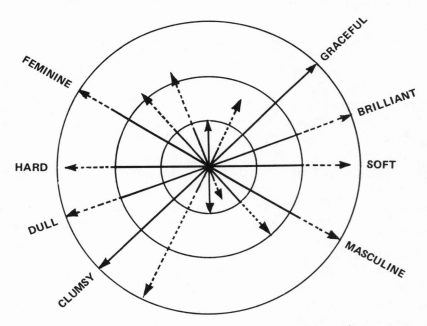

"Stretching" the self-concept. Movement in one direction inevitably stretches the opposite polarity.

concept. I have to teach myself to invade that part of me which I do not approve of. There are various techniques involved in this process. First, I must uncover that part of myself which is disowned. Second, I need to come into contact with the disowned part of myself. This is the preliminary step —getting in touch with how I keep secrets from myself. I might put a part of me on the couch, representing my secretive self, and that part might say: "I am mysterious and I am interesting. You should appreciate me because I keep you from exposing your tenderness and I protect you." And the other part, sitting in a chair, might say: "Yes, but don't we pay a price for that?" Then I go back to the couch and say, "Yes, a lot of the time I find myself alone when I don't want to be alone, and I stew in my secretiveness."

Once I feel kinder toward and more fully understanding of my secret self, I can relate to another person who tries to penetrate that inner territory or threatens that part of me. I call this whole process stretching the self-concept, creating more room in one's picture of the self. The more broadly I know myself, the more comfortable I am with myself.

One of my clients experiences severe anxiety, falling victim to a part of himself that says: "You are not worth living. You are a bad person; your life is bad. There isn't anything good about you." He cannot take ownership of this mean, sadistic attitude as part of his own character. He always experiences "it" as suddenly accosting him, as if "it" came from outer space. As he is working with me, he realizes that the "bad" part of him developed very early in his life. As a child, every time he left his house the other kids kicked, beat and teased him. Slowly, he began to identify with these children, and after a while they taught him to be his own critic, his own enemy. Now, as an adult, he doesn't need his angry friends. He does the job himself, kicking himself in the ass every day.

Once he was able to come in contact with this introjected critic-sadist, he could feel more sympathetic toward this unacceptable part of himself. Now when he feels self-critical, he can address himself to the critic: "Hey, you have really suffered. You are the part of me that was beaten. I am sorry you

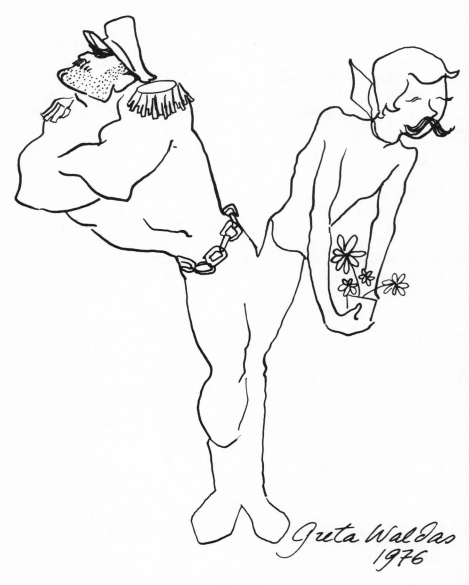

*The curious result of the stretching process is that the polarities of
the characteristic will become more evident, more solidified.*

took this job on for yourself. Isn't it time you stopped being so hard on me? After all, you know I am a decent human being."

One may think that if this man accepts the reality of his criticism and sadism, he will become a sadist. This is a fallacy. The more this man accepts his punitive, sadistic self, the less the possibility that he will act on his sadism in the future. The curious result of the stretching process is that the polarities of the critic will become more evident, more solidified. Thus, if for him the polarity of critic and sadist is acceptor and healer, then his acceptance and healing qualities will become more genuine and real with others, as well as with himself.

On the other hand, the less aware he is of these negative aspects of himself, the more he will find himself acting out these parts. I remember a young man who came to see me because he was horrified by his behavior. When I inquired further, he said, "I don't know what got into me, but I hit my baby boy so hard I broke his leg. And yesterday I threw the cat against the wall." This young father had no contact whatsoever with his own sadism. It was totally disowned. "It" popped out of him like a foreign object, beyond his control.

A person who is always considerate and kind may not be in touch with his resentment or anger, or with his sorrow about the pain which was inflicted on him. It is very difficult for such a person to accept his rage. Sometimes the only way he can handle rage is to be a better human being to others than anyone has ever been to him. He does not handle the consequences of being a victim, and it is inconceivable to him to identify with the victimizer.

Let me give you another example. We cannot agree to do something fully unless we have a choice to say, "No." A woman complains because she's agreed to give her time to solicit for a worthy cause when she doesn't have the extra time, or when she feels that she's done it so many times before that someone else should do it this time. She can't say "No" because she knows someone should do it, or maybe because she won't look good if she refuses. So she says "Yes" and feels resentful or makes a martyr of herself. She's not doing the job because she really wants to. It would be better for the woman to say, "Look, I know this is a worthy cause and I understand your problem in getting volunteers, but I've done this many times before, and I'm tired and busy, and I will not do it this time." If she could learn how to say "I won't" genuinely, she would have much more pleasure saying "I will" when she does accept the job another time. The "I won't" stretches the fullness of the "I will."

INTERPERSONAL CONFLICT

Interpersonal conflict often arises out of intrapersonal conflict. This occurs when an individual represses his awareness of some part of himself and then projects it onto someone else: It is easier to see the evil in another than in oneself. The devil is a grand projection of our inner evil and God of our inner goodness. It is easier to fight with someone else than to fight with oneself, to "resist the devil" than to cope with one's own evil intentions. Fighting with oneself is a lonely business and anxiety-provoking. It is less painful to attack a part of oneself by blaming the other person for being that way, especially if the blame is not open and above board.

Sometimes we attack parts of others which are lovely but too frightening to ourselves. Let us say that I have a part of me that really likes to cuddle, to hold someone and rock or sing to them, but I learned along the way that a "mature" man doesn't do that, or that it's aesthetically ugly, or that if I do I am going to get in trouble. So here is a lovely thing to do, but if I wanted to do it, I would be uncomfortable. Then I see a mother holding her 12-year-old son and rocking him, and I say, "Look at her, she's making a piece of jelly out of that boy; she's weak; she doesn't know how to handle her son. She should put her foot down and stop giving him all that sympathy." I would be disapproving: "What's the matter with you? Why are you so soft?" The result may be an argument.

Out of my own expertise as an "exhibitionist," I tend to be particularly sensitive to another person's exhibitionism. When

I am not aware of showing off, I tend to be attracted to that behavior in another person: One showoff knows another. If I want to have a constructive conflict, a creative conflict, I had better get in touch with that part of myself first; for by being in touch with that aspect of my inner life, I take the venom out of my potential anger.

If someone I dislike exhibits behavior that is so repugnant to me that I disown it in myself, then I cannot be objective about that behavior. I can't be clear about it; I just feel pissed off. For example, some students report to me that a colleague of mine didn't show up for a teaching session. I should be the last person in the world to hear such criticism, because I disapprove of my own tardiness. I feel guilty if I am just a little late. When my colleague arrives, I tell her, with all my righteousness, that I don't like what she did, it is shitty behavior, and it is incompetent. The result is that everybody in the room gets angry with me. If I were a little kinder to myself about my own tardiness, I might be more reasonable with my colleague and take time to get more information before passing judgment on another.

I think that recognizing one's own polarities affects one when falling in love. We often fall in love with the person who represents the dark polarities in ourselves. Let us say that I am a woman who does not experience certain parts of myself. I don't have self-confidence. I feel I am not inspired. I experience myself as a rather dull person. I am sure I am not creative. Then I meet a man. He takes me out; he is lively and exciting. He says, "I'm going to turn this world upside down." He seems creative, shows me some of the things he has done, and I fall head-over-heels in love with him. He is a delight. He perks me up. He makes me feel good. It is as if a lost piece of myself has suddenly come back to me—there it is! And often the language of love is exactly like that: "He's a piece of me. I'm not complete without him. He makes me a whole person."

It is a beautiful feeling, but there is always a problem with that kind of situation. Maybe the man isn't everything she thinks he is. He might have other characteristics which she

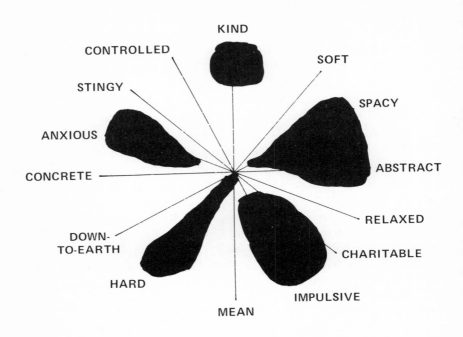

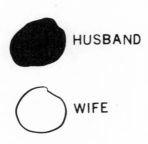

Husband and wife often divide up polarities, each filling an "empty" or "dark" polarity in the other.

may not want to see. Or if she sees him only as a missing part of herself, she may later resent that part of his life with which she can't have direct contact. For example, she might feel like, "If you are carrying the creative me out there in the world and having fun, and I'm a drab housewife sitting at home and not really using myself, then I resent you. I'm jealous of you. I feel like that piece of me should be right here." But how can that be possible when he is a separate human being?

Husband and wife often divide up polarities, each filling an "empty" or "dark" polarity in the other. Therefore, it takes two people to make a complete person. This is a confluent relationship, a state in which people are living in the same psychological skin. This is true both dynamically and in terms of concrete behavior. Conflict often occurs when one partner attacks in the other the polarity which is dark, troublesome or unknown in himself.

Projected polarities can either be dark, unknown and troublesome (ego-alien) or dark, unknown and supportive (ego-

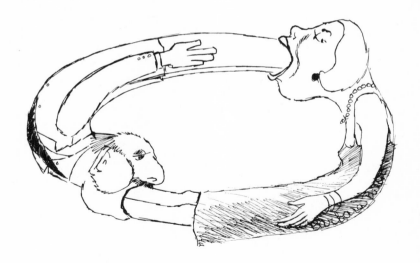

Conflict often occurs when one partner attacks the other in the polarity which is dark.

syntonic). If the husband behaves impulsively, the wife may define him as the "lively one." She may like that about him, in part, because she has some appreciation of how nice it would be for her to have that quality. This is an example of the projected dark and supportive polarity. However, it is also possible that she is frightened by her own impulsiveness and, therefore, his impulsiveness upsets her. When he behaves in this way she becomes anxious and angry with him, and accuses him of thoughtlessness and flightiness. She can deal with him effectively only if she can appreciate her own repressed flightiness.

My theory about the way to have a good marriage between these two people is for the wife to get to know her own creativeness, her own liveliness, to know in herself all the things that she admires and adores and appreciates and pleasures in him, and vice versa. Let us say that her husband fell in love with her softness, her giving, her support. He should learn to be in touch with his own softness, his own ability to give, and his own self-support, and he should learn about his own capacity to support others as well.

What you would have is not two overlapping circles of polarities in which each takes care of the other, but two whole human beings who can love each other out of the full awareness of their own selves. The husband could then say to his wife, "Out of my sense of softness, I appreciate your gentleness and delicacy. I value those qualities in myself." Instead, what I hear with so many couples is a resentful, "Talk to him about that, he's the creative one." After ten years of marriage, the attractive characteristic is no longer a nice thing. It is something she dislikes in him.

When talking about their new home, one husband said to me, "Talk to her about redecorating the house, she's the decorator. I don't know anything about colors and fabrics." Now what happens if the husband decides he's going to take an interest in the decorating? This special contact between two differentiated beings can be exciting, but won't the wife resent the fact that he is now stepping into her territory? As long as there is differentiation, there is going to be conflict, but it is a healthy conflict. For instance, the husband may say, "I think we should upholster this chair bright red." His wife might answer, "You're crazy. How can you think that when there's nothing bright red in this room? I think it should be orange." He might answer, "Well, I never thought of that. That's a point, but there's a little bright red in that pillow." Suddenly, there is a productive starting point of continued interaction between two strong, thoughtful people.

Take the case of Joan and Bob. Joan has returned to work after many years of staying in the home caring for her family. Another man might find his wife more interesting if she expands her interests, but Bob wants to be known as the breadwinner in the family. He resents the fact that Joan is now sharing this role and taking away from his sense of importance in the family. The man who feels secure in his own competence, who knows his own goodness as a person, will not begrudge his wife's experience of competence in her own world. But Bob feels like a little guy who is not doing well enough; he has little sense of of his own worth. Joan goes out into the world and develops an interesting life when his life is downright dull. Bob can't allow himself to enjoy her pleasure because now she has the goodies and he feels threatened. Gone are the days when Bob could say, "Staying at home is what you are capable of. I can go out and do more." Now, if I say to Bob, "You're really a competitive guy. You feel like you have to be better at everything than she is," his response may sound like this: "I'm not competitive. What's this craziness you're telling me?" He then might rationalize the necessity for Joan to stay home.

A feeling of inferiority is the first cousin of competitiveness. As long as I feel inferior I will have to protest my competence to everyone. If I feel adequate in my own growth, I'm not going to make comparisons. I am going to say, "Well, I'm not a nuclear physicist, and I'll never be one, so I'll let John be the nuclear physicist. I will not be threatened just because he is a successful scientist. I would like to learn something from him; certainly he can enrich my life with his knowledge. And he can learn about my accomplishments as well, if he desires."

That is the difference between a mature relationship and a

competitive one, where you don't get anywhere as long as the parties don't take ownership of their own inner experiences. Chances are that Bob, who says his wife should stay at home, has certain parts in himself which he is not in touch with at all. It doesn't have to be the fear of being emasculated; it could be just plain stinginess. It might be his stinginess that says, "I'm not going to share her with the rest of the world."

A similar conflict may occur between Bob and his 18-year-old daughter. He has been known to say, "You are my daughter and I want you to call me at ten o'clock and let me know where you are," or "That skirt is too short for you; it should be longer." What he is saying to his daughter is not, "I want to teach you how to be a woman or a responsible person." He is saying, "You belong to me. You are mine. You are my possession." Bob is not aware of his stinginess, nor is he aware of his righteousness.

The wife of a therapist-client had the feeling that if she became a psychologist, her husband would somehow put her down or be critical of her work. As we worked on this problem together, she realized that she is competitive with her husband. Not only does she want to be a psychotherapist; she wants to be as good as her husband, even though he has had more than 15 years of experience. She deprived herself of studying in that field for many years because of the feeling that her husband wouldn't support her efforts and ability.

Eventually, she returned to school and, as a student, helped her husband with a couple in therapy. After about five or six meetings she told him, "You know, I'm discovering that you're nice to work with. You don't threaten me; you don't criticize me; you let me be myself. I can talk and you don't jump in; you let me have my own space in the process." What the wife was doing was projecting her own self-criticism onto her husband. She was very hard on herself so she assumed that he would be hard on her. She had grown up with people who were hard on each other all the time, and had internalized that experience and kept it sitting inside her like an undigested lump.

WORKING WITH CONFLICT

I call my method of working with conflict between people, "leaning into the accusation." The first step is to teach each person to become aware of the dark side of himself. Self-therapy is always good preparation for creative conflict. The second part of this process involves each person considering: 1) how I can hear your concern about me; 2) what I can do about that concern without making you defensive or incurring your wrath, and thereby putting me on the defensive even more; and 3) how we can work that concern in such a way that you don't feel like you're crazy for accusing me or for seeing that part of me; in other words, acknowledging that your concern has validity even if it does sting me a bit.

For example, an employer walks up to his busy secretary's desk and starts a long conversation. In the midst of their talk, she says, "You're talking so much. Maybe you have spare time for a conversation with me, but I'm trying to type. You want me to talk to you and yet you still expect me to do all this work." His first instinct may be, "How can you say that to me? You're a bitch. You're unkind. You have no consideration for me." An alternative would be for the secretary to make a statement to her boss which would acknowledge his experience, not just her own: "You know, when I get all excited about an idea, I interrupt my husband while he is working on his annual report and start telling him about what's happened to me. I know you are excited, but I have to get this typing done for you."

The approach I use in therapy is to say, "As an expert in interrupting, I feel like you're interrupting me," or "As an expert in interruption, I know what interruption is all about." As soon as you are able to take ownership of your experience of the problem, I no longer feel that you are saying I am a terrible human being.

If a mother talking to her children can take ownership of something they have done by saying, "I remember when I was your age and did the same thing you're doing now," it can be more effective than saying, "Well, you're young; you've got a lot to learn. I know better than to do things like that." Essentially, when you put yourself into the space in which the other person lives and speak out of that part of you, then you will be heard.

Sometimes there is so much accumulated wrath between people—what the transactional analysts call "collected stamps"—that even if you teach them a way of talking to each other, they cannot do it. There is a piling up of one injustice after another over a long period of time, until suddenly the person feels so filled with anger that he leaves and never comes back. The sudden disappearance of a spouse or any member of a family is an example of this phenomenon. The fantasy of the person who leaves might be: If I were to express my anger I would go crazy or the house would disintegrate. I would kill the children. I would destroy everything.

I have a client who became so enraged with his girlfriend that he threw the furniture out the window. This is a brilliant, lovely couple, but I suspect that lovely, quiet people are the most frequent stamp collectors. T.A. therapists say that when your album is filled with stamps, you can cash it in for a separation, divorce or suicide attempt (which is another way of punishing the other person), or by becoming catatonic and not saying a word to anyone. One of my clients came in the other day and said, "I ran away from home." She is a grown woman with two children and she had run away from home for a week. This was her way of cashing in her book of resentment stamps. All of us have these feelings sometimes—a yearning to find the Shangri La out there, to move toward relief from accumulated difficulties.

When there is a great store of anger, I like to give the person an opportunity for its safe expression in the consulting room. Mary and Jack are having a hard time talking. Jack is furious with her because she has had an affair. He is the pure, good guy. (I might mention that you can suspect the virtuous man or the pure, righteous wife, because if he or she is so rageful about the spouse's behavior, he/she can often be implicated in collusively helping the spouse out in that fashion.) I ask Jack to scream at his wife or to pound on some pillows with his fists.

Sometimes you need to have them scream at each other before they can be level-headed enough to relate at a more advanced level of confrontation—such that Jack could express, "As somebody who has always longed to have an adventure, I really feel like you've got a lot of nerve! I could never permit myself to be so bold." I am not saying that this is always the reason for the rage in such an instance, but it is one good possibility. Neglected spouses often set up an affair for the husband or wife because they themselves want to do it, but don't have the courage to try. When the spouse acts out, they can then get into their righteousness about how terrible and sinful the other is, rather than carefully examining what brought them both into the situation.

Several years ago I came across a dramatic example of collusive acting out. A 13-year-old girl had had sexual intercourse with her father. The family was referred to me by the court. The girl, Robin, was brought to the office by her mother. I overheard the mother and daughter arguing in the waiting room as if they were competing mistresses. The information I gathered from each member of the family amounted to the following events: The mother had refused to have intercourse with the father for three months and when Robin and Dad were at home one day, Mom decided to leave the precocious daughter alone with her frustrated husband. When the mother came home, Robin and her father were in the bedroom. While Robin was crying for help, Mama, who was in the next room, turned a deaf ear. To round out the complexity of this situation, the father had a subnormal I.Q. Here is a situation where the mother, who had sexual problems, got the daughter to take sexual responsibility with her husband. Robin bore the guilt for the situation and the court punished the father for being a horrible person. Yet there was clearly a cooperative effort in this conflict. Had the parents taken ownership of their sexual problems, as well as their feelings of inadequacy, incest could have been avoided. As long as there is openness in taking ownership of one's own problems, there is less chance of getting into deep trouble with someone else.

After having vented their accumulated anger, the couple can begin to engage in a more or less orderly process of exploring a sensitive situation under the guidance of a therapist. Here is an outline of this process which is followed by a demonstration of how it works; the couple are myself and Florence, my wife.

1. Each person makes a list of several qualities which upset him or her about the other person, e.g., "You are stingy" or "You are insensitive."

2. One confronts the other using *one* item, e.g., "I have really been bothered by your insensitivity."

3. The accused person shares the body response aroused by the confrontation, e.g., "My jaws and fists are clenched and my muscles taut."

4. Leaning into the accusation—the accused person makes an effort to take some ownership of the accusation, e.g., "I am insensitive when your mother visits," giving as many examples as possible of the behavior, in this case insensitivity, toward the other person.

5. The accuser expresses what he or she heard, e.g., "I heard you say . . ." This step is crucial because couples rarely hear each other during arguments.

6. The accused reports ways in which he or she acts out the polarity of the accusation, e.g., ways in which he or she is sensitive.

7. The accuser reports what he or she heard the other person tell about exceptions to the rule (and can remind accused of items that were forgotten).

8. The accuser takes ownership of projection, e.g., "As an expert in insensitivity, I am insensitive to you when you drink too much and when I have spent too much time with the kids."

9. The accused reports what he or she heard.

10. Each person shares feeling about the preceding process.

Florence's Difficulty with Joseph's Grandiosity

F: One of the things I have difficulty with is your grandiosity, particularly when you relate things that you have done or when you talk about some of your experiences.

J: When you said that, I could feel it in my chest. I felt a tightness in my chest. I wasn't breathing. I held my breath as I listened to you. I heard you say that you don't like my grandiosity. You don't like it when I exaggerate or play up things that I do or have done. Is that right?

F: That you may have experienced—not necessarily what you may have done.

J: That I may have experienced—is that right?

F: That's right.

J: Okay, so I heard you. What I want to do now is see if I can find some examples to substantiate what you said to me. I think that I've exaggerated my father's success as a dentist. I have exaggerated or over-dramatized some of the things that have happened to me in my life in Europe. I think I've over-dramatized some of my accomplishments, like the number of things I've written, for example. I over-dramatize when I tell about something that's happening in the family to friends—an argument or something that's happening with the children. I over-dramatize to the children about how much money I make. I think that in the past—not recently—I've over-dramatized my sexual experiences and my sexual prowess.

F: Let me see if I heard you accurately. I've heard you say that you've over-dramatized your life experiences in Europe. You've exaggerated your father's success as a dentist. And I heard you say that, in the past but not recently, you've dramatized your sexual prowess, and I heard you say that you've over-exaggerated how much money you make to the children. I've heard you say that you've exaggerated or over-drama-

tized the number of things you've written. I don't
think that's true. That's one thing I didn't feel.

J: I'm not talking about lies. I'm talking about dramatization. I'm not a liar.

F: No, I'm not talking about lying. You haven't over-
dramatized what you've written or how much you've
written. I don't feel that fits.

J: Now, I'm going to tell you ways in which I don't dramatize myself or my experiences. Let me see, right now
I feel I'm not very dramatic; right now, at this moment when I'm talking to you, I feel I'm "under-
playing." Most of the time when I see people in therapy I don't over-dramatize. There are times when
there are little peaks in which I may use a certain
expression that sounds dramatic, but most of the time
I'm pretty quiet and sedate. I don't over-dramatize to
other people how much I love you and the children.
That's important. I don't over-dramatize to other people how hard I work and what varied ways I live my
life. It's a new concept, a new way of thinking of
myself, so it's not like I have ready-made answers for
you. Oh, I don't over-dramatize my accomplishments
or my feelings or my needs to our friends. I can just
be there and be natural, be myself. Although that
doesn't mean that I don't use my influence or that I'm
not aware of my power.

F: It's not the power or the influence that distracts me.

J: It's the theatrical quality of it. Well, I think that as I
become more mature and more aware of myself, the
more solid I feel inside, the less in need I am of
making something more powerful by being theatrical, so, all in all, I feel like in the last ten years I've
managed to become more solid. I'm also more in
touch with my sadness. The less I'm aware of my
bravado, the more I'm aware of my sadness. I want to
know if you heard me.

F: Okay. I heard you say that, right here and now, you're
not grandiose; you're very natural. That you're not
grandiose about the way you love me and the chil-

dren. I heard you say that you're not dramatic or
grandiose when you are with your friends, that you
use your power and your influence, but in a way
that's appropriate rather than in a dramatic way.
You're not grandiose about the variety of things you
do or the way you live your life. What else did you
say?

J: I said I feel more solid; I really feel that you heard me.
It is so nice to talk about this problem sanely. Now, I
want to tell you the ways in which my grandiosity or
my dramatization works for me, and ways in which it
doesn't work for me. I feel that when I am out of
town and I'm doing a workshop, there's a part of me,
my grandiosity, that works for me. I feel I can do
anything. And àt those times, when I feel that sense
of grandness, or of theater, I do some very creative
things and some unusual things. I create an atmosphere of liveliness and excitement for other people in
my workshops. Another exciting thing about my
dramatization is that I have a tendency to use dramatization in my work. I've developed ways of working
with dreams as dramatic experiences; I like to use
music and spontaneous movement and improvisation with movement, as well as other forms. The way
it doesn't work for me is that somehow if I don't do it
right or I'm not appropriate with it, I turn you off,
and you're important to me. I don't want to turn you
off. And I suspect that I do that with my friends;
sometimes I overload the dosage of my dramatizing
and it shuts other people off and their creativity and
their capacity to be innovative, because I fill the
space with my excitement and my drama and my exaggeration. So that's what it doesn't do for me—it
doesn't allow me to engage more clearly and fully
with other people. That's it.

F: Okay. At this point I need to take ownership of the
ways in which I am grandiose or I exaggerate or I'm
overly dramatic.

J: Or you could take ownership of how you're not grandi-

ose enough—take ownership of the whole grandiosity issue.

F: A way that I can think of that I am overly dramatic
is the way I talk about school, for example, and that
whole bit about what I'm doing now. I make a big to-
do about how tired and how busy I am, and how
much work there is and all those terrible papers,
when, indeed, I have control over that and can do
something about it other than just making such a big
fuss about it, being dramatic about it. Another way
I'm grandiose is in my sense of feeling like I could do
much better with money, for example, than you do. I
don't know that I could do any better in handling it
than you do.

J: Indeed, you don't know that I would do worse than
you would do.

F: Okay.

J: What are some ways in which you're not grandiose
enough?

F: I tend to underplay most of what I do. For example, I
had some clients that I was very successful with last
year and could think of ten different ways why I was
successful with them and not say that it was really
something that I did that made a difference; but I
could say, "Well, their circumstances changed," or
"Some uncle came in from heaven," or something
like that changed the whole way the therapy went,
rather than saying that I was influential. So I could
take more credit for that. Another way I'm not grandiose enough is that I don't even give myself enough
credit, for example, for the papers that I write as
being well done.

J: Yeah, you underplay a lot.

F: I am apologetic about my writing, in a way. Even after
I get a lot of outside reinforcement that they were,
indeed, good papers, well written, informative, and I
know that I've learned from them, I still tend to underplay them. I tend to be not grandiose enough in

terms of not being bold enough; in terms of choosing
clothes and decorating, I don't trust my boldness. I
tend not to be grandiose in talking about things that
I've done. For example, at the Couples Workshop I
didn't say anything about what I had done or what
kind of experience I had.

J: At the workshop you didn't share the experiences you
have had that were important.

F: Or what experience I've had in doing this kind of
work. And I have had some experience which did
allow me to do the work in a fairly competent way.
See, even the way I say, "in a fairly competent way"
—I think I was competent in what I did. I was learning, but I was competent in what I did. Even just the
way I think about it, talk about it, is an example of
my lack of grandiosity. I'm not grandiose when I
consider how competent I will be. I have a lot of
doubts about my future competence, rather than
thinking in a very positive way that, chances are,
with experience and the skills that I will learn, I will
be a competent therapist. But I don't think that way,
and I think I need to be more grandiose about that.
It's much easier for me to think of ways I'm not grandiose than it is for me to think of ways in which I am
grandiose or overly dramatic.

J: Okay, I want to make sure that I heard you take ownership of your grandiosity. I don't remember the very
first thing you said. Do you?

F: About my grandiosity?

J: I'll tell you what I do remember. I remember that you
said you're grandiose about how well you think you
can manage money, compared to me. You said that
you're grandiose about school, that you make a big
fuss and that you dramatize the things that need to be
done, that you need to do in school. On the other
hand, you under-dramatize and understate the things
that you do in school that you do well, like writing
papers. And you also understate the clothes you

wear. You under-dramatize most everything that you do, really. You understate most everything that you do, you said. The other day at the workshop, you did not dramatize how competent you are and what you do know and how much you have accomplished.

F: In the introductory phase, when we were asked how long we've been doing this and what we have done, I didn't say anything. I mean, I did my work in the workshop, but I didn't say anything in the introductory phase.

J: I'm curious. Do you feel like the more you're able to dramatize yourself and what you are doing, the more comfortable you'll feel about my dramatization? Do you think that will have an influence?

F: Well, I see the balance changing, rather than necessarily my feeling differently about your grandiosity.

J: How do you mean, the balance?

F: Well, I see you becoming more solidly grounded and not having to do that so much. It's not so much the grandiosity as the exaggeration that bothers me. And I don't see you as needing to do that as much. And as I feel better about myself and what I can do and what I do do, I think that I can be more bold about my own experience and expression.

J: You may even exaggerate sometimes!

F: Yeah, I may even exaggerate.

J: So where are we right now?

F: I feel very good. I feel like I'd almost like to do this around a lot of issues, like I realize I've done this with three things that bother me about you and you haven't had a chance to deal with some of the issues that bother you about me.

J: Wait, I'll get my chance!

F: What bothers you about me? What do you feel right now?

J: Well, I feel like we disarmed the whole notion that being accused by you, or being told that you're displeased about something is going to devastate me, or devastate both of us. I appreciate it. I feel relieved.

F: You're right. Dealing with these issues has been, for me, very helpful because both other times, and now too, I don't feel like I'm coming away hurt and you don't feel like you're going away hurt. I feel like you really heard me and I was able to be honest with you about what could be a very delicate and potentially explosive kind of experience. I really dig this way of dealing with issues that bother us.

J: I want to get this thing in perspective before we move on. You don't like my grandiosity. You don't like it, in part, because it is distasteful to you and because I push you and others away with it.

F: At the same time, I don't like it because I don't give myself permission to show off or even to simply share my own accomplishments. I suppose that if I could have some of your drama, I would feel more satisfied with myself and less resentful of you.

J: I appreciate that. In return, I am willing to pay more attention to my own exaggerations. If I don't fill the room with my bullshit, perhaps you can begin to express yourself more freely and openly.

F: You don't bullshit.

J: Here I go—exaggerating again!

Very early in a relationship, couples need to learn methods of dealing with "getting stuck." If we could teach them some basic skills of fighting creatively, we might be able to save potentially good relationships which are beginning to deteriorate. The above model is one vehicle of dealing with accusations or displeasures with each other. Its strengths are obvious:

—Each person learns to present a resentment.
—Each person learns to listen to the other instead of rehearsing a retaliatory scenario.
—Each person learns to take ownership of his own projections.

—Each person learns to be respectful of the other's experience and self-validation, without losing self-esteem.

—Outcomes of such discussions do not result in greater animosity; both párties feel some sense of integration of differences.

The weakness of this model is that usually a couple cannot do it independently, without a "teacher," an intermediary. Each person often behaves as if his very life is at stake and tends to clobber back unfairly or, perhaps, to crumble, feel hurt and withdraw. An intermediary can also encourage expression of feelings without danger of destructive acting-out between the parties. The teacher or therapist can say, "Okay, this is enough. Now that you have blown off some steam and moved around and around without getting anywhere, are you ready to try something different? This will take some discipline, but the payoff is great."

Let me give a simple example of being stuck. Joel does something and Martha feels hurt. The only thing she may have learned about healing herself is to withdraw. Martha goes to the bedroom. It is now dinner time and dinner is on the stove. Joel feels guilty and puts dinner on a plate, which he takes to his wife. He apologizes, but all Martha does is sulk. In the meantime, Joel is standing there with his "present." Not getting a response from Martha, Joel throws the dinner against the wall and leaves, feeling depressed. They end up not talking to each other for several days.

When people get into conflicts with each other they seem to give up most of their talent and creativity. They don't think clearly; they hit below the belt; they lose their imagination. They most certainly don't use their humor. If one of them could see something funny in the midst of the conflict, the whole thrust of the swords could be broken. Conflicts have a tendency to be circular; the patterns repeat themselves over and over again. The couple jumps on a merry-go-round and doesn't know how to get off. Too often there is no resolution, just a truce. The idea of some of these techniques is not only to achieve a truce, but to arrive at a resolution that is creatively novel. Another characteristic of non-creative conflict is its lose-win quality. When one partner loses and the other wins, the whole partnership loses. Everybody wins in creative conflict resolution.

Humor can be learned by taking a conflict that has already been resolved and talking about how the couple *could* have played with it, had some fun with it, without getting as serious and upset. For example, Florence could begin bragging about me with outrageous lies to the kids at the dinner table. If I am in the right place, I can join in and add to her stories. The outcome is that we all laugh at my exaggerations and I have learned a lesson for myself. In the case of Joel and Martha, I imagine Joel standing there with the plate of food; suddenly he begins to sing his favorite aria from La Boheme or to recite a love poem to Martha. She bursts out in laughter. The ice is broken and they begin to speak about the problem.

It is always important, however, not to mask one's feelings and to express one's anger or sadness openly. Constant suppression of anger results in somatic symptoms: cardiac problems, asthma, stomach difficulties, colitis, migraine headaches. The trick is to have a life balanced between self-control on the one hand and expression on the other. One needs to be respectful of one's internal rhythm.

Some of the above issues are illustrated in part of a session Florence and I had with a young couple. Nina, who recently gave birth to their second child, resents her husband, John, for his constant sexual approaches. They have an agreement about making love in the morning when both of them feel fresh and rested. He takes the agreement literally, while she thinks of the morning broadly and considers it more significant when John is demonstrative with his feeling and tenderness.

> *John:* I feel like I have no right to be angry with such a wonderful, lovely wife and mother, and so that makes me all the madder and gets me immediately into withdrawal, and I want to curl up and go to sleep.

Joseph: In an earlier fight there's a good example of not really having a clear understanding of what "morning" means. A lot of the time I think you go on very inadequate information about what the other person is feeling or thinking.

John: Morning has meant earlier.

Nina: There have been times when we both awakened and were rested and we had a good time.

Joseph: The other thing that I think you didn't get into, generally because one doesn't think about these things, is just because you say you would prefer to make love in the morning doesn't mean that next morning or every morning, that it's a contract that you would be willing to make love every morning.

John: (To Nina) I really didn't think that you were being resistant at all. I didn't get any strong feelings of "go away." If you had said, "Go away . . ."

Nina: I really wasn't because I wanted to get it over with as soon as possible.

Joseph: That's a third difficulty you have, which is your passive-aggressive stance: "I'll do what will please him and get it over with, but I'll resent him for intruding on me." It's a Catch 22.

Nina: Yeah. I knew I was doing it and that's what made me mad.

Joseph: At yourself.

Nina: Yeah, at myself. That's how I got into the "I'm being bad" thing.

John: As soon as you said, "Look how inconsiderate you are and how little sleep I got, and here you are pushing me," that's when I really got mad at myself for being so inconsiderate and pushing you when you'd got so little sleep. So that's a perfect time for me to get the hell out of the house before I really started feeling bad about myself.

Joseph: Those are like general perimeters for fighting. Another thing we talked about is your withdrawal as a way of healing, a two-purpose number: Number one is that you're healing yourself and taking care of yourself, and number two is that you're punishing her for being such a bitch to you.

John: Yeah, *you* worry about it. It's *your* problem. *You* can sit and stew about it.

Joseph: But if it were as simple as just accomplishing punishing her, it wouldn't be so bad. The problem is that you wind up feeling shitty, too. There's no way you can avoid feeling bad.

Florence: Yeah. You both get into the same kind of double bind in a different way. You withdraw and end up feeling badly, and you do what you don't want to do and end up feeling badly anyway.

Nina: I withdraw before the fight takes place and he withdraws afterwards.

Florence: It sounds to me like you don't fight; that's no fight.

Nina: Even yesterday, you lit into me and I thought it was ridiculous and then we postponed the whole thing and then I lit into you and . . .

John: Then I curled up. Then you finally came over and said, "You're feeling sorry for yourself."

Joseph: And then you snapped out of it.

Florence: And she said it was okay, but you didn't really deal with the pressures that get you into the thing.

John: Something that hit me an hour before work is that we pay attention to what I'm feeling bad about, but I'm not always aware about what I'm feeling bad about until the situation is all over.

Florence: It sounds like something triggers it off rather than your starting out feeling badly about something.

John: Yeah, it's not until I'm curled up there for a while that I know how bad I'm feeling about myself.

Nina: It seems that some of my problem is related to bitching about things that are bothering me, because that would just reinforce his ideas that being a housewife is a terrible thing to be, having two kids is awful.

Florence: He feels that having two kids is too much anyway.

Nina: Yeah.

Joseph: Say that first part again.

Nina: (To John) If I'm feeling sorry for myself I don't let you know it; if I'm really tired or even if I do bitch I don't feel like I'm getting any support from you.

(To Joseph and Florence) I'm storing all that shit up; then when he asks something of me I think is too much, it overflows. What I'm doing is useless in his eyes, anyway.

Joseph: In your set-up there's room for only one person to be feeling sorry for himself, is that right?

Nina: Yeah, like I'm supposed to be so happy because, after all, I wanted to be a housewife and I wanted two kids, and I wanted a big house, so how can I possibly bitch about it. So I feel guilty about doing it. Now, probably a lot of it was not created by John at all; that's my mother's influence.

Joseph: Why should you have to carry the burden of selling John a piece of propaganda in addition to the actual problems you have to deal with as a couple?

Nina: I feel I'm really trying to talk John into the idea that it's nice to have two kids, which it is from time to time, but it's not always a picnic.

Joseph: So, had you been able to let go of having to persuade John how nice things are, you might have been able to say, "Yeah, you know at times this family can be really shitty. I agree with you."

Florence: But you keep telling yourself, Nina, "I should appreciate what I have. I wanted this and now I have everything I wanted and I should feel good all the time."

John: Yeah, because I don't hear you bitch at all.

Nina: I know.

Joseph: Would you like to start practicing bitching?

Nina: I guess just everything . . . like the illnesses are really upsetting me, and that I guess I'm beginning to resent the tension.

Florence: Try not to say, "I guess." Just say, "I resent."

Nina: Yeah, I resent not getting enough sleep. I resent feeling pressured to look absolutely gorgeous. I resent worrying about whether or not I have enough breast milk because I've been trying to diet. I resent feeling pressured to lead a normal social life and leave the house when I don't really want to leave the house, or not being able to leave the house when I do want to leave. Very often when we've made plans, I'm tired when it's time to go out. I resent not being able to share the joys of having the kids when I really have a good time with them, either because John is out or because he doesn't want to have anything to do with them. And I resent that, in the future, he's not going to be participating with the kids, that he's gonna just let me do it all.

Joseph: You resent fantasies you have of what the future will be.

Nina: Yeah. I resent even having them because then I feel guilty about them.

Florence: You have quite a list there, and you sound angry as well.

Nina: I think I blamed John for some of these situations, like not getting enough sleep.

Joseph: Would you like to get into blaming him? "I hold you responsible for this, and this, and this."

(Nina is so nice. She holds so much of her anger in. I am giving her permission to express her resentments and her blame openly and freely and directly to John. I am assuring Nina that she will not continue blaming but rather allow herself to be openly negative before she can show John her love and her genuine caring.)

Nina: I blame you for making me feel ugly and I blame you for making me feel like it's my duty to spend all the time I can with you and therefore lose sleep. And I blame you for pushing for so many activities. And I blame you for not offering to take the kids, to take over and take them for a while and not give me a bunch of shit about it. And I blame you for being sick

for the last three weeks. I blame you for making me
feel that the future's going to be awful with two kids.
(To Florence and Joseph) He looks like he hasn't
crumbled yet and that makes me feel good.

Joseph: Have you got any more? If you can't think of
more, just make it up.

(The more extreme the negative polarity is, the more fully
she can grow to become positive in the future, to love
him.)

Nina: I blame you for not appreciating how nice the kids
are. I think I blame you for not appreciating me, too,
how cute and nice I am.

Joseph: (To John) See if you can feed that back to Nina. I
want to be sure she is aware that you can hear her.

John: You blame me for putting demands on you that
keep you from getting sleep. You blame me for not
taking the kids. You blame me for causing your fantasies about how bad it's going to be with the kids. You
blame me for not appreciating how cute the kids are.
You blame me for not spending time with them and
not appreciating how cute and nice you are . . . (His
list is fairly complete.)

Joseph: That was pretty good. Would you take it one step
further and take each item and lean into it and lean
into her accusations? "You blame me for this, and
from such-and-such experiences I can understand
how you would feel that way." Think of how many
things you can think of to support her anger with
you. That's the part that gets skipped in your arguing
—each of you leaning into the other person's
experience.

John: What is "leaning into"?

Florence: Acknowledging.

John: My first reaction was to say, "Yes, but," and then I
thought, "What am I doing?" I want to give her the
opportunity to tell me what she's resenting about me.
I can learn from that. I can see why you are angry
about my illness for the last two months (because it's

mostly stupidity on my part that got me that way), that's a legitimate claim. I can see why you blame me for making you feel fat and ugly, because I come out with snide remarks. I can see where you can blame me for not seeing when the kids are really cute, because I don't see very often when they are, and a lot of times I don't acknowledge it when I do see it and tell you how much I enjoy the good parts—when Lenny smiles at me and when Joanna and I are playing. I don't say anything about that. And I can see why you blame me for not making you feel cute and nice. Then, later, when I do say something nice to you, you probably don't even hear it because I've made snide remarks. And I do make a lot of demands on your time. And I do push you to do things.

Florence: (To John) How does that feel to you, to acknowledge Nina's complaints.

John: Strange. I didn't flip into feeling bad about myself. (To Nina) It was like I could see your point of view, and I didn't feel like I was apologizing for the way I was—that's the way I was.

Joseph: So, it didn't flip into being a win/lose situation, or a lose/lose situation. Both of you have a sense of validity of your own experience. What is it like for you to be heard by John and for him to support some of your feelings?

Nina: It's really different and it's good. But it makes me also very impatient to do something about it. It makes me very objective, very much like, "So, if you know what's going on with me, let's correct it."

John: That's where I start feeling like shit. Right there.

Nina: With my impatience to correct it?

John: When you say, "If you know about it, why don't you do something about it?"

Florence: It's as if he is acknowledging what his demands do to you, but you, in turn, are not acknowledging that, although he knows about it, it's hard for him to do something.

Joseph: It takes two to tango. The correction of those things requires one more step that involves both of you.

(To Nina) Like, "Okay, now that I feel heard by you, let's see if we can take these things one by one and figure out a way of being responsive to these matters." And, "How can we plan on having you take care of the children once a week without feeling resentment."

Nina: See, this is where I get scared, too. Because even if I've been heard and he understands the problems, I am afraid to ask for anything from him.

Florence: What stops you?

Joseph: Whenever you stop yourself from asking, you also make it more difficult for him to ask you for something in the future as well.

Florence: (To Nina) But what stops you from taking that step? What would stop you from saying, "Okay, it feels more comfortable or better for me if we make love in the morning." What stops you from saying, from establishing some sort of more specific information-giving?

Nina: At this point, with the information we've got, and he understands why, it seems like it should be pretty easy, but it's still hard because somehow there's this pattern in my head that once you know something, then it just follows that you shouldn't have to ask. If he knows what's going to make me feel better, why not do it? My father wouldn't have had to be asked. He would have taken care of me and done anything to make me feel better.

Joseph: The old Oedipus is back! Because no one loves her like daddy does. Nobody!

John: I don't want to have to measure up to your Dad's adoration and performance.

Florence: I think that what is important now is the business of, "He knows, so how come he doesn't act on it?"

Nina: Yeah. Whatever was good for me was provided without ever having to say, "Do it," or "I want you to do it." As long as I could make the need apparent, if I knew it was apparent to the other person, it was done.

Joseph: And it's certainly very nice when that happens. I know couples who have the opposite problem— everything needs to be negotiated and every need must be discussed. Everything is a mini-contract, a business deal.

Florence: Yeah. Do you want to have spinach for dinner, or do you want to have cauliflower? It gets down to that point when there is no decision, no matter what energy is wasted.

Joseph: You probably take for granted many things with each other—that the other person does recognize little things that give you pleasure and joy. Still, there *are* things that you will have to make explicit to get what you want. You can't read each other's minds.

Florence: You can't be all bitch and you can't be all nice guy. It's just not reality. But I also think it really is a skill.

Nina: Somehow, when I do make demands, it's kind of like me doing it and him taking it and crumbling.

Joseph: The crumbling is a conditioned reflex. He can learn how not to crumble. It is the only skill in his repertoire that he has to get a rise out of you, and he is going to learn other kind of skills. Another skill is simply to respond and get a rise out of you from being responsive: "Hey, I was heard. Come over here and I'll give you a big hug." That's a higher ego level of getting a rise out of you than withdrawing. You can get more goodies for yourself that way, John.

Nina: I guess right now I want to hear from John. I want you to tell me that you support me and my trying to do this, trying to be honest and explicit with you.

John: What do you mean by that?

Florence: You're not going to clobber her over the head.

Joseph: If she says about your sexual overture, "I didn't

mean 4:30 in the morning; I meant 8:00 in the
morning."

John: Or even, "Not now." Yes, I am willing to support
her effort to be honest and explicit with me.

Nina: You are not going to make my life miserable for the
next 24 hours. You're not going to automatically zap
me. I'm feeling terrifically unsupported.

John: I am hurting a little and I am supporting you as
much as I can.

Joseph: I have two pieces of homework for the two of
you. John, I'd like you to do with Nina what Nina did
with you, sometime during the week. You know, tell
her your list of resentments and check out if she is
able to hear you this time. Also, have Nina lean into
and validate your feelings. The other bit of homework is this—I'd like for you, Nina, to get back to the
position of being in charge of the sexual business. I'd
like to see Nina become the aggressor and get for
herself what she really wants when she wants it.

I feel that many good relationships—marriages, friend-
ships, employer-employee interactions, business partner-
ships, any two-person system—can be saved by teaching people how to make trouble creatively. Most of the time people
are so heavily invested in defending their esteem and their
need to be right, that they sacrifice important relationships for
the sake of "pride."

Too often, couples who live together never learned the use-
fulness of disagreements. They came from parents who pro-
tected them from "bad feelings" by arguing in hushed voices
behind locked bedroom doors while their children slept at
night. (Fighting has been one of the principal middle-class
taboos.) The children had no model to respond to; even poor
models are useful because they can be pushed against,
shaped, modified.

A similar disability exists on a grander scale. Just as couples
"play house" and act polite with each other, corporate lawyers
play games with union representatives; the halls of Congress

are filled with formal rhetoric while conflicts of the people in the streets remain unsolved. On the grandest scale, nations engage in polite negotations while planning to annihilate each other. Examples from world history are too numerous— and obvious—to mention.

If we can develop a comprehensive yet simple model of creative conflict resolution, then we can teach little kids how to fight in the classroom. We can instruct high school students in methods of constructive disagreement with their teachers, parents and friends. I can imagine every newly elected congressman, senator, president and diplomat taking a creative conflict workshop before taking office and filling their daily work schedules with useless, formalized, by-the-book bullshit. Who knows? We might have a better to world to live in after all.

Chapter 9

Art in Gestalt Therapy

The creative intention is a yearning in one's body,
A desire to fill the container of life.
This yearning expresses itself in energy, movement,
   rhythm.
The activity of creation, its expression, is a loving
   assertion of life.
Creation is an act of thankfulness or an act of
   cursing.
It is a privilege of tasting, seeing, touching life, a
   celebration of being—
or a pleading for a meaningful exit.

J.Z.
1/1/76

The reason drawing or painting may be "therapeutic" is that, when experienced as process, it allows the artist to know himself as a whole person within a relatively short period of time. He not only becomes aware of internal movement toward experiential wholeness, but he also receives visual confirmation of such movement from the drawings he produces.

This chapter begins with sharing my own experience of making art in creating a painting. The second section, "Every

Person is an Artist,"* elaborates how I have communicated my experiences and growth as an artist to others in the form of an art workshop. The final section delineates three levels of creative process as experienced by the workshop participants.

MOVEMENT, RHYTHM AND GROUNDING

All creative activity begins with movement. The body's propensity is to traverse space, to be in continuous transaction with the environment. It is difficult to make art while cemented behind a small desk. I need to get on my feet, to experience my energy.

Bent slightly at the knees, my legs begin to move in a walking motion. I feel energy building in my pelvis as I let the weight of my body rest fully on one leg, then the other. My hips rotate from one side to the other, allowing my body to experience its grace and flexibility.

Now I am aware of my breathing: My belly sticks out as I inhale, my diaphragm descends into my abdomen. As the air enters my lungs, my chest expands and I feel like stretching: Arms move into the air sideways. My breathing is slow and full.

Mental imagery emerges from this physical liveliness. I begin to revolve in slow motion, imagining my body as a fluorescent sculpture turning in a dark, thick space. My arms break the darkness with thick, glowing lines, like the strong brush on Franz Kline's canvasses. My fingers brush the space with fine lines, five at a time, hanging horizontally in space like curved platinum wires.

My body is a sculpture and in my imagery it makes impressions in space as it moves. Its mass moves through the air, fills in parts of the space, and moves on. My body is a breathing sculpture, drawing in the outside world and then exhaling it— continually disrupting and remaking space.

Music enhances my process. Its rhythm confirms my inner flow and encourages my energy to build, to grow.

*"Artist" as defined here is anyone involved in a creative process.

Having etched space with my fingertips, I pick up a piece of charcoal and transfer the lines to a flat surface, a large sheet of newsprint. My inner rhythm says, "Give all, give all . . . let the lines break the edges of the paper. Let the force of your body strain the paper; don't be afraid of tearing it. Just move and make marks. Participate in the primal dance of creation. Join the first hunter creating images of his prey on cave walls . . ."

The paper is filled with thick, black lines—some whole, others broken—from one edge to the other. The paper has fallen prey to my energy.

Now I use both hands simultaneously. I close my eyes to shut off the criticism of my inner parent. The lines write themselves. I am the instrument. The primal experience of "art" has begun. It is an organic, sometimes orgiastic experience. In the process, my adult brain flexes to recover my inner child—the original rhythm, the carelessness, the sense of abandon, the trust of being for its own sake. I am a body impacting itself on space.

As I stay with my process, I begin to change shapes, add colors, develop masses which relate to each other in space. With eyes open, the image unfolds as my hand moves over the paper. At some point I allow myself to engage the drawing intellectually: "This is a shape of a woman's body . . . well, not quite . . . there are no arms . . . she is all breasts and buttocks . . . that's okay . . . I'll develop the arms moving in space somehow. Pink and yellow and orange. Like sun in a late summer afternoon. The woman goddess, the maker of babies, the voluptuous mother-earth, the nourishment of life . . ."

This thinking process modulates the changing of shapes in relation to the background. The first lines were fragmented, floating in the center of the paper, tracer lines of a lost child. Now they boldly expand into solid rich masses of color, ruthlessly invading the space. An act of assertion. I am here with all my energy. No apologies. Just like that. My energy is transformed into a rich, fine tapestry of autumn color.

At first the color hangs aimlessly and purely between the lines. Later, colors begin to overlap, mix and change the simple linear structures. A painting evolves from simple lines,

lines which grew from raw, undifferentiated energy. As my process continues, colors are rewoven and the image changes. Again it is a human form. She reminds me of the female figures on the sides of ancient temple walls in India. Her bosoms are full, tilted slightly as they respond to turned hips. One leg is bent at the knee and firmly planted on the ground; the other leg and the arms are in the air. A festive figure. Festive colors. She surprises me as she slowly emerges from my drawing.

I remind myself, once again, that this outcome is not precious, not the finished product of "professional" effort. Just a stage. A learning. Another sign along the road. A pleasure to experience. I may or may not treasure it. Tomorrow, when I look at it with cool eyes, I may realize the changes that need to be made. But now it is love at first sight.

This painting is a projection of myself, a part of my inner life superimposed on a surface. I imagine that I am the painting. I let the painting speak for me: "I am your mother, Joseph. I am all the mothers of the universe combined in one. I am the archetypal mother who loves her child. I am the warmth of your life, the pleasure of being fully alive. I affirm everything in you. I don't require anything to love you. Just be what you are and it is enough . . ."

In this way, I take full possession of my work. It is an object out there and it is also a chunk of my inner life. I take ownership of this figure on paper and the very process of doing so enhances and enriches me. I feel a sense of completeness.

In making something whole, I discover my wholeness. Wholeness is a way of moving in the world, a way of experiencing myself. Wholeness grows out of jerkiness and fragmentation. Like an infant who starts life with awkward movements, wholeness develops as an organic act of faith. The parent does not look and say, "This is an imperfect being." It is assumed that there is a whole being there, in the process of emerging, nourished in acts of goodwill. So wholeness emerges in me as an adult artist. It grows out of an implicit assumption that I and my work will undergo a metamorphosis from fragmentation to integration, from contradiction to unity, from tentativeness to rootedness, from a surface quality to

richness, from lack of awareness to substance, from flightiness to presence.

Art. Faith in my breathing and movement. Faith in my arms
and hips, in the energy thrusting forth over and over again.
Faith in the eyes that appreciate simple lines and mixed pig-
ments. Art. A natural process of holding on to the innocence
of childhood.

EVERY PERSON IS AN ARTIST:
GESTALT ART WORKSHOP

For the past ten years I have been developing ways of using
artistic productions in Gestalt therapy groups. My methods
are based on generating awareness of one's energy, one's capacity to appreciate rhythm and movement. I try to teach people how to support and ground themselves as the basic step
toward getting in touch with their artistic capacity.

Any production can be experienced as a dance, and for this
reason I use music to enhance the process, which an individual can then take ownership of, not only on a visual level, but
at deeper layers of sensation.

My workshops last for a weekend, about 15 hours, and include many media. Here I will concentrate on creating with
chalks and clay. The remainder of this section is a transcript
of my instructions to workshop participants and their responses to the process in which they are involved. At times
this dialogue is interrupted to clarify the conceptual framework and intent of portions of the workshop.

Primal Creations: Chalk Drawings

"There are several areas which I would like to work on with
you this evening. One area has to do with energy, with the fact
that you need to be in contact with the parts of you that are
hurting. Those parts may not be easily contacted. The reason
is that you may experience an area as being 'tied-up,' rather

than painful. Functionally, it's the same place. If you can get hold of the part of you in which you are tight and get into that part, you will recover your energy. In order to do anything, to be in contact with yourself, to grow, or to paint, you need to become aware of where your energy is stuck and how you can liberate it.

"Another area which is very important for a creative experience is process. Allow yourself to have faith in the full range of experiences as you are working, rather than becoming stuck with some precious goal that, if not fulfilled, makes you upset and angry with yourself. This weekend the emphasis will be on process. Process will be facilitated by the music I use, the contact you have with me, and your contact with yourself, as well as with one another.. Have respect for your own process. Be patient with yourself as you work. Allow yourself to love what you're doing even if you're doing something marvelously ugly. If you are stuck with making something beautiful, concentrate on ugliness. Get into your polarities. But most of all, have faith in your process because it gets you where you need to go.

"The third area has to do with theme. If you have been in workshops before, you've probably asked yourself, 'What kind of theme do I want to develop for myself?' You may respond, 'I want to deal with my complexities,' or 'I want to deal with my sexuality.' Then, no matter what you do, you can just dig that particular theme and develop it in any way you wish. If you work together you can work on each other's polarities. So now we can start."

❈   ❈   ❈

After the participants have been oriented to the purpose and process of the workshop, I spend considerable time helping them ground their bodies and locate their energy. Each three-hour segment of the workshop starts in this way. It is a kind of meditative ritual before the work begins. The ritual says: "I must be fully here and I must be physically rooted before I can be present for this experience."

* * *

"What I'd like you to do is to find a comfortable place on the floor and just settle yourself. Work from a position of maximum support. Allow your body to be fully supported by the ground so that you don't waste energy pushing against yourself. You can use this energy to facilitate the unfolding of your feelings, and later, to move into your creative process.

"For some of you it may be a little difficult if you're not used to this kind of exercise. Try it anyway. Close your eyes and concentrate on your breathing. What I'm trying to do now is get you juiced-up, find where your energy is stalled. If you are experiencing any particular tensions—in your neck or shoulders or back—see if you can just move that part a little. Attend to distractions in your body. As you are doing that, pay attention to your breathing, because breathing is your basic support system. Make yourself aware of the air entering your body; as exhalation begins, attend to the parts of your body that are involved and follow the exhalation all the way to the end. Now check out your body, asking yourself, 'Where is my energy? Where am I generating energy at the highest level?' Or, if you can't locate that energy, ask yourself, 'Where am I frozen? Where am I tight?'

"If you are frozen in a particular place, think of some action, some way in which you can exercise the muscles where the tightness lives. In other words, put those muscles to use in some way. Generally speaking, the frozenness is skeletal-muscular, and if that is so, think about a movement. You may want to stretch, to kick, to jump, to move your pelvis, to rotate your head, or to open your mouth wide and make sounds."

* * *

Participants are asked to get into their mobility by concentrating their energy on moving from inner activity outward. Music facilitates this process. They are encouraged to move at their own pace and in their own idiosyncratic way. All movement is good. All spontaneous activity is nurtured and supported.

At this point, participants are beginning to experiment in various ways.

✿   ✿   ✿

"Good. Good. You may want to leave the original position you are in. If you're stiff in your thighs or buttocks, get off your ass and move around or do something that makes mobility possible. Dig exploring. Whatever you do, don't rush it. Slow yourself down enough so that you can let your awareness catch up with your movement.

"I have this notion that all of art is a form of dance. If you are frozen inside, if you're not allowing yourself to get into your energy and movement, it is very difficult to make art. Just exercise your symptoms in space, rather than inside your body.

"Imagine that you are moving in slow motion. Attend to your muscles and tendons. (Music begins.) After you locate your energy, allow it to radiate to other parts of your body. Imagine the energy spreading all over your body as you are breathing. Whatever you do, you need to learn to do it out of maximum support."

Sylvia: This music makes me feel very sad . . .

"Stay with your sadness. Move your body out of your sense of sadness. Allow yourself to vibrate with the sounds. Imagine the sounds are entering your skin, your hands, your belly. Imagine the sounds vibrating in every part of you. If you get tired of standing, lie down on your back and work with your legs . . . move your legs and arms.

"Now, whatever part of your body you are moving in space, imagine that you are making lines with it. Your body is luminescent and moving in a thick, dark, open space. With your arms, your ass, your toes, or your tummy, you are making line sculptures in this thick, liquid space. Imagine you are coloring it. Wherever you move your body, you are creating surfaces and lines, masses in space, very beautiful and colorful and graceful. All of you look very graceful to me. Just allow yourself to dance with your hands. Use a full range of movement. Try not to get too localized."

✿   ✿   ✿

Slowly, people begin to experiment with small gestures. They are not asked to move in any particular way. Thus, each person can be respectful of the emerging energy in his own body. Usually, movement emerges from the tips of hands and feet or the head and shoulders. Later, people get on their feet, moving larger and more centrally located parts of their bodies. Each person is encouraged to attend to the dosage and method of movement comfortable for him. No two people look alike, yet the total group looks graceful, as if performing an ancient ritual.

The energy derived from the activity of the entire body can now be directed to the more specific activity of making something with one's hands. The person feels the support to go one step further, to use the body as an instrument in the creation of something visual—visual in the sense that he can look at his own creation constantly.

Participants are asked to "draw" by first moving the chalk in the space above the paper, while staying with their energy. With newsprint and chalks in front of them, they begin to make expressive movements with hands and arms above the paper. They are encouraged to stay loose and let themselves "hallucinate" or visualize forms and lines. Then they are asked to pick up a black chalk and make marks on the paper using the music as a propellant, a vehicle of rhythm. The music is constantly changing—Gregorian chants, Bach, the Beatles, experimental music, classical guitar. They work with eyes closed, using both hands. I continuously encourage and support their work.

✿   ✿   ✿

"Listen to the music. Get in touch with it before you start drawing. When you feel the music, when you experience yourself in it, begin to put your experience down on paper. Make some marks which represent your experience. Do not consider the work of others; it is totally irrelevant to you. Experiment with forms, colors and lines. Do not worry about translating the music literally. Let go. There are no right or wrong drawings. The important thing is that you stay with your energy and your breathing. Let yourself experiment freely. Close your eyes and play with the movements of your hands. You do not have to sit; you can stand above the drawing and move freely."

* * *

After some time they are given more colored chalks and can choose to use them in the production as they please. At this time, the emphasis is on continuous expression and the filling of space with interrelated forms, rather than just lines.

* * *

"Try holding the chalks in both hands and, with your eyes closed, make large marks on the newsprint. Cover the paper with marks. Change the paper with each new piece of music and continue the process, concentrating on the kinesthetic sensations rather than on the 'goodness' of the visual forms. Stay with the process."

(Half an hour later) "You may now open your eyes and make forms filling the total space of the paper consciously and deliberately. Avoid treating your production as something precious. Stay loose and permit yourself to use 'ugly' colors. Don't be afraid to 'spoil' your picture. The picture can always be 'fixed' or you can start a new one."

> *George:* Are you sure I don't have to fill in neatly between the lines? That's what my first grade teacher made me do. (Laughter from the group.) Once I was asked to draw a dog. After I was through (the class waited because I was 'slow'), the teacher looked at my paper, burst into laughter, and said it looked more like a duck. I was hurt . . . it is such a relief just to let go and make colors on paper. Just to be me and not care . . .
>
> *Marc:* I like to smear and rub the chalks . . .

✿   ✿   ✿

Now they have been drawing with the chalks for several hours.

✿   ✿   ✿

"So far, you have just been warming up and getting loose, working with your eyes closed and both hands at the same time. Perhaps now you can begin to think about a theme. You can invent an 'arbitrary' theme, or you can work in the here and now, like Sylvia drawing her sadness. Think about the feeling you have inside of you. Imagine what shapes, colors, configurations, and textures your feeling contains, and begin to do a piece of work which would reflect this inner feeling.

"Try not to become too critical of yourself, to go back to first grade and say, 'I've got to do it the way the teacher wants me to.' or 'This has to be done well.' Don't do it well, do it freely, do it badly. Give yourself that kind of freedom. But ask yourself, 'In what color am I drawing? What kind of line—a broken line or a smooth line? Am I really like a square, like a block? Am I grey or yellow or blue? Or maybe I'm colorless.' Just begin to explore. Pick out the colors and lines and surfaces that you need here and now to experience your theme. I'll use music again to stimulate your work."

✿   ✿   ✿

Eventually, each person exhibits his drawing and describes it in the first person. This keeps people from over-objectifying the drawing, and at the same time, encourages them to take ownership of their feelings.

✿   ✿   ✿

Martha: I am black and condensed. I am tight. I am in pain. All the world's pain is in me. I have no color, no dynamism. I wish I were dead.

Fred: I am full of stuff. Lots of color and excitement. I don't know what my structure means or where it is going.

Joseph: Or where who is going?

Fred: I don't know where *I* am going. I know there is a lot of activity in me, but I don't have a direction. I am still in process.

Joseph: That's good. You have plenty of time to explore your goals as you move from one piece to the next. Be loving with your process. That's fine.

Dorothy: Right now I am ugly. I am exploring my ugliness. I am a mixture of purple and brown and puke green.

Joseph: You want to puke?

Dorothy: I don't feel it in my stomach.

Joseph: When you begin to feel it in your belly, let me know. In the meantime, please continue.

Dorothy: I am made of ugly colors, but there is a lot of richness in me . . . sort of like the earth. I am the earth. I have a lot of stuff . . . that makes things grow. (Aside: I wonder if I am pregnant.) I am also beautiful because underneath my muddy layers there is a lot of clarity and sweetness. I am glad that Dorothy made me.

The Experience of Mass: Sculpture

"I would like you to get into your breathing. Close your eyes. Now, I'd like you to search for where your sense of energy is at this point. Get in touch with the place where you feel the energy perking, or where the energy is stuck. See if you can coordinate your breathing with that place inside of you which feels warm, juicy, excited, vibrant, radiant. Breathe from that part of you Now, see if you can allow the energy to radiate into your arms.

"Once again, imagine that the atmosphere around you is thick, full of color, touchable, palpable. I am going to play some music. This time, begin to move your arms, and imagine that you are shaping the environment. Imagine that it is thick and moldable. Begin to move your body, constantly keeping in touch with your energy. Imagine that the density of your environment is getting thicker and more difficult to mold, and you really have to shape it with force. You have to breathe and push to get this thing into the shape you want.

"As you are moving your hands, also use them on yourself. You are part of the density. Treat yourself as another kind of density, another piece of sculpture—a living, breathing, warm piece of sculpture—and begin to explore and mold your own body—face, head, chest, arms, legs, feet. Explore how intricate your body is: where it is soft, where hard, where flexible. Some parts of your body you can be rough with, squeeze hard, use almost all of your energy. With other parts of your body you want to be very gentle and delicate.

"As you do this, concentrate on the parts of you that feel typical of you. Try to begin to correlate your experience of yourself in the world with how your body feels. What is it about your body that makes you who you are? Is it your face? Is it how your face is shaped? Is it the hardness, the toughness, the strength? Or is it the gentleness, the delicacy, the fragility? Whatever quality it is, search for it in your body. Formulate an 'image' of yourself.

"This kind of exercise asks you to integrate your sense of mass and bulk with your sense of who you are. Take your time and let yourself do that. Begin to formulate some shapes in your head that represent you. What kinds of shapes, what kinds of masses do you identify with? What sort of shape are you?

"When you are ready, I'd like you to open your eyes long enough to reach out for a piece of clay nearby. Close your eyes again and begin to explore this particular surface. Find out what the material will do—stretch, twist, poke, break it—understand it. . . . Now, begin to move into the shape, molding a shape you can identify with.

"If you're really into painting, and the clay feels very strange to you, you can explore the same problem in your painting. Don't get turned off just because it's clay. You can work the same issue in your painting. You have a choice.

"Those of you who want to explore the clay, please close your eyes. Stay with the sense of exploring another density, another shape, another part of the solid environment. You can add to it and make it as big as you want.

"Begin to relate the clay to parts of your body. Roll up your shirt and touch the clay to your tummy, or to your face. Keep referring back to your body with your hands so that you are constantly going back and forth between your body and the piece you are molding. They are just different kinds of densities. Give yourself a chance to stop for a moment and 'check in' with your body. Touch your face or some other part of your body before you go back to the sculpture so that you are constantly relating your own body to the sculpture you are making.

"If you haven't bothered to look at your piece, open your eyes and explore it visually to see what you want to do with it. What is your attitude toward it? I hope that it is non-judgmental, because what you make is what you are."

Les: For me, it was a really neat experience just touching all parts of my body: putting my fingers into my mouth; flipping over and feeling my back; feeling the softness, the hardness; very lightly touching, then touching very hard so I could feel the bones underneath; flexing a muscle, then relaxing, and feeling the difference there. I spent a long time feeling my body. When I saturated myself with my own touching, I felt the clay and it was a shocking experience, the coldness of the clay. I had to discover the clay. It was just all lumped with holes and ridges . . . and the wetness of it. A totally different experience than touching my own body. Then I started to manipulate the clay and work it.

Joseph: Touching the clay as lovingly and respectfully as you've touched your body can be an important experience. There is a lot in common there . . . where you've come from, where you're going . . .

Les: As I was molding the clay, I was aware of little

pieces of it falling off, and very conservatively, I was picking them up and putting them back on. Then I gave myself permission to let them fall. I was trying to let the clay emerge from my experience. I became aware that it was falling apart in pieces, so I began to mold one piece that fell off. As I was doing that, I noticed that Greg was molding a body. As I looked at mine, I realized that I was shaping a male torso. I was very much in touch with my own body and began to sculpt it. I would never have gotten there thinking I could mold a man. I thought it was beyond my realm of potential. I began to take risks in putting detail into my man; I even put a penis with the balls on it, and the muscles. I was very pleased with my own creation.

Joseph: You have done a fantastically significant thing existentially. You started molding your life. Try describing what you have made in the first person.

Les: I am a man. My feet are large. They are well grounded. I am well grounded. I can stand and I am not easy to push down. I have broad shoulders. Although I have a little penis, it works well for me. I take ownership of shaping my life. I am making my life. I am responsible for my life.

Joseph: You sound very potent.

Marilyn: (To Les) The part that really impressed me was how an accident was used. When you put away your man somebody stepped on it and it was broken in three pieces. The fellow who stepped on it said, "I was really feeling bad about hurting it until I saw how you were putting it back together so tenderly and carefully." And you said, "It was just as fragile as I made it."

Les: I was having trouble getting the trunk to stick to the pelvic area and the legs attached to the whole thing.

Marilyn: But then when you owned it—that you are just

as fragile as you make yourself—it was so beautiful, because you are not fragile.

Les: And I was also willing and able to receive help in putting myself back together from somebody who knew how to work with clay. And that was important to me.

❖   ❖   ❖

At the end of the workshop, the pictures and sculptures are exhibited. Each person takes the group to his productions as if on a museum tour, telling about his experiences. Later, we talk about the kinesthetic and visual pleasure and pain with the whole group. We deal with issues like the courage to make something, what we learned about ourselves, and the pleasure of being in the ongoingness of the experience, the creative process.

PROCESS: STAGES OF DEVELOPMENT

Over the years, I have noticed that no matter what the music is or what I say to the participants, they progress through three stages of development as they work. These stages relate the person's inner experience of self to the appearance of his or her developing work. A person who produces something visually disjointed and scattered feels that way inside. The scattered person also has difficulty expressing that feeling verbally; his language tends to be as disjointed as his work. The individual who makes something whole and complete feels a fullness and a sense of integration within himself. The integrated person also verbally expresses his feelings more smoothly and poetically.

While I believe these stages apply to any creative process, I have focused on the process of drawing.

First Stage

At this point, there is a tendency to cling to the rhythm of the music as a way of breaking through resistances to "drawing." The productions are fairly crude and primitive, although there is often a sense of order, especially if the material is handled with both hands. The drawings have a rhythmical symmetry. The marks are often floating in the center of the paper, tentative and not anchored to the edges. The person is testing himself on the medium and making sure that what he is doing will be not criticized or "put down." He often looks around to check out what others are doing. There is a high level of excitement in the room, fed by each person's expanding energy.

> *John:* I am tempted to see if the others are as silly as I am. I feel a little competitive. I don't mind if *all* of us make fools of ourselves.
> (Later) I am in touch with the rhythm of the music, with my own rhythm.

Second Stage

The productions get bold, covering more space. People still prefer to make lines, but they fill the paper from edge to edge. More confidence is expressed in the process. The person is "lost" in his work, fully involved in his own experience. The place could be too cold or too hot, or the person may feel thirsty—no matter. The work goes on.

In the drawings themselves, a figure/ground relationship emerges: Shapes begin to move out of a previously homogeneous background; areas become more solid. The person's inner process is reflected in the production. He is rising out of an overwhelming undifferentiated energy into a clarity of awareness.

Greg: I made this!

Ursula: It is wonderful!

Joseph: Try that in the first person, Ursula.

Ursula: I am wonderful!

Bev: I am feeling like I'm beginning to dig into my own substance. I'm letting the drawing become more substantial.

Susan: I'm not so afraid of space in this one. I've tightened up, but then I didn't freak out on all that extra space out here. I was excited by that. I'm excited by my space. And it doesn't seem very linear at all. Last night I had that little line—remember that funny, skinny line that was winding itself around? And it was very skinny. In this painting I broadened my line and it became a wave that flows in and out. In that one I brought myself together and became more riveted. I also allowed myself to be more spacious and it's sort of a contrast and much more exciting. It's much more exciting if I let myself be both my men and women . . . and then with just a few movements up like this I somehow exploded. It became deep colors, and then I became part of what I am in the country. I've been living in the fields for the last two weeks, literally walking across the fields every morning in the fresh dew. I know I've always had that feeling of wanting to portray something that was so whole and so full. But every time I tried, it was impossible. Now I get the feeling, when I look at those fields, of the splendor of it. I am richness and growing and flowering. There are lines and there are spaces in me. I am overwhelmed with me.

Third Stage

The person is beginning to experience a sense of completion. His energy is more controlled and modulated. He looks more thoughtful; he stands away from his work, eyeing it and tilting his head. The person examines himself respectfully, analytically; the cognitive process becomes more active.

The productions express more highly developed themes. Spaces are filled with rich detail. There is an integration of parts such that the whole piece hangs together. The art work moves into a complex, counterpunctual structure.

The person experiences himself similarly. He is more discriminating of a variety of inner feelings, forces, and polarities. He feels thoughtful and respectful of his inner richness. Often, he experiences a combination of renewal and exhaustion—and astonishment at having produced something complete, whole, integrated, beautiful, new.

Dick: I am a bird emerging out of a blurry sky. I am flying high; my wings are strong; my body is gliding smoothly through space. I feel clarity and strength.

Margaret: There are many parts of me emerging. Some of me is half formed; some parts are only hints of what is to come. Other parts, like my turmoil, my pathos, are full, complete, and present.

Sonia: I am fascinated with how comprehensive and complete I am, how I fill all the space of life, my humanness. I always thought of myself as a simple ninny until I started these drawings. I am discovering how intricate and interlaced I am.

Ed: I feel filled up inside when I look at this drawing . . .

Cynthia: The full scope of underwater life in the ocean . . . or all the magnificent micro-organisms in a drop of water . . . I feel my full scope, my own inner detail.

Bruce: I can really feel the Gestalt emerging. I am looking at myself with a sense of detail and respectfulness.

Miriam, an artist, described the total process as follows:
"In the beginning I felt slightly uncomfortable and not sure of what I wanted to do. I stared at the paper and asked myself what color I wanted to use. Did I want to 'violate' this white

paper with something which was still not fully formed within me? I felt no intimacy with the materials around me and I experienced no relationship between the materials themselves. All things seemed to be separately there and I felt almost imposed upon to do something with them. I felt uncomfortable. I experienced resistance.

"As images began to form and my excitement mounted, I allowed myself to make a first commitment to apply the colors to the paper. I realized that I was not pleased with the drawing but I also began to feel more comfortable with the actual process of creating something, of applying color, of moving my hand with the color on the paper, of executing the drawing. I developed rhythm, an agreement among myself, the chalk, and the paper—a sense of unity, a sense of friendliness so that the movements of applying the color became more fluid, comfortable and congruent with my feelings.

"By the time I reached my peak, the analyzing of complementary colors, the arrangements of spaces, the application of the color to the paper, even washing my hands—all of these actions became fluid, comfortable and almost automatic, no longer requiring strained, deliberate consideration. I experienced a fluidity of feeling, of movement—a rhythm within me. I became one with my work.

"Where in the beginning of the series I experienced doubt, conflict, alienation from myself and the medium, and a general sense of strangeness and discomfort, I experienced myself more fully at the end. Although I may still be critical of my final production, I have a sense of completion, of wholeness, of comfort, and of being pleased with myself."

❊   ❊   ❊

Creation is a process, not a single act or experience. The process appears to have certain lawful characteristics which apply both to the inner feeling of the artist as a person and to the intrinsic character of his work.

The aesthetic "goodness" of a drawing or sculpture is facilitated by the total process, rather than by the striving for a specific outcome. The artist's initial resistance to work, as well as his insistence on making good his first attempts, plays an important role in hampering this process.

In the process of drawing, the person allows himself to express his excitement fully until he feels internally satisfied and complete. His drawings show the same characteristics as his changing feelings—from fragmentation to fluidity to wholeness. Thus, the figure-ground formation of awareness in the person is congruent with the visual figure-ground formation of his drawings. The completed drawings, aside from their aesthetic value, become a concrete confirmation of his capacity to become an integrated human being.

Chapter 10

Castanedian Vision

One day I was walking along Tinker Creek thinking of nothing at all and I saw the tree with the lights in it. I saw the backyard cedar where the mourning doves roost charged and transfigured, each cell buzzing with flame. I stood on the grass with the light in it, grass that was wholly fire, utterly focused and utterly dreamed. It was less like seeing than like being for the first time seen, knocked breathless by a powerful glance . . . I had been my whole life a bell, and never knew it until at that moment I was lifted and struck.*

Over the years I have found that most people suffer from functional blindness. Not only do we not notice the subtle visual aspects of our world; we often overlook the obvious. In my work I use my eyes a lot; sometimes they help me search out what the person's language does not tell me. This chapter is meant to sensitize you to your visual world. But it is meant to do more than that. It asks you to consider your potential power to see what is not ordinarily available to most people, to let the magician inside of you look through your eyes.

*Dillard, A. *Pilgrim at Tinker Creek.* New York: Bantam Books, Inc., 1974.

In Gestalt therapy, we start an encounter seeing the client clearly at his surface. The surface alone can tell us a great deal. It contains many hints about the person's interior life. Castanedian vision makes a creative leap beyond this initial visual encounter. It cuts through the person's surface into his center, his essence. It is as if my own center becomes a power-house of light, of clarity directed toward the other person's center.

In Carlos Castaneda's *Tales of Power,* the old man, Don Juan, says to Carlos: "I'm afraid that you are confusing issues. The self-confidence of the warrior is not the self-confidence of the average man. The average man seeks certainty in the eyes of the onlooker and calls that self-confidence. The warrior seeks impeccability in his own eyes and calls that humble-ness. The average man is hooked to his fellow men, while the warrior is hooked only to himself. Perhaps you are chasing rainbows. You're after the self-confidence of the average man, when you should be after the humbleness of a warrior. The difference between the two is remarkable. Self-confidence en-tails knowing something for sure; humbleness entails being impeccable in one's actions and feelings."*

Castanedian vision is grounded in this impeccability, this complete attentiveness to the vision of one's inner "warrior." Castanedian encounter is a "center to center" encounter. At those rare moments when one is so well grounded that one can laser-beam into another person, one can break some standard rules of preparation and grading and quickly enter into dialogue with the the other person's inner experience. Intuition is. not guided by hard and fast principles; rather, it emerges from an interior well of archetypal wisdom. The vi-sion which grows out of this well is accurate, compelling, uncompromising. Experiments evolving in this process are powerful, electric and take both myself and my client by surprise.

I share my thoughts about this sort of vision more as a hope for ascending, inspiring experiences in psychotherapy, than

*Castaneda, C. *Tales of Power.* New York: Simon and Schuster, 1974.

as a presentation of well-tested experiences and meticulously formulated ideas.

EVERYTHING IS PROJECTION AND
NOTHING IS PROJECTION

As I gaze at the fuzzy red carpet of my office, it begins to shimmer at the edges. In the realm of physics, the red carpet may or may not be shimmering at its perimeter. There are people who believe you can measure such phenomena. If it isn't shimmering by some objective measure, then people may say that I am "projecting." I can only process things visually at the level at which my organism is capable of processing these things. So I am a shimmering person somewhere between my retinas and occipital cortex or between my toes and hypothalamus. And if a man doesn't have a shimmering inside him, his rug will stay neat at the edges.

In a sense, everything is projection. You can take in only with what you have. Your AM radio will not play FM music. It will be faithful to AM stations only.

Culture would not exist without man's lofty projections. Nor would it be in danger of disappearing without his destructive projections. I am deeply grateful for the projections of Copernicus, Leonardo da Vinci, Shakespeare, Columbus, Michelangelo, Mozart, Leoncovallo, the Wright brothers, Jesus of Nazareth, Einstein, Alexander Graham Bell, Van Gogh, Bach, and many other fellow human beings who leaned into their projections. The world was enriched by their lofty inner images.

There is a difference between pathological and creative projections. The psychotic person has no sense that what he sees out there has a relationship to the nature and quality of his internal equipment, to his own "nature" as a human being. His projection is just as "real" as the other guy's; unfortunately, he cannot own his miracle-making or his anger, his homosexuality or his secretiveness.

"If one is put in a situation where one emits a response but does not have the opportunity to take responsibility for it—to integrate it—one, to some degree, increases pathology. For example, projective testing, as it is done today, actually increases pathology because in it the person is asked to emit responses without giving him a chance to integrate them."* Sagan's view is remarkably close to mine, even though we have had no contact. The psychologically disturbed person emits responses which he is not able to integrate, to own. His responses are suspended without being anchored in his psychological life.

The creative projector knows that his production was born of a dialogue within himself. This dialogue is then concretized. Because he knows the roots of his images, the creative projector has less chance of feeling at the mercy of the environment. He experiences his own power in the environment. He can modify his productions with his intellectual integrity and learn from his own experience. He can develop and sharpen his artistry from one production to the next.

It is only after this sense of control develops that he can afford the luxury of "giving up control"—allowing the painting to paint itself. He lives in a powerful state of respectful receptivity. It is this passive, yet powerful sponginess, this reverence and intense dialogue, which Carlos Castaneda experiences in his Journey to Ixtlan: "Don Juan spoke to me almost in a whisper. He told me to watch every detail of the surroundings, no matter how small or seemingly trivial. Especially the features of the scenery that were most prominent in a westerly direction. He said that I should look at the sun without focusing on it until it had disappeared over the horizon.

"The last ten minutes of light, right before the sun hit a blanket of low clouds or fog, were, in a total sense, magnificent. It was as if the sun were inflaming the earth, kindling it like a bonfire. I felt a sensation of redness in my face."+

Castaneda, like Annie Dillard, set the environment ablaze

---

*Sagan, E. "Creative Behavior." Explorations, November 1965.
+Castaneda, C. Journey to Ixtlan. New York: Simon and Schuster, 1972.

with his inner vision. Yet their inner experiences were sparked by their environment, for nothing is fully projected. Everything I see is determined in some measure by what is out there. As someone said recently, "If you feel paranoid, someone is probably out to get you."

I remember an Indian psychiatric resident who had a paranoid schizophrenic episode. At the time, I was a graduate student in a large psychiatric hospital. I remember clearly how the chief psychologist constantly joked about the Indian's poor English behind his back, months before the psychotic episode. And I recall how the hostile, twitchy chief of psychiatry joined my boss at lunch to gossip about the resident's behavior. So, if the Indian had a sense of being alone and unsupported, and if he felt plotted against, they drove the feeling home. They were out to get him and they did. This particular illness, like most others, turned out to be a cooperative effort—in this case, between the resident and his superiors.

Often, there is even creativity in madness. If the resident saw my boss as a witch on a broom, it was because he was able to distill, to visually condense the most relevant part of this woman's behavior with him. Had he been able to take ownership of his own anger and accuse her to her face, thereby "hurting" her, he might have spared hurting himself.

A Gestalt therapist should be constantly in touch with his own projections and those of the people with whom he works. Therapeutic changes occur when pathological projections are converted into creative ones. For example, an obsessional person complained about his "homosexual" fears. He became intensely anxious when he glanced at other men's crotches. This made him feel that the whole world knew that he was a perverse, sick, disgusting man. I made an effort to have him take ownership of his projections by asking him to look at everything in my office and to convert all objects into "sexually perverse and sick" images. I said to him, "You have my approval to make as many 'homosexual' images as you wish. Enjoy yourself." The man gorged himself with "visual perversions." Looking at a photograph of two jumping children he said, "These are two homosexual boys and they are going to suck each other off." Then, turning to the window, he said, "See that little innocent old man walking down there? Well, he has a fourteen-inch penis." He took his time to convert everything, including the ashtrays, sculptures and furniture, into sexually-loaded imagery.

At the end of his pornographic orgy, I asked him what he was feeling. "I am not anxious," he responded. "It is as if my anxiety fell away. I am a man. An imaginative man . . . as I am in other parts of my life, I am also sexually imaginative. Like a magician, I can change things with my eyes and my brain. I am bright." I was moved by his response. By leaning fully into his sexual imagery, he felt less victimized by the "out there." He began to come into dialogue with and take ownership of his sexuality.

TWO FORMS OF LOOKING

Gazing

In a position of gazing, one is calm and not distracted. One feels supported by his body and the surface on which he is resting. His eyes are serene and unfocused. They move slowly from one object to another; the motion is not forced or studied, but random. The eyes rest on one thing—or perhaps in spaces between things—without considering goals or making assumptions. It is a form of scanning, allowing objects and patterns to assert themselves. One feels alert and clear, without the need to cling to any particular thought.

Gazing requires a form of breathing called "retinal breathing." I imagine that I am both inhaling and exhaling through the surfaces of the retina, the rods and cones in my eyes. I concentrate especially on the inhalations, sucking the visual field "out there" in through my pupils. I believe that this kind of breathing concentration engorges the visual aparatus with additional oxygenated blood. At the same time, the pupils dilate, causing the imagery to become slightly fuzzy. The slight loss of sharpness causes me to apprehend the whole without becoming distracted by irrelevant details. This is a form of visual loving.

I am with a client, Marc. I am looking at him but not seeing, listening but not hearing the words—just sensing the melody of his voice. When I become fatigued, my eyelids slowly roll over my eyes like those of a lizard. I still hear his voice. With my eyes closed I visualize a little man, a homunculus. He has an enormous head, most of which is taken up by the mouth. I see his mouth spurting out millions of bubbles, crystalline spheres. Each bubble is filled with several precious words. The bubbles are filling the office, replacing the air, and the little man is beginning to asphyxiate. I experience a sensation of tightness in my chest. Now I open my eyes. My client is still talking about his fears off the top of his breathing, and his voice is weak. His chest is not moving very much; his body looks lifeless.

"Marc," I say to him, "I just had this hallucination about you. You were filling the room with words and running out of air. I figure we have to work on your lifelessness now. What do you think?"

Marc replies, "I have a pain in my chest."

When we began to work on his chest pain and breathing, the therapy hour came to life. Sometimes I am not interested in the moment-to-moment content of another person's words. Often, I find myself least creative as a therapist when I get sucked into an exchange of verbiage and semantic hairsplitting. Little energy is generated in me and there is minimal change in the other person's perspective.

When I move into a state of gazing, my ego boundary is clearly separated from the other person's world. There is no confluence. I am an independent agent. I have complete freedom from the other's limited and specialized categorization of experience. When I am not seduced into the client's literal meanings, I can invent new metaphors of his world. Or I can see his metaphors as kernels of a new vision when he is blind to his own linguistic artistry. Don Juan tells Carlos to put himself in a position in which he, Carlos, need not give explanations to others. In this way, "Nobody is angry or disillusioned with your acts. And above all, no one pins you down with their thoughts."*

At the same time, gazing gives me a sense of the equal beauty or ugliness or value of the world around me. I can homogenize everything and then let something emerge as figure from the undifferentiated ground. The other person can be "the whole world" and I can allow different parts of him to become figural at random. I am fascinated and focused and disinterested, all at once. I begin in a dialectic state, a rhythmic homogenizing, and then focus in. If, at the same time, I care for him, if I value his experience and feel for his suffering, then my gazing stance gives me power.

I go back to my hallucination of Marc, ". . . the bubbles fill the space around him . . ." and realize that he deadens himself not only by holding his breath, but also by diluting his experience with his ample verbal outpouring. When I ask him to concentrate silently on his breathing, his face fills with color, almost as red as my shimmering crimson rug. Within minutes his body looks more lively; there is more tone in his muscles. I can't see his muscles directly, but I can feel the increased tone in my own arms and legs. I trust my sensory receptivity.

The attitude of gazing does not carry judgment or evaluation. It is not an attitude of visual prodding or analyzing. I allow the other person to float in his own experiential space and I give myself the same privilege.

When I move from gazing into a more focused attitude, the visual punctuality is firm and clear. My looking rhythm moves from homogenized equalization to clear-edged analysis, and later to a ground-glass equalization again. One attitude strengthens the other.

Some years ago I was observing another psychologist interview a man. As soon as the man walked in and sat down, the therapist asked how old he was when he first had polio. The man was surprised that he had noticed. The therapist's mo-

*Castenada, C. *Journey to Ixtlan.* New York: Simon and Schuster, 1972.

mentary gazing was followed by a clear picture of a subtle left-sided weakness in his body; his left arm was bent slightly forward at the elbow. The gestalt of polio at age five was later verified.

In another situation, a man, whom I will call Sean, came in for a second therapy session. At once I felt that I was in the presence of a person with a hypertensive condition of some sort. Sean looked somewhat like an astronaut who is experiencing high G pressure on his body in a stress situation. The films that we ordinarily see show astronauts with their faces distorted and bloated out of shape by the pressure in their environment. This image came to me while gazing at Sean. His upper lip and the area around his mouth looked tense and puffed up, as if his blood was surging against the outer skin. His face looked as though he had just undergone strenuous exercise without the release of tension. It was very pink and muscularly frozen, especially around the chin.

In short, Sean looked as if he was creating pressure against himself, as if he was pushing against his own efforts without relief. I asked him, "Do you have high blood pressure?" He replied, "It was diagnosed recently, but it's not a serious condition. How did you know?" I shared my vision with him, and we proceeded to work on his high level of tension and anxiety.

My internist tells me that there is no way of identifying hypertensive disease by looking at a person, and that I had a good chance of guessing my client's problem, since about 20% of the population suffers from high blood pressure. What is of interest to me is that the matter brought itself to my attention without any discussion with Sean about his physical health.

Lasered Focusing: The Castanedian Experience

I am sitting opposite a woman and we are focusing on one point between each other's eyes. In this case, I am not gazing at all—my eyes do not move freely and my eyelids do not move over my eyeballs. I stare without closing my eyes. After some time my eyes begin to itch and I concentrate on the itch without blinking. When I feel tearful, I let myself "cry." The crying is not accompanied by feelings of sadness or grief, yet there is a fullness of feeling in my chest.

The woman in front of me has a round face with large brown eyes which change as I am staring between them. First, they look cold and morose. I visualize a murderess and think to myself, she could kill without a moment's hesitation. I check myself out—"Joseph, you could kill without a moment's hesitation," I say to myself. "Does not fit much right now, just a trifle. Last year I felt that way for days." With some sense of comfort and matter-of-factness I say to her, "As an expert in cold-blooded murdering, I now see a feelingless murderess." She begins to cry. She tells me about her destructive fantasies toward her husband; in her fantasy she uses a butcher knife to cut off his genitals.

The therapist can tune into feelings and images inside others which are already inside of him—if only on a fuzzy, undifferentiated, or archetypal level. Jung pointed out that the more frightening the vision is, the less assimilated it is inside the person. If the vision is a complete surprise, then one knows that it must have roots which are not directly related to one's personal history. These visions can be imagined as transpersonal genetic recordings in the brain cells. They are not visual "miracles." They constitute a full range in human visual experience. I call them "Castanedian visions." All I need is to let go of my cause/effect thinking and let myself hang loose. Eyes have their own wisdom.

I continue staring at the point between her eyes. This time her whole face becomes fuzzy and its image pulsates. Her eyes change several times: soft-hard, hard-soft, then hard-calm, hard-murderous, and again hard-calm and hard-murderous. Suddenly her face turns into a large cat's head—a second cousin of the cold-blooded eyes but somehow there is more calm and natural grace in the hallucination of the cat's head. I feel a little frightened. I say to myself, "I often feel like a cat: touching people's lives and moving on without much hesitation." I share my vision with the woman, making sure she knows I take ownership of my own hallucination: "As an expert in touching people's lives lightly and moving on, I see you as a cat." We then share our cat-like natures. The exchange is thick with feeling.

I ask the woman to act like a cat with me. The notion of being a cat visibly excites her, as if a truth button has been pressed inside her. She gets down on her hands and knees, moving around the room gracefully and stealthily. She looks comfortable and natural as she brushes by me ever so lightly. She makes a tiger-like growl at me. I tell her that I feel slightly teased. As we work, she remembers how, when she was seven, her father played with her on the floor. Later, when she began to show signs of puberty, her father stopped playing with her. There was no more touching. As she spoke, her eyes became murderous again.

"Imagine your father is here," I said, "and tell him how angry you are with him." She started to talk. Words turned into screams, and screaming became the pounding of fists on a pile of pillows. She pounded for a long time, beads of perspiration running down her forehead into her eyes. As she slowed down, I noticed that her right hand began to stroke one of the pillows. She started sobbing softly. "Papa," she whispered, "I love you very much. I wish you would hold and stroke and play with me like you used to."

"Have you ever asked your husband to hold and stroke you?" I asked. Without turning her face toward me she quietly said, "It's easier for me to comfort him; that way I can stay aloof and in control. But I think I can begin to ask for comforting from John. I think I am ready for it now, Joseph. Joseph, would you hold and comfort me?" I held her for a long time.

Months later she told me, "My butcher knife fantasies have not come to me while I make love. It is as if something inside me let go. I seem to give myself more fully to the whole experience. I seem to be more assertive and aggressive in my lovemaking." Experiments generated out of my spontaneous visualizations or those of others usually yield powerful emotional experiences for people. Often these experiences create significant changes in their lives.

It is exceedingly important that one allow oneself to be surprised in daily life. That he not be habit-bound or jaded. That he always have a sense of wonder about his own life and the lives and words, gestures and images of others. One must always be ready for surprises. As old man Don Juan put it: "When nothing is for sure, we remain alert, perenially on our toes . . . It is more exciting not to know which bush the rabbit is hiding behind than to behave as though we know everything."*

*Castaneda, C. *Journey to Ixtlan*. New York: Simon and Schuster, 1972, p. 35.

Appendix

GESTALT THERAPY

EXISTENTIAL-PHENOMENOLOGICAL PRINCIPLE	GESTALT METHOD
The organism's ongoing phenomenological world is its "reality." Pathology: Discrepancy between this phenomenal self and the rest of the organism (visceral-sensory, etc.) (Rogers).	Staying in the present with the experiencing person. Principle of non-interpretation. Attending to discrepancies between words (content) and appearance (form) or actions, thinking and feeling (cognitive and visceral), self-concept and total organism.
The organisms's need satisfaction cycle is in fluid rhythm as in the figure-ground relationship (Köhler). Pathology: Organism disrupts its own need satisfaction rhythm (Perls).	Facilitating sensation, awareness, excitement and contact in relation to needs. Repeated exposure to sharper awareness of needs and their satisfaction.
All parts of the organism are dynamically interrelated and each part can only be understood in relation to the other parts. Pathology: Organism relies heavily on few modalities in effort to preserve phenomenal self (Goldstein).	Attending to body and to physical support systems: breathing, posture, movement, muscular stasis of armor. Attending (helping client to) to physical accompaniments of functional processes.

Effective learning (or relearning) takes place in the total organism (both the phenomenal self and the visceral-sensory-motor self). Pathology: Disruption of the cognitive-motor axis: person can't "act on his ideas."

Focusing on specific sensory-cognitive-motor blockages. Use of experiment for purpose of sensory-motor integration (Polster: "synaptic experience" or insight).

Every person exists in a continually changing world of experience. The organism is in process. Pathology: Fixedness in unfinished situations; fixedness of daily experiential world (to preserve self-concept) (Rogers).

Staying with the ongoing, with process. The use of fantasy, dialogue (empty chair), dramatization, experiments to complete old business. Dislodging introjects.

The person's existential urgency, his being-in-the-world, is experienced in the here and now. Pathology: In effort to "hold on to" oneself, the person creates stasis and cannot flow experientially from moment to moment.

Emphasis on what is experienced in the moment. Locating, describing, enriching all that supports the person in the flow of the therapy hour. Insights are generated by starting on the experiential "surface" (the obvious) and allowing person to make own inferences.

The organism's habit-forming hardware gives it experiential stability. The person clings to his self-concept. Pathology: the person immobilizes himself in a rigid self-concept system (Learning theory).

Exploring and locating polarities (opposing forces) in the personality. Use of experiment in the integration of polarities. "Stretching" self-concept (Zinker).

The rigid self-concept is supported by rigid postural-muscular armor. The armor develops functional autonomy. Change in self-concept must be accompanied by armor modification (Reich, Rolf).

Locating and dislodging of armor. Relearning muscular functions in more fluid, self-supporting directions. Expression of "resistance" loosens armor in the same motoric system that permits satisfaction of blocked needs. Use of tension systems for resolution and integration.

Bibliography

Allport, G. *Becoming.* New Haven, Conn.: Yale University Press, 1955.

Bach, George and Peter Wyden. *The Intimate Enemy.* New York: William Morrow & Co., 1969.

Baron, Frank. *Creative Person and Creative Process.* New York: Holt, Rinehart & Winston, 1969.

Berg, J. H. Van Den. *The Phenomenological Approach to Psychiatry.* Springfield, Ill.: Charles C Thomas, 1955.

Berdyaev, Nicolas. "Master, Slave and Free Man." In *Four Existential Theologians.* Garden City, N.Y.: Doubleday & Co., Inc., 1958.

Bion, W. R. *Experiences in Groups.* New York: Basic Books, 1961.

Bryson, Rebecca B., et al. "The Professional Pair." *American Psychologist,* 1976, *31*:1.

Buber, Martin. *Ten Rungs: Hasidic Sayings.* New York: Schoken Books, 1962.

Castaneda, Carlos. *The Teachings of Don Juan: A Yaqui Way of Knowledge.* New York: Ballantine Books, 1969.

———. *A Separate Reality.* New York: Simon and Schuster, 1970.

———. *Journey to Ixtlan.* New York: Simon and Schuster, 1972.

———. *Tales of Power.* New York: Simon and Schuster, 1974.

Cummings, E. E. *Six Nonlectures.* New York: Antheneum, 1971.

Dillard, Annie. *Pilgrim at Tinker Creek.* New York: Bantam Books, 1974.

Fagen, J. Anne and I. Shepard. *Gestalt Therapy Now.* Palo Alto, Calif.: Science and Behavior Books, 1970.

Fantz, Rainette. "Polarities: Differentiation and Integration." Gestalt Institute of Cleveland, Ohio, 1973.

Franck, Frederick. *The Zen of Seeing.* New York: Vintage Books, 1973.

Fromm, Erich. *The Art of Loving.* New York: Harper & Brothers, 1956.

Gallant, Leonard. "The Role of Anger in Hypertension." *Mind and Medicine,* 1975, 2:4.

Gendlin, Eugene. "The Process of Experiencing in Psychotherapy, Client-centered Therapy with Schizophrenic Persons." APA Convention, 1962.

Ghiselin, Brewster. *Creative Process.* New York: Mentor Books, 1952.

Gibran, Khalil. *The Prophet.* New York: Alfred Knopf, 1960.

Goldstein, Kurt. *The Organism.* Boston: Beacon Press, 1963.

Gordon, William. *Synectics.* New York: Collier Books, 1961.

Harman, Robert. "Goals of Gestalt Therapy." *Professional Psychology,* 1974(May), 178-84.

Hartford, M. E. *Groups in Social Work.* New York: Columbia University Press, 1971.

Herrigel, Eugene. *Zen in the Art of Archery.* New York: Vintage Books, 1971.

Hora, Thomas. "Existential Psychiatry and Group Psychotherapy." In *Psychoanalysis and Existential Philosophy.* New York: E. P. Dutton & Co., Inc., 1962.

———. "The Process of Existential Psychotherapy." *Existential Inquiries,* 1962, 1:1.

Isenberg, Sheldon. "Variations of the Gestalt Prayer." (Unpublished poem, Chicago, July 25, 1975).

Kaufmann, Walter (ed.) *Existentialism from Dostoevsky to Sartre.* New York: Meridian Books, 1956.

Kempler, W. *Principles of Gestalt Family Therapy.* Oslo, Norway: A. J. Nordahls Trykerri, 1973.

Koestler, Arthur. *The Act of Creation.* New York: Dell Books, 1964.

Koffka, K. *Principles of Gestalt Psychology.* New York: Harcourt, Brace & World, 1935.

Kohler, W. *Gestalt Psychology.* New York: Liveright Publishing Corp., 1947.

Kopp, S. B. *Metaphors from a Therapist Guru.* Palo Alto, Calif.: Science and Behavior Books, 1971.

Latner, Joel. *The Gestalt Therapy Book.* New York: Bantam Books, 1974.

Lederer, William and Don Jackson. *The Mirages of Marriage.* New York: W. W. Norton & Co., 1968.

Lowen, Alexander. *The Betrayal of the Body.* London: Collier Books, 1967.

Maslow, Abraham. *Motivation and Personality.* New York: Harper & Bros., 1954.

———. *Toward a Psychology of Being.* Princeton, N.J.: D. Van Nostrand Co., Inc., 1962.

———. *The Farther Reaches of Human Nature.* New York: Viking Press, 1971.

May, Rollo (ed.) *Existential Psychology.* New York: Random House, 1961.

McKim, Robert. *Experiences in Visual Thinking.* Monterey, Calif.: Brooks/
    Cole Co., 1972.
Moreno, J. L. *Who Shall Survive? Foundations of Sociometry, Group Psy-
    chotherapy and Sociodrama.* Beacon, N.Y.: Beacon House, Inc., 1953.
———. *Psychodrama: Foundations of Psychotherapy, Volume 2.* Beacon,
    N.Y.: Beacon House, Inc., 1959.
Nevis, Edwin, Sonia Nevis and Elliott Danzig. *Blocks to Creativity: Guide
    to Program.* Cleveland, O.: Danzig-Nevis International, Inc., 1970.
Ornstein, Robert E. *The Psychology of Consciousness.* San Francisco: W.
    H. Freeman & Co., 1972.
Perls, Fritz. *Ego, Hunger and Aggression.* San Francisco: Orbit Graphic
    Arts, 1966.
———. *Gestalt Therapy Verbatim.* Moab, Utah: Real People Press, 1969.
———, R. F. Hefferline and P. Goodman. *Gestalt Therapy.* New York:
    Julian Press, 1951.
Polster, Erving. "Encounter in Community." In A. Burton (ed.), *Encounter.*
    San Francisco: Jossey-Bass Inc., 1969.
——— and Miriam Polster. *Gestalt Therapy Integrated.* New York: Brun-
    ner/Mazel, 1973.
Pursglove, P. D. *Recognitions in Gestalt Therapy.* New York: Funk and
    Wagnalls, 1968.
Ram Dass. *The Only Dance There Is.* New York: Anchor Books, 1974.
Read, Herbert. *Art and Alienation.* New York: World Publishing Co., 1963.
Reich, Wilhelm. *The Function of the Orgasm.* New York: Orgone Press,
    1942.
———. *Character Analysis.* New York: Orgone Press, 1949.
Richards, M. C. *Centering.* Middletown, Conn.: Wesleyan University
    Press, 1962.
Rogers, Carl. *Counseling and Psychotherapy.* New York: Houghton Mifflin,
    1942.
———. "A Process Conception of Psychotherapy." *American Psychologist,*
    1958, *13,* 142–149.
———. *On Becoming a Person.* Boston: Houghton Mifflin, 1961.
———. *Carl Rogers on Encounter Groups.* New York: Harper and Row,
    1970.
Sagan, E. "Creative Behavior." *Explorations,* 1965 (November).
Satir, V. *Conjoint Family Therapy.* Palo Alto, Calif.: Science and Behavior
    Books, 1967.
Stephenson, D. (ed.) *Gestalt Therapy Primer.* Springfield, Ill.: Charles
    C Thomas, 1975.
Stern, Karl. "Death Within Life." *Review of Existential Psychology and
    Psychiatry,* 1962, *11*:2, 143.
Straus, Erwin W. "Symposium: Existential Psychology and Psychother-
    apy." *American Psychologist,* 1962, 7:6.
Ungerer, Tomi. *The Underground Sketchbook.* New York: Dover Publica-

tions, 1969.

Wann, T. W. (ed.) *Behaviorism and Phenomenology.* Chicago: University of Chicago Press, 1964.

Wertheimer, M. "Gestalt Theory." *Social Research,* 1944, *11.*

Zinker, Joseph C. "An Attempt to Clarify Concepts of Existentialism and Phenomenology in Personality Theory." Unpublished paper, 1959.

———. "On Public Knowledge and Personal Revelation." *Explorations,* 1968 (October).

———. "Beginning the Group Therapy." *Voices,* 1970 (Summer), 29-31.

———. "Dream Work as Theater: An Innovation in Gestalt Therapy." *Voices,* 1971, 7:2.

———. "The Phenomenological Here and Now." In *Integrative Therapie,* Neuss, Germany, FPI Publications, 1975.

———. "Creative Process and the Creative Life." Unpublished manuscript, Cleveland, Ohio, 1973.

———. "Gestalt Therapy is Permission to be Creative." *Voices,* 1974, 9:4.

———. "On Loving Encounters: A Phenomenological View." In D. Stephenson (ed.), *Gestalt Therapy Primer.* Springfield, Ill.: Charles C Thomas, 1975.

———. "The Case of June: The Use of Experiment in a Case of Frigidity." In C. A. Loew, et al. (eds.), *Three Psychotherapies.* New York: Brunner/Mazel, 1975.

——— and Charles F. Hallenbeck. "Notes on Loss, Crisis and Growth." *Journal of General Psychology,* 1965.

——— and Julian Leon. "The Gestalt Perspective: A Marriage Enrichment Program." In Otto A. Herbert (ed.), *Marriage and Family Enrichment.* Nashville, Tenn.: Abington Press, 1976.

Index

Act of Creation, The (Koestler), 23n, 75n
Agapeic love, and therapy, 6
Alien gradations, 145
Alter-ego role, in group process, 172–73
Analogies
  direct, 55, 56
  fantasy, 54–55
  personal, 54
  symbolic, 54
Arica school, transpersonal therapy, 121
Arieti, Silvano *(Creativity)*, vii
Around the world experiment, 146, 147–49
Art, in Gestalt therapy, 236ff
  developmental stages, 251ff
    first, 250, 252
    second, 252–53
    third, 253–55
  movement, rhythm, and grounding, 237ff
    faith in, 240
    in painting, 237ff
    wholeness of, 239
  workshop, 240ff
    chalk drawings, 240ff
    sculpture, 247ff,
Art and Alienation (Read), 9, 9n
Artist, definition of, 237n
Artist, therapist as. *See* Therapist as artist
Assumptions and roots, 76ff
Awareness-excitement-contact cycle, 90–92

Balbot, Barbara, drawings of, 45, 125, 190, 209
Baron, Frank *(Creative Person)*, 23n
Behaviorism, and Gestalt psychology, 123
Behaviorism and Phenomenology (Watt), 123n
Belville group, 186ff
Betrayal of the Body, The (Lowen), 26n, 103n
Bibliography, 271ff
"Blind spots," in self-awareness, 200
Blocks to Creativity (Nevis), 62n
"Broken wheel" group, 163
Buber, Martin
  on love, 6, 6n, 8
  Ten Rungs: Hasidic Sayings, 6n, 8n

Carl Rogers on Encounter Groups (Rogers), 158n
Castaneda, C.
  Journey to Ixtlan, 260, 260n, 268n
  Tales of Power, 258, 258n
  Teachings of Don Juan, The, 74n, 75n
Castanedian vision, 257ff
  functional blindness, 257
  looking, forms of, 262ff
    gazing, 262ff
    lasered focusing, 265ff
  projection, 259ff
    all as, 259
    giving up control, 260
    pathological, 259–260, 261
    therapist's, 261

Catatonic schizophrenic, expression of anger, 106
Cerebral hemispheres, 60
Chagall, Marc, and prayer, 16
Character Analysis (Reich), 87n
Client-centered therapy, individuals associated
  with, 86n
Cognitive map, 11, 12, 76
"Collected stamps," 214–215
Compulsive mode of experience, 119
Computing function, 84
Confluence, defined, 46
Conversion hysteric, and sensation, 100
Counseling and Psychotherapy (Rogers), 78n, 87n
Courage to Create, The (May), vii
"Creative Behavior" (Sagan), 260n
Creative leap, 21ff
Creative Person and the Creative Process, The
  (Baron), 23n
Creative Process (Ghiselin), 47n, 49n, 57n
Creative stance, 37ff. *See also* Creative therapy
Creative therapist. *See also* Creative therapy
  creative integration, 60
  integration of modes, 59–60
  qualities of, 57–58
Creative therapy, 5ff
  Gestalt as, 17ff
    experiment, 18–20
    roles of therapist, 17–18
  as growth process, 8–9
    art making, 9
    risk taking, 9
    specialization, 8
  as loving encounter, 5ff, 7
    agapeic love, 6
    authentic love, 6
    being loved, 7
    "brotherly love," 6
    creative tension, 6
    "grandparently love," 6
    integrity, 6
  as problem solving, 9–11, 12
  as projection, 13ff
    creative, 15–16
    dialogue with self, 13
    escapism, 15
    examples, 14
    pathological, 15
    and psychotherapy, 15
  as Tao learning, 11–13
    deficit learning, 11–12
    trajectory of growth, 13
  as transcendental/religious experience, 16–17
    art as prayer, 16
    empathy, 15–16
    narcissism, 17
Creativity (Arieti), vii
Creativity, blocks to, 62ff, 67ff
  custom-bound, 64, 68, 72,
  fear of failure, 63, 68
  frustration avoidance, 63–64

fear of unknown, 64
impoverished emotional life, 66, 70–72
impoverished fantasy life, 64, 70–72
need for balance, 64, 72
over-certainty, 63
reluctance to exert influence, 65
reluctance to let go, 66
reluctance to play, 63, 73
resource myopia, 63
sensory dullness, 67, 68, 69
unintegrated Yin-Yang, 66, 68
Creativity, nature of, 3–4, 21. *See also* Creative
    therapist, Creative therapy, Creativity, blocks
    to
Cultural behavior patterns, 110
Cummings, E.E.
    on identity, 76–77
    on self-determination, 89–90
    Six Nonlectures, 77n, 90n
    on time, 79

Daseinsanalyse
    in Gestalt therapy, 88
    meaning of, 86–87
Dass, Ram *(Only Dance There Is),* 32n
Depression, 42–43
Dillard, D. *(Pilgrim at Tinker Creek),* 257n
Dreams, and group therapy, 170ff, 187ff.
"Dream Work as Theatre," (Zinker), 171n

Ego-alien polarities, 209
Ego, Hunger, and Aggression (Perls), 87n
Ego-syntonic and alien gradations, 145
Ego-syntonic polarities, 209–210
Ego-syntonic reality, 197
Empathy, 15–16, 46
Empty chair experiment, 149ff
Enactment experiment, 146ff
Energy, generating and transforming, 24ff
    blockage of energy, 24–25
    expression of, 26
    "pumping up," 28
    resistances, 24, 26
Exhibitionism, 206–207
Existential philosophers, 86n
Existential therapists, 86n
Experiments in therapy, 123ff
    defined, 123
        goals of, 126
        types of, 123–127
    elegance of, 153–155
        developmental readiness, 153
        imagery, 153–154
        pacing, 153
    evolution of, 127ff
        awareness, 136–37
        choice of experiment, 141–142
        consensus, 131–132
        development of theme, 140
        enactment, 142–145
        focus, 138–139
        grading, 132ff, 136, 145
        groundwork, 129–131
        insight and completion, 145–146
        preparatory self-support, 139–140
    two classic
        around the world, 146
        the empty chair, 149ff

Fagan and Shepherd, *(Gestalt Therapy Now),* 123n
Fantz, Rainette ("Polarities"), 33n

Farther Reaches of Human Nature, The (Maslow),
    75n
Figure-ground phenomenon, 92–93
"Float thoughts," 55
Freud, Sigmund. *See also* Psychoanalysis
    on art and creativity, vii
    on free association, 46
    on motivation, 86
    on psychotherapy, 8
    and the unconscious, 201
Frigidity, 33–34
Functional blindness, 257
Function of the Organism, The (Reich), 87n

Gestalt prayer, 160–61
Gestalt Psychology (Kohler), 92n
Gestalt therapy. *See also* Goals of Gestalt Therapy,
    Creative therapist, Creative therapy
    and "acting out," 105
    conception of, 117
    Daseinsanalyse of, 88. *See also* Daseinsanalyse
    experiments of, 88ff. *See also* Experiments in
        therapy
    individuals associated with, 86n
    influences upon, 87–88
    and other therapies, 104–105, 123
    and phenomenology, 123
    principles of, 275–276
    and symptoms, 118
"Gestalt Therapy" (Kepner and Brien), 123n
Gestalt Therapy (Perls et al.), 80n, 83n, 87n
"Gestalt Therapy" (Wertheimer), 92n
Gestalt Therapy Integrated (Polster), 29n
Gestalt Therapy Now (Fagan and Shepherd), 123n
Gestalt Therapy Verbatim (Perls), 80n
Ghiselin, Brewster
    Creative Process, 47n, 49n, 57n
    quoting Jung, 47
Goals of Gestalt therapy
    awareness-excitement-contact cycle, bridging
        interruptions within
        action and contact, 108–109
        awareness and mobilization of energy, 101ff
        contact and withdrawal, withdrawal and
            sensation, 109ff
        defense mechanisms, 98
        mobilization of energy, 97
        mobilization of energy and action, 105ff
        sensation and awareness, 100–101
        withdrawal and sensation, 98–100
    discovery of new concepts, 116–118
        and experience, 117
        relation to psychoanalysis, 117–118
    expansion of experiential range, 118–120
        meta-needs, 120
            defined, 120
            frustration of, 120
        meta-therapy goals, 121–122
"Goals of Gestalt Therapy" (Harmon), 90n
Goethe, creating *Faust,* 47
Goldstein, Kurt
    influence on Gestalt therapy, 87
    The Organism, 35, 35n, 87n
Gordon, William J.
    "hedonistic response," 46–47
    making the familiar strange, 54
    Synectics, 32n, 46, 47n, 48n, 54n, 57n
Grading 132–133, 145. *See also* Experiments,
    evolution of
Group exercise, defined, 167
Groups. *See also* Gestalt therapy
    and dreams, 187ff
    existential aspects, 186ff

experiments, 167ff. *See also* Experiments in therapy
  defined, 167
  emerging issues and experiments, 174ff
  group exercise, 167
  from individual experiences, 170ff
  therapist's qualities, 169
  Gestalt process, 161ff
    active contact, 163–164
    awareness, 162–163
    experiment, 164
    ground rules, 165
    present experiment, 162
    principles, 164
  "mechanics" of experimentation, 180ff
    energy and timing. 183–184
    group cohesiveness, 184–186
    preparation and grading, 181–183
    techniques and creations, 180–181
  process models
    Carl Rogers, 157–159
    old Gestalt, 159–161
    psychodrama, 161

Hamlet (Shakespeare), 37n
Harmon, R. L. ("Goals of Gestalt Therapy"), 90n
Harris, Cynthia, on retroflection, 103n
"Hot seat"
  "top-dog/under-dog," 19
  in group therapy, 160
Hypnosis, demonstration, 98–99
Hysteria, 108–109

"If onlys," 106–107
In the Wilderness is the Preservation of the World (Porter), 23n
Introjection, 98

Jackson, C. W.
  on Gestalt groups, 165, 165n
  lecture, 166n
Jones, Ronald (in *Real Time 1*), 195n
Jouney to Ixlan (Castaneda), 260, 260n, 268n
Jung, Carl, on creativity, 47

Kafka, Franz, state of amazement, 47
Kepner and Brien ("Gestalt Therapy"), 123n
Koestler, Arthur (*Act of Creation*), 23n, 75n
Koffka, K.
  figure-ground, 92
  Principles of Gestalt Psychology, 92n
Kohler, W.
  figure-ground, 92
  Gestalt Psychology, 92n

Lowen, Alexander
  The Betrayal of the Body, 26n, 103n
  on energy, 26
  on respiratory patterns, 102–103
LDS, and bridging withdrawal-sensation, 99

Manic-depressive, fear of inactivity, 111
Maslow, Abraham
  The Farther Reaches of Human Nature, 75n
  meta-needs, 120
  self-actualization, 38
  Toward a Psychology of Being, 7n, 38n, 120n
May, Rollo (*Courage to Create*), vii
Meta-needs, 120
Metaphors, and group process, 170
Meta-therapy, goals of, 121–122
Miles, Dwight, on work, 40
Modes of thought/feeling, 59–60

Moreno, J.L.
  "now and here," 161
  Who Shall Survive?, 161n
Multilarities, 197

Narcissism, and therapy, 17
Nevis, Ed and Sonia
  on blocks to creativity, 62ff, 67ff. *See also* Creativity, blocks to
  on grading, 132–33. *See also* Grading
  "Ways of Heightening Contact," 166n

Obsessive-compulsion, 101
Oedipal situations
  and conflict, 232
  and Gestalt therapy, 162
  and group process, 162
On Becoming a Person (Rogers), 78n, 87n
Only Dance There Is, The (Ram Dass), 32n
Ontoanalytic therapists, 86n
Ontology, 86
Organism, The (Goldstein), 35n, 87n
Organismic self-regulation, cycle of, 90
Ornstein, Robert
  on cerebral hemispheres, 60
  The Psychology of Consciousness, 61n

Perls, Fritz
  on computing function, 84
  Ego, Hunger, and Aggression, 87n
  Gestalt Therapy Verbatim, 80n
  working with groups, 19, 159
Perls, Fritz, et. al. (*Gestalt Therapy*), 80n, 83n
Permission to be creative, 3ff
Phenomenological Approach to Psychiatry, The (Van den Berg), 83n
Phenomenology, 76ff
  content validity, 85
  final integration, 93–95
  and Gestalt therapy, 123
  goal of Gestalt therapy, 94
  here-and-now therapies, 86ff
  ownership, 84–85
  process, 83–84
  sensation, 78–79
  space, 83
  time, 79ff
Pilgrim at Tinker Creek (Dillard), 257n
Polar forces, 35. *See also* Revolutionary molding
Polarities and conflicts, 195ff
  healthy conflict, 195
  interpersonal conflicts, 202, 206ff
    competition, 211–212
    dark polarities, 207ff
    exhibitionism, 206–207
    love, 207, 209
    marital polarities, 208, 209
  intrapersonal conflicts, 200–202
  and self-concepts
    healthy, 198
    pathological, 199
    stretching, 202ff
  polarities and understanding conflict, 196ff
  working with conflict, 213ff
    blame, 230–231
    "collected stamps," 214–215
    creative trouble, 234
    expression of, 225ff
    grandiosity, 217ff
    humor, 225
    incest, 215–216
    one marital approach, 223–224
    oedipal, 232
    passive-aggressive, 226–227

resentments, 229
self-pity, 228
sexuality, 232–234
stages, marital context, 216–217
support, 233
"Polarities: Differentiation and Integration"
    (Fantz), 33n
Polster, Erving
    interaction with Zinker, 116
    multilarities, 197n
Polster, Erving and Miriam (*Gestalt Therapy
    Integrated*), 29n
Power, impeccability and, 74–75
Primal scream, 20, 39
Principles of Gestalt Psychology (Koffka), 92n
"A Process Conception of Psychotherapy" (Rogers),
    78n, 84n, 87n
Projection
    and conflict, 195, 206
    painting as, 239
    taking ownership of, 223
    in therapy, 8
Psychoanalysis
    acting out, 105
    as lateral learning, 117–118
    the unconscious, 201
Psychodrama, 161. *See also* Groups, process
    models
Psychology of Consciousness, The (Ornstein), 61n
Psychophysiological cycle, 90–92
"Pumping up," 28
Pythagoras, and aesthetics, 48

Rationalizations, 106–107
Read, Herbert (*Art and Alienation*), 9, 9n
Real Time 1 (Jones in), 195n
Reenactment experiment, 146ff
Reich, Wilheim
    Character Analysis, 87n
    The Function of the Orgasm, 87 n
    influence on Gestalt therapy, 87
Repression. *See also* Creativity, blocks to
    of anger, 173
    as a block, 98
    and conflict, 195, 206
    between sensation and awareness, 101
Resistance, and irrelevant comments, 57
Resource myopia, as creative block, 63
Retinal breathing, 262
Retroflection, 26n, 98, 103
Revolutionary molding, 21, 29ff
    context and metaphor, 31–32
    novel integrations, 33–34
    resistance to, 34–36
        blocking, 35
        polar forces, 35
Rhythm, disturbances of, 109ff
Rogers, Carl
    Carl Rogers on Encounter Groups, 158n
    Counseling and Psychotherapy, 77n
    experiential purity, 167
    group process model, 157–159
    On Becoming a Person, 7n, 77n, 87n
    on phenomenology, 77–78
    "A Process Conception of Psychotherapy," 77n,
        84n, 87, 87n
Rolfing, 39
Roots and assumptions, 76ff
Rubenstein, Arthur, 5, 40

Sagan, E. ("Creative Behavior"), 260n
Satir, Virginia, on therapy, 17

Schizophrenic, catatonic, expression of anger, 106
Schizophrenic sensations, 100
Self-actualization, 38, 39. *See also* Maslow,
    Abraham
Self-concept, 202ff
    healthy, 198
    pathological, 199
Sensory dullness, as creative block, 67
Shakespeare, William *(Hamlet)*, 37n
Simkin, James
    model of groups, 164
    structured approach, 167
    work with groups, 159–160
Six Nonlectures (Cummings), 77n, 90n
Superego, and conflict, 201. *See also* Creativity,
    blocks to
Synectics (Gordon), 32n, 46, 47n, 48n, 54n, 57n

Tales of Power (Castaneda), 258, 258n
Tao learning, 11–13
Teachings of Don Juan, The (Castaneda), 74n, 75n
Ted, operation of, 137, 145
Ten Rungs: Hasidic Sayings (Buber), 6n, 8n
Therapist, creative, 36. *See also* Creative therapy,
    Creative therapist
Therapist as artist, 38ff. *See also* Creative therapy,
    Creative therapist
    capacities, abilities, techniques, 48ff
        birth of an insight, 51
        creative integration, 60
        development of an insight, 50
        direct analogy, 56
        mourning, stages of, 48ff, 58–59
        resistance, 57
    essences, values, attitudes, 38ff.
        confluence, 46
        detached involvement, 46
        empathy, 46
        goals of, 4ff
        humor, 41ff
        innovation, 41
        playfulness, 40–41
        risk taking, 47
        "tracking", 47
Therapy, creative. *See* Creative therapy
Therapy as art, 37–38. *Se also* Therapist as artist,
    Creative therapy
Toward a Psychology of Being (Maslow), 120n
"Tracking," defined, 47
Transactional analysts, 214

Underground Sketchbook of Tomi Ungerer
    (Ungerer), 28n
Ungerer, Tomi, 28n

Van den Berg, J.H. (*Phenomenological Approach to
    Psychiatry*), 83n

Wakefulness cycles, 110
Waldas, Greta, 91, 204
Walters, Barbara. 5n, 40
Watt, T. W. *(Behaviorism and Phenomenolgy)*,
    123n
"Ways of Heightening Contact" (Nevis), 166n
Wertheimer, M.
    figure-ground, 92
    "Gestalt Therapy," 92n
Who Shall Survive? (Moreno), 161n
Wolpian desensitization, 121
World of Marc Chagall, The (McMullen), 16n

Yin-Yang, unintegrated, 66, 68, 71